CSWE's Core Competencies and Practice Behaviors Covered

Competency	
Professional Identity	
Practice Behavior Examples...	
Social workers serve as representatives of the profession, its mission, and its core values	
Social workers know the profession's history	
Social workers commit themselves to the profession's enhancement and to their own professional conduct and growth	
Social workers advocate for client access to the services of social work	1
Social workers practice personal reflection and self-correction to assure continual professional development	1, 2, 3, 4, 5, 6, 7, 8, 9, 11, 14
Social workers attend to professional roles and boundaries	6
Social workers demonstrate professional demeanor in behavior, appearance, and communication	
Social workers engage in career-long learning	6, 7, 14
Social workers use supervision and consultation	1–14
Ethical Practice	
Practice Behavior Examples...	
Social workers have an obligation to conduct themselves ethically and engage in ethical decision-making	6
Social workers know about the value base of the profession, its ethical standards, and relevant law	
Social workers recognize and manage personal values in a way that allows professional values to guide practice	4
Social workers make ethical decisions by applying standards of the National Association of Social Workers Code of Ethics and, as applicable, of the International Federation of Social Workers/International Association of Schools of Social Work Ethics in Social Work, Statement of Principles	5, 6, 13
Social workers tolerate ambiguity in resolving ethical conflicts	5
Social workers apply strategies of ethical reasoning to arrive at principled decisions	6
Critical Thinking	
Practice Behavior Examples...	
Social workers know about the principles of logic, scientific inquiry, and reasoned discernment	
Social workers use critical thinking augmented by creativity and curiosity	1, 10, 12
Critical thinking requires the synthesis and communication of relevant information	
Social workers distinguish, appraise, and integrate multiple sources of knowledge, including research-based knowledge, and practice wisdom	4
Social workers analyze models of assessment, prevention, intervention, and evaluation	1, 2, 3, 5, 6, 7, 8, 9, 10, 13
Social workers demonstrate effective oral and written communication in working with individuals, families, groups, organizations, communities, and colleagues	1–14

Adapted with the permission of Council on Social Work Education

CSWE's Core Competencies and Practice Behaviors Covered in This Text

Competency	Chapter
Diversity in Practice	
Practice Behavior Examples...	
Social workers understand how diversity characterizes and shapes the human experience and is critical to the formation of identity	6, 12
Social workers understand the dimensions of diversity as the intersectionality of multiple factors including age, class, color, culture, disability, ethnicity, gender, gender identity and expression, immigration status, political ideology, race, religion, sex, and sexual orientation	
Social workers appreciate that, as a consequence of difference, a person's life experiences may include oppression, poverty, marginalization, and alienation as well as privilege, power, and acclaim	
Social workers recognize the extent to which a culture's structures and values may oppress, marginalize, alienate, or create or enhance privilege and power	3
Social workers gain sufficient self-awareness to eliminate the influence of personal biases and values in working with diverse groups	
Social workers recognize and communicate their understanding of the importance of difference in shaping life experiences	
Social workers view themselves as learners and engage those with whom they work as informants	
Human Rights and Justice	
Practice Behavior Examples...	
Social workers understand that each person, regardless of position in society, has basic human rights, such as freedom, safety, privacy, an adequate standard of living, health care, and education	
Social workers recognize the global interconnections of oppression and are knowledgeable about theories of justice and strategies to promote human and civil rights	
Social work incorporates social justice practices in organizations, institutions, and society to ensure that these basic human rights are distributed equitably and without prejudice	
Social workers understand the forms and mechanisms of oppression and discrimination	
Social workers advocate for human rights and social and economic justice	
Social workers engage in practices that advance social and economic justice	
Research-Based Practice	
Practice Behavior Examples...	
Social workers use practice experience to inform research, employ evidence-based interventions, evaluate their own practice, and use research findings to improve practice, policy, and social service delivery	
Social workers comprehend quantitative and qualitative research and understand scientific and ethical approaches to building knowledge	
Social workers use practice experience to inform scientific inquiry	
Social workers use research evidence to inform practice	

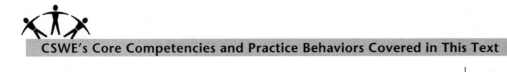

CSWE's Core Competencies and Practice Behaviors Covered in This Text

Competency	Chapter
Human Behavior	
Practice Behavior Examples...	
Social workers know about human behavior across the life course; the range of social systems in which people live; and the ways social systems promote or deter people in maintaining or achieving health and well-being	1, 7
Social workers apply theories and knowledge from the liberal arts to understand biological, social, cultural, psychological, and spiritual development	3, 14
Social workers utilize conceptual frameworks to guide the processes of assessment, intervention, and evaluation	1, 2, 3, 5, 8, 13
Social workers critique and apply knowledge to understand person and environment	2, 7, 8, 10, 12
Policy Practice	
Practice Behavior Examples...	
Social workers understand that policy affects service delivery and they actively engage in policy practice	9, 12, 13
Social workers know the history and current structures of social policies and services; the role of policy in service delivery; and the role of practice in policy development	
Social workers analyze, formulate, and advocate for policies that advance social well-being	
Social workers collaborate with colleagues and clients for effective policy action	7
Practice Contexts	
Practice Behavior Examples...	
Social workers are informed, resourceful, and proactive in responding to evolving organizational, community, and societal contexts at all levels of practice	9, 11
Social workers recognize that the context of practice is dynamic, and use knowledge and skill to respond proactively	4, 9
Social workers continuously discover, appraise, and attend to changing locales, populations, scientific and technological developments, and emerging societal trends to provide relevant services	
Social workers provide leadership in promoting sustainable changes in service delivery and practice to improve the quality of social services	2, 12

Competency	Chapter
Engage, Assess, Intervene, Evaluate	
Practice Behavior Examples...	
Social workers identify, analyze, and implement evidence-based interventions designed to achieve client goals	
Social workers use research and technological advances	
Social workers evaluate program outcomes and practice effectiveness	
Social workers develop, analyze, advocate, and provide leadership for policies and services	2, 4, 11, 12
Social workers promote social and economic justice	
(A) ENGAGEMENT	
Social workers substantively and effectively prepare for action with individuals, families, groups, organizations, and communities	
Social workers use empathy and other interpersonal skills	4, 10
Social workers develop a mutually agreed-on focus of work and desired outcomes	9
(B) ASSESSMENT	2, 3, 4
Social workers collect, organize, and interpret client data	
Social workers assess client strengths and limitations	2, 3, 6
Social workers develop mutually agreed-on intervention goals and objectives	4, 9
Social workers select appropriate intervention strategies	5
(C) INTERVENTION	6, 9
Social workers initiate actions to achieve organizational goals	
Social workers implement prevention interventions that enhance client capacities	
Social workers help clients resolve problems	
Social workers negotiate, mediate, and advocate for clients	
Social workers facilitate transitions and endings	5, 6
(D) EVALUATION	5, 6
Social workers critically analyze, monitor, and evaluate interventions	

Clinical Social Work Supervision

Practice and Process

Robert Taibbi
Mary Washington College

PEARSON

Boston Columbus Indianapolis New York San Francisco Upper Saddle River
Amsterdam Cape Town Dubai London Madrid Milan Munich Paris Montreal Toronto
Delhi Mexico City Sao Paulo Sydney Hong Kong Seoul Singapore Taipei Tokyo

Editorial Director: Craig Campanella
Editor in Chief: Dickson Musslewhite
Executive Editor: Ashley Dodge
Editorial Product Manager: Carly Czech
Editorial Assistant: Nicole Suddeth
Vice President, Director of Marketing: Brandy Dawson
Executive Marketing Manager: Jeanette Koskinas
Senior Marketing Manager: Wendy Albert
Marketing Assistant: Dasle Kim
Digital Operations Manager: Felicia Halpert
Production Project Manager: Maggie Brobeck

Production Editor: Brian Mackey
Editorial Production and Composition Service: Chitra Ganesan/PreMediaGlobal
Interior Design: Joyce Weston Design
Art Director, Cover: Jayne Conte
Cover Designer: Suzanne Duda
Cover Art: Kubais/Fotolia
Printer/Binder: Courier Companies, Inc./Westford
Cover Printer: Courier Companies, Inc./Westford
Text Font: Minion Pro Regular 10/12 pts

Library of Congress Cataloging-in-Publication Data

Taibbi, Robert.
Clinical social work supervision : practice and process / Robert Taibbi.
    p. cm.
   Includes index.
   ISBN-13: 978-0-205-77693-1
   ISBN-10: 0-205-77693-0
   1. Social workers—Supervision of   2. Social case work.   I. Title.
   HV40.54.T34 2013
   361.3068'3—dc23

2011049941

10 9 8 7 6 5 4 3 2 1

PEARSON

ISBN-10:   0-205-77693-0
ISBN-13: 978-0-205-77693-1

Contents

3. Laying the Foundation—Part 2   31

Preface

It seems that in the past few years clinical supervision has been coming into its own. Becoming a supervisor is no longer the relatively simple and logical move up the workplace ladder that it was many years before. State licensing and governing boards nationwide are both delineating and increasing the mandatory prerequisites for becoming an approved supervisor, established supervisors are increasingly required to receive ongoing continuing education in order to remain current in this shifting and varied terrain, and agencies see supervisory oversight as primary defense against ethical and liability concerns.

But in many ways this new focus on supervision, and particularly clinical supervision, is old news in the social work field. Supervision has always been an essential component of social work practice. Not only has it been seen as a necessary means of ensuring that clients and communities receive quality services, it is through the supervisory relationship that social work clinicians have been welcomed, inducted, and trained in the art and craft of doing clinical practice. This book follows in that tradition.

The vision of this book from the onset was to step outside the typical textbook format—those tomes tightly packed with literature reviews, theory, and surveys of supervisory models—and instead offer a text that was user-friendly and, above all, practical in real-world application. Undergirding this effort has been 3 broad themes that I want to briefly highlight here, and then track throughout this text.

The first theme is my belief that good supervision, like good clinical work, is not a one-size-do-it-right process, but ideally a reflection of the creative mix of the supervisor's personality and supervisory skill. When these 2 aspects blend together well, the supervisor is said to develop her own supervisory "style," something that is much more expansive and effective than the sum of its parts. The reflective questions at the end of the chapters and the case examples presented throughout are ways of encouraging you, the reader, to consider and experiment with defining and developing your supervisory style and voice so that you can become the most you can be.

The second theme is that clinical supervision is more than that move up to middle management and its new world of budgets, record compliance, and staffing. Clinical supervision is the application of a supervisor's clinical skills to a new population, namely, the clinicians she serves. This is not to say that supervision in any way becomes therapy, but rather that a supervisor's clinical skills in assessing individuals and finding creative ways for them to overcome and grow beyond their stuckpoints are part and parcel of her everyday role, and not to be pushed to the supervisory back burner.

Finally, the last message is that what drives good supervision is the same one that drove most of us into social work to begin with—that is, that we want to make a difference, we want to do good, and we want to make a positive impact on people's lives—and a good supervisor has the opportunity to do precisely that. Not only can he shape the workplace, but through his sensitivity and mentorship within the supervisory relationship, shape the clinician himself, and in turn, those whom the clinician sees and serves. The developmental model presented here is, I believe, a way of contouring and multiplying the potential power of this unique relationship.

In reflecting upon my own shaping over the years, I realize how much I am exceedingly indebted to both those who have served as my supervisors and those whom I have had the privilege of supervising. I am grateful to all of them for what they have taught and given me. I'd also like to thank the many reviewers of this project for their feedback during this manuscript process—Ruby Gourdine, Howard University; Lisa Jennings, California State University, Long Beach; Stacey Kolomer, University of Georgia; Anita Lightburn, Fordham University; and Linda Long-Mitchell, University of Georgia.

Get Connected with MySearchLab

Provided with this text, MySearchLab provides engaging experiences that personalize, stimulate, and measure student learning. Pearson's MyLabs deliver proven results from a trusted partner in helping students succeed.

Features available with this text include the following.

- A **complete eText**—Just like the printed text, you can highlight and add notes to the eText online or download it to your iPad.

- **Assessment**—Chapter quizzes, topic-specific assessment, and flash cards offer and report directly to your grade book.

- **Writing and Research Assistance**—A wide range of writing, grammar, and research tools and access to a variety of academic journals, census data, Associated Press newsfeeds, and discipline-specific readings help you hone your writing and research skills.

MySearchLab can be packaged with this text at no additional cost—just order the ISBN on the back cover. Instructors can also request access to preview MySearchLab by contacting your local Pearson sales representative or visiting www.mysearchlab.com.

1

The Challenges of Social Work Supervision

Competencies Applied with Practice Behaviors — in This Chapter				
☒ Professional Identity	■ Ethical Practice	☒ Critical Thinking	■ Diversity in Practice	■ Human Rights & Justice
■ Research-Based Practice	☒ Human Behavior	■ Policy Practice	■ Practice Contexts	■ Engage, Assess, Intervene, Evaluate

It's Monday morning, you're checking your voice mails, and you're already off to a rough start. The first message is from a supervisor at Social Services. She is calling to let you know that Tom, one of your seasoned staff, cancelled his home-based appointment with a family at the last minute on Friday, again. The family is getting annoyed and wants to stop therapy. Please call her. She's worried about what might happen with the family if they were without treatment. You're worried as well. Tom has been coming in late and has taken more sick time than usual lately. Something's going on. You make a mental note to call him and schedule a meeting.

The next message is from your boss left at 6 a.m. this morning—not a good sign. He needs your budget reworked again and wants you to shave down expenses by another 5%. He needs the new figures by 3 p.m. this afternoon. And, he says, rumor going around at the regional meeting last Friday was that there may be a surprise state records audit coming sometime this week—make sure your folks have their records up to speed. Oh, one more thing, he says almost as an afterthought, make sure there are fire escape maps posted in each of the halls in your section. It's a new requirement by the licensure folks. Ugh.

Finally there is message from Jodi, one of your newest staff. She wants to know if she can catch you early morning before she runs over to the clinic. And as you are listening to her message you see her pacing outside your office. Jodi has been on the job only a few months straight from graduate school. She's smart and energetic and anxious. She has seemed a bit stiff and formal in supervision so far, and has never before asked for any time outside of her weekly supervision time. While you're feeling a bit rushed for time, you decide it's important to support her reaching out and invite her into your office.

She begins by apologizing for bothering you and you assure her it's fine. What's up, you ask. Well, she wants to talk to you about a mother she has seen just a few times who needs help with parenting. Jodi's feeling frustrated. At the last 2 sessions the mom agreed to do the homework Jodi suggested—setting clear bedtimes and sticking to them, thinking about possible rewards for the kids' good behavior—but has followed through with none of it. And in the last session the mother several times made reference to Jodi's being single by making "since you don't have children"-type comments. Jodi admits that she didn't know how to respond and ignored the mother's comments.

You know how Jodi feels; you had been there yourself when you first started. You ask Jodi what she thinks is going on. She bites her lip. Probably, she says, the mom doesn't trust her because she seems young, and just because she is new. You nod in agreement but are thinking that her comment is also a possible parallel statement—that Jodi herself doesn't trust you yet—and make note to check this out with her later. You both start brainstorming ways of building trust and reducing the client's resistance, and you're pleased that Jodi is able to put her anxiety aside and initiate ideas. All of a sudden the fire alarm and lights start blaring and flashing, catching you in midsentence. "Let's go everyone—outside!" you hear Sue, the other supervisor, yell to her staff.

You quietly sigh. Yup, it's going to be one of the those days.

THE CHALLENGES OF CLINICAL SUPERVISION

Welcome to the world of clinical social work supervision. Not all days are like this, of course, and even this one may end up on a good note. What makes clinical social work supervision, particularly in an agency setting, both invigorating and meaningful, and at times frustrating and difficult, are its unique challenges. Some of the major ones will be outlined here, and discussed further in later chapters:

Balancing Quality Assurance with Staff Support

Number 1 on any supervisor's job description is ensuring high-quality clinical services. You hire social workers who have good clinical skills, and then continually monitor and evaluate their work and records to ensure that clients are effectively receiving the services they need. You are the enforcer of standards. Your position gives you the power to request, demand, and expect a certain level of performance, and you have the authority to fire someone who isn't able to comply. It is this part of your job that prompts you to talk to Tom about his cancellations.

But supervision is more than accountability and toughness. The other side of the supervisory coin is support, even nurturance, that comes in the form of teaching, listening, empathizing, and advising. You are the person clinicians, like Jodi, come to, to help them make sense of what they do. You are one they seek out when they feel confused, angry, or emotionally drained from the work. Whether you want to be or not, you are the resource and role model for how to be in the job. You create a unique professional relationship that works only if there is openness and trust on both sides.

And this is the challenge: the ability to successfully blend these complementary and at times seemingly conflicting roles of enforcer and supporter. Being a good supervisor is analogous in many ways to being a good parent, a good coach, a good leader. Like good clinical work it requires skill and art, clear thinking, and emotional sensitivity. It's this achieving and maintaining this balance that will be discussed throughout this book.

Representing Management While Advocating for Staff

As a clinical supervisor you are part of management, but at the same time you represent and advocate for your staff. You live in that middle zone where you selectively pass down information and directives from above, while staying alert to staff needs and selectively passing them up. It's another balancing act that requires both skill and sensitivity.

You're not alone, of course, in feeling caught in the middle. The director, for example, feels the same pulls—answering to the board of directors while advocating for the entire staff, representing the agency while weighing larger community needs and the always-changing political and fiscal currents. The confluence of all these dynamics creates a tension that moves up and down the organizational line, and one that you must be able to moderate.

Wearing Multiple Hats

Though your primary roles will center around clinical quality assurance (QA) and support, your daily tasks are likely to be much more than this—budget issues, performance evaluations, hiring new staff, maintaining staff morale, representing the agency or service on intra and interagency committees, doing public relations, and even the occasional interior design (moving cubbies, choosing chairs, deciding the location of new phone lines). Most of this was never covered in graduate school, nor are they tasks that you necessarily have any particular aptitude for, but they are part and parcel of your job, and you need to figure out how to do them. On a good day these tasks can provide you with welcomed variety; on others they seem like one more thing on your plate, and an unwelcomed distraction.

Professional Identity

Practice Behavior Example: *Practice personal reflection and self-correction to assure continual professional development.*

Critical Thinking Question: Supervisors must carry out a variety of roles. Reflecting on your past experience, how well are you able to transition among roles?

Supervising Staff at Different Levels

Jodi, with her limited experience and high anxiety, requires a different type of supervision than someone like Tom, who is more skilled and experienced. One size does not fit all. To be a good supervisor you need to be astute and flexible. You need to be able to accurately assess a clinician's needs, provide the type and level of support he requires, and adjust your style as the same clinician changes and grows over time. If you are doing the same things at Day 1 of supervision at Day 300, either your clinician is not going to grow or you're going to be left behind, and you certainly will not be effective in your role. Learning how to shift gears and determine the best type of supervision that is needed is what will be discussed in detail.

Supervising Staff You Didn't Hire

It's your first day on the job as supervisor, and you meet Janet who has been working at the agency for almost 25 years and is, in fact, counting down her time until retirement. Immediately, you sense that Janet is set in her ways—she's not open to new ideas; she seems to shake her head or ignore most of what you say. In her mind she's seen a lot of supervisors like you. She just wants to be left alone and finish out her time.

Because you usually inherit your staff rather than choosing them as you might in the corporate world, you're likely to have to work with folks like Janet. And if you are a relatively new supervisor, you might feel intimidated by her. She can remind a bit of your mother or mother-in-law. You find yourself walking on eggshells around her. There's a strong temptation to do what she wants, avoid the struggle, and leave her alone. Your challenge is to somehow override your anxiety, and approach, rather than avoid her, and build that professional relationship.

Understanding That Clinical Supervision Is More Than Being a Senior Clinician

It's always easier to stay within professional and personal comfort zones. This creates a particular challenge for new supervisors, and some established ones, who are struggling to make the shift from clinical work to clinical supervision. Rather than thinking like a supervisor and focusing on the needs of the clinician, they continue to think like clinicians and join with them and continue to focus on the needs of the clients. They are essentially doing therapy by proxy, shaping the treatment the way they see fit, rather than helping clinicians to utilize their unique skills and style to become creative change agents.

Although there certainly are parallels between clinical supervision and therapy, clinical supervision requires a very different mind-set and skill-set. While one of the goals of supervision is to ensure quality services

---

Critical Thinking

Practice Behavior Example: Analyze models of assessment, prevention, intervention, and evaluation.

Critical Thinking Question: If you were to develop a supervisory model based upon a clinical theory, how would your model look? What do you see as the greatest strength of your model? How would it shape the supervisory process?

to clients, it is the ineffective supervisor who makes the client her primary focus. Quality client services come only through the shaping of quality clinicians. For the supervisor it is the clinician who is now, in fact, her new client. The work happens not "out there," but in the room, within a dynamic supervisory relationship and session process.

MODELS OF CLINICAL SUPERVISION

Like clinical social work practice with its wide variety of treatment approaches geared toward helping clients meet the challenges of life, clinical supervision has its own array of models to help supervisors manage the challenges that they face. Bernard and Goodyear (2009) have catalogued 3 major approaches to clinical supervision: therapeutic, social role, and developmental models. Therapeutic supervisory models arise from the psychotherapeutic foundation upon which they are based. These include psychodynamic models (Frawley-O'Dea & Sarnat, 2001), person-centered models (Tudor & Worrall, 2004), cognitive-behavioral models (Ellis, 1989), and narrative models (Parry & Doan, 1994). In these models the principles of the therapy are applied to the supervision process itself. A psychodynamic supervisor, for example, might focus heavily on the nuances of the supervisor–supervisee relationship and its impact on the clinician–client relationship, while a cognitive approach would focus on supervisee cognitions and misperceptions.

Social role models, in contrast, focus on the roles that supervisors take—teacher, facilitator, consultant, administrator (Kadushin, 1992; Bernard, 1997)—or functions, such as advising, supporting, modeling, and evaluating. In these models the approach, rather than grounded in the therapeutic school, is grounded in the activities of the workplace and profession. Supervisory skills come in understanding when and how to shift roles to best meet the needs of the clinician.

Finally, developmental models look at professional development as moving through predictable stages. The Integrated Developmental Model of Stoltenberg, McNeill, and Delworth (1998), for example, maps out 4 developmental levels, each with their own characteristics and challenges and interventions by the supervisor. Other developmental models look at personal/professional change over the life span from untrained work with others to master clinician and supervisor (Ronnestad & Skovholt, 2003).

The model that will be followed falls heavily within the developmental camp and, like Integrated Developmental Model, has 4 stages each with their own characteristics, goals, tasks, and challenges. But the model also draws upon therapeutic models such as psychodynamic theory with its use of parallel process (Ekstein & Wallerstein, 1958), systems theory with its focus on patterns of interactions, and even transactional therapy with its use of the Karpman or Drama Triangle (Karpman, 1968), as well as incorporating social role theory by linking specific roles and functions to each of the 4 stages.

Table 1.1 provides an overview of the model that will be discussed. The following chapters will look more closely at each stage.

Table 1.1   **Overview of 4-Stage Model**

	Stage 1	Stage 2	Stage 3	Stage 4
Supervisory Role	Teacher	Guide	Gatekeeper	Consultant
Characteristics	*Know what don't know;* reactive; overwhelmed by content	*Don't know what know;* settling down; focus on process; more proactive	*Don't know what don't know;* blind spots; anger/power; counterdependence; loss/grief	*Know what know;* supervisor as peer/consultant; individuation/ integration
Goals	Develop trust and safety; reduce anxiety; assess skills; orient to agency and work	Manage session process; increase self-awareness; explore patterns	Exploration/ experimentation; maintain boundaries; awareness of style	Problem-solve cases; aware of strengths/ weaknesses; define/integrate professional role/ style
Tasks	Teaching skills; pairing/observing staff; develop supervisory plan	Role-playing; live observation and recordings; co-therapy; written exercises	Group supervision; supervisory training; teach adjunct approaches/extended learning	Expand job responsibilities; create leadership opportunities
Challenges and Dangers	Overresponsibility; spoon-feeding; remains anxious— rigidity/burnout; clinical incompetence	Encouraging dependency; impasses; blurred boundaries	Too confrontive; impatient; rebellious; dual relationships/ abuse of clients	Boredom/stale; inefficiency; blurred boundaries between supervisor and clinician

CORE PRINCIPLES OF THE 4-STAGE SUPERVISORY MODEL

The model that will be used is grounded in social work agency practice and, like any model, is based upon certain principles and assumptions. As you read these, compare and contrast them against your own.

Individuals Naturally Change and Grow Over Time

Your own personal life, and more importantly those of your supervisees, is never static; and if you are doing a good job, neither are your supervisees' professional lives. As they master skills, learn about themselves and their style, and face new challenges, their needs will be constantly changing.

Clinical supervision, therefore, needs to be dynamic. As was said earlier you can't provide the same supervision at Year 2 to Tom that you did at Year 1, nor the same supervision to Tom as to Jodi if you are to continue to meet your supervisees' needs. You need to be flexible and adapt your approach and focus to accommodate the moving psychological landscape: that is, the clinician. If you can't—if you try to fit everyone you supervise into the same box, if your response or approach is always the same one note—not only will you eventually feel frustrated and ineffective, but your supervisees will be tempted to roll their eyes and think at some point that what you have to say is no longer particularly relevant. They will look to others for support and clinical inspiration. Not only will the supervisory relationship wither, you will be effectively out of the administrative loop, and you will lose your ability to effectively do quality control.

Human Behavior

Practice Behavior Example: Know about human behavior across the life course; the range of social systems in which people live; and the ways social systems promote or deter people in maintaining or achieving health and well-being.

Critical Thinking Question: Social workers are sensitive to the way individuals change over the life course. Consider how you have changed the most in the past 5 years. The past year. How do these changes help you work with others?

We Can Map Individual Change Through Developmental Stages

Just as knowing the stages of their children's development helps parents put their children's behavior in context, anticipate what is to come, and support them in appropriately shifting gears, so too does your own knowledge of the stages of clinical development. It gives you lens through which you can view clinicians' behaviors, a way of evaluating the progression of your supervisory relationship. Just as a road map is no substitute for actually traveling the road, having the map and seeing what comes next can help reduce your anxiety by giving you something to hold on to when you fear that you are getting confused or lost in the supervisory process.

It Is Not Individuals Who Help Us Change, but Our Relationships with Those Individuals

You as a supervisor, by role, by job description, have clearly defined power. But as supervisor who has a good and valued relationship with those you supervise, your influence is increased a thousand-fold. Think about the people who have made a difference in your life—a grandparent or parent, a teacher, a coach—someone who inspired you, who saw potential that you could not, who encouraged you when you wanted to give up. It wasn't these individuals themselves who made the difference. It was the relationship they had with you. Their advice, their encouragement, only took hold because the relationship was safe and strong.

There has been much written in recent years about "bully bosses," and surveys over time have highlighted that one of the top reasons that people leave their jobs is because of poor relationships with their supervisors. Staff don't usually cite this as the reason for leaving. Instead, they will talk about higher salaries, or that the commute is killing their family life, and all this may be true. But the reason that they are looking for a new job at all is often connected to feeling unsupported, criticized, frustrated by their everyday relationship with their supervisor. You obviously can control only your half of a relationship, but in some ways yours is larger than half. It is your responsibility to do whatever you can to create a safe and sound relationship, one that is positive and encouraging, one that is sensitive to the clinician's changing needs, one that is based on honesty and openness so that if problems arise they can be addressed, rather than swept under the rug and ignored.

Individual and Relationship Change and Growth Happens Within the Process

Process versus content—it's an age-old split in the social work and clinical field—the river versus the flowing of the river, complaints versus the act of complaining, what versus how. As will be discussed throughout, process almost always trumps content as a clinical and supervisory focus because process is relationship in action. Where professional and personal relationships bog down, where problems truly become problems lies not in a poor solution—the content, the outcome—but in a faulty process, the means by which 2 people go about discussing and interacting around the problem. How they choose to talk about something is usually more important than what they ultimately talk about. How 1 person responds to what another person says, and how the other person, in turn, responds, determines the outcome. The process between 2 people is how relationships form and grow.

Your power as a supervisor, just like a clinician's power with a client, lies only in the room, right now, in the interactions between you both together. What happens after—what the clinician later does when she sees her client in her office, what her client does once he eventually gets home—you and the clinician have virtually no control over. What you can control is you. What you can help shape is what is unfolding immediately before you: the process. The content—what you say—is never the goal, but the means. It is how you affect and influence the person sitting across from you. Only by successfully managing the process do you create change.

This means that for you as a supervisor not only does the buck stop with you, but it starts with you as well. You need to be the one to set the pace, to initiate, monitor, and change the interactional patterns between you and the clinician. Because you're responsible for the quality of your interactions with your staff, you want to model honesty, clarity, and integrity so your staff can learn to do the same. You want to talk about the process itself—I'm feeling confused; you're quiet, did you just feel I was being critical; you sound angry just talking about it—rather than, like them, too easily getting lost in the content of details and facts, or worse yet, heaping on content as a way of masking and managing anxiety.

Your Professional and Personal Lives Always Overlap

In social work, unlike say computer repair or plumbing, problems and solutions are never cut and dried. Your own reactions are part of the mix, and despite your best efforts, objectivity becomes a relative term, and the lines between the personal and professional are always in danger of becoming blurred. Clinical theory not only provides a path for you to follow, but gives you something to hold onto to help you contain your personal reactions. Rather than objectifying and potentially dehumanizing your clients, your clinical lens helps prevent you from overhumanizing your role. It allows you to stay the empathic outsider who is better able to see the blind spots that clients cannot.

The same is true when providing clinical supervision. As supervisors you are always in danger of overidentifying with the clinician or the client, of losing perspective, and of undermining effective treatment and quality supervision. You need a supervisory model that can be leaned upon, one that gives you a consistent frame for both your reactions and those of your supervisees. Knowing, for example, the characteristics of the developmental stages helps you separate out what is common and normal in a Jodi or Tom from what is unique in them. Knowing yourself and using your clinical skills allows you to make sense of the unfolding dynamics of the relationship, and to fully utilize your personal strengths. The frame allows you to relax and move creatively within it.

The Supervisor's Challenge Is to Help Clinicians Be Flexible and Creative, and Develop Their Own Unique Styles

There's both a practical and a philosophical side of this goal. The practical side is that clinical flexibility allows you maximize the use of your staff. This is important, particularly in multiservice agencies. You want a generalist—someone who is able to work with Susan's families when she goes on maternity leave, as well as handle calls from Henry's geriatric clients when he is on vacation—rather than a specialist who is only comfortable working with depressed moms or men who have anger issues. This flexibility in staff and staffing allows you as a manager to deliver services effectively and efficiently.

Practically, you also want to help clinicians feel creative because it is this sense of creativity that leads to good staff morale. Just as staff often leave their jobs because of poor relationships with their supervisors, they also are prompted to leave when they feel that their skills and talents aren't being utilized. Unfortunately this is often an inherent danger in many work settings, namely, that while clinicians will grow with experience and your guidance, there are few career-ladder options. In order to help prevent your staff from feeling frustrated and clinically stagnated, your challenge is to find ways of putting their increasing talents and skills to use.

The more philosophical argument is linked to nature of the profession itself. Because clinical social work is not computer repair or plumbing, the use of self is at the heart of what makes the therapy process so unique and powerful. The best therapist is the one who is not only skillful, but able to combine these skills effectively with her unique personality and perspective. Just as clinicians work to empower and develop the talents of the clients they work with, your job is to provide the guidance and nurturance that clinicians need to transform the raw materials of knowledge, skill, and self into unique and effective clinical practice.

Critical Thinking

Practice Behavior Example: *Critical thinking augmented by creativity and curiosity.*

Critical Thinking Question: Social workers combine critical thinking with creativity. How does creativity play into your work?

Reaching these goals—of flexibility, creativity, uniqueness of style—all have at their core a willingness to take risks, to find the solutions that lie only outside comfort zones. But even in a profession built upon risk and change, taking risk can be a challenge for those new to the field. To help shape creative, empowered clinicians, you as a supervisor need to take the lead in creating opportunities for acceptable risk-taking. With your support and encouragement, you can help your clinicians move beyond their own bounds, and discover what lies within them.

These 6 principles will be discussed in more detail in the chapters to follow. Again, compare and contrast them with your own beliefs about supervision and clinical work.

GOALS OF THIS BOOK

It is hoped that this book will be a handbook to help you navigate the waters of clinical social work supervision. It deliberately does not have scores of references; it is not meant to be a comprehensive, survey-like text of the variety of models and research in the field. Its focus, instead, is on the practical and pragmatic, providing you with the thinking and tools to conduct effective, everyday clinical supervision in the workplace.

While clinical supervision is, like a cousin, related to therapy by the same deep roots, similar culture, and shared experiences, the overriding goal of your journey is to help you see clinical supervision as having a unique mind-set with its own important purpose. Good supervision is more than supportive listening, more than mundane record-checking, more than prudent advice-giving. The good supervisor, like the good clinician, utilizes particular skills, but has honed those skills upon the strength of her personality and innate talents. She is also able to use the fullness of herself, is willing to enter the process and take risks, and sees as the ultimate goal not only good social work, but the evolution of what one can become and be.

One of the primary goals of this book is to present you with a model of clinical supervision that you can use as a map of what is to come, how to think about it, and most importantly how to respond. A 4-stage developmental model of clinical supervision that defines the clinical challenges, goals, tasks, and challenges of each stage will be presented. The overriding premise is that if you know what to expect, you can change your supervisory approach to meet the clinician's changing needs.

The other equally important goal is to help you think about, and ultimately develop, your own supervisory style. Just as it is valuable for the good clinician to meld theory, skills, and personal strengths into a cohesive clinical style, it is important that the clinical supervisor do the same. It is hoped that through case examples and critical thinking questions you will take the opportunity to compare your own thinking to what is described, to consider your own principles, values, and priorities, and to become more clear about your own supervisory approach.

Finally, the last goal of this book is to provide you practical information about navigating the practical aspects of doing the work of a clinical supervisor. Management skills, the everyday tasks of a supervisor—handling evaluations, hiring and firing, liability and ethical issues, record-keeping, time management—those aspects of job that make the difference between feeling satisfied and empowered and feeling deflated and discouraged will be discussed.

BOOK FORMAT

The book is essentially divided into 3 parts. In the first we will look at some core concepts that will serve as a foundation for discussing other aspects of the model. Specifically we'll talk about the 3 primary ways of managing anxiety, the concept and application of parallel process, and a presentation of the Relationship Triangle and its usefulness in understanding personality traits of many clinicians, as well as the development of the supervisory relationship over time. We'll also talk about learning styles and common leadership styles and their strengths and weaknesses.

With this foundation in place we will then move on to exploring the 4-stage developmental model. We'll look at each stage one at a time, explore their characteristics, the supervisory goals and tasks, their challenges and dangers. We'll also be following the development of one social work clinician as she moves through each stage to illustrate her changing thinking and focus over time. After covering this broad terrain, we will discuss specific tools and techniques to use in supervision, as well as look more closely at the unfolding and management of the supervisory process itself.

In the last section we'll discuss the practical issues of the work—time management, the use of group supervision, the format and process of supervisory sessions, the use of specific supervisory techniques, the fine line between supervision and therapy, the challenges of new supervisors, supervising interns, evaluations, record-keeping, the hiring, accountability, and firing process, liability, and ethical issues. Finally, we'll close with some suggestions on self-care for the supervisor.

Along the way you will find case examples and stories that illustrate the ideas and hopefully help you bring them into your work, and many of the critical thinking questions are aimed at helping you begin to become aware of your assumptions, values, strengths, and challenges as you begin the process of supervising others. Hopefully, you may be surprised at what you may discover.

Let's begin our journey.

The following questions will test your application and analysis of the content found within this chapter. For additional assessment, including licensing-exam-type questions on applying chapter content to practice behaviors, visit **MySearchLab.**

1. The 3 primary models of clinical social supervision are
   a. Cognitive, psychodynamic, solution-focused
   b. Administrative, supportive, educational
   c. Therapeutic, social role, developmental
   d. Developmental, psychodynamic, behavioral

2. Following a social role model of clinical supervision a supervisor would focus on
   a. Changes in the clinician's growth over time
   b. Successfully moving between administrative, supportive, clinical aspects of her job
   c. Having the supervisory framework parallel that of the clinician's therapeutic focus
   d. Characteristics and challenges as the clinician moves through stages

3. Sam seems hesitant and uncomfortable in supervisory sessions. If you decide to focus on the session process you would
   a. Say to Sam that he seems to be feeling uncomfortable with you
   b. Ask Sam to describe his new cases
   c. Ask Sam what topics he feels he needs training on
   d. Not say anything and let him start the session

4. In her session with Tom, Susan, the supervisor, empathizes with him over a difficult case he is struggling with, but also brings up the fact that his paperwork is late. This is an example of
   a. Distinguishing between policy and procedure
   b. Balancing needs for QA with supervisory support
   c. Being an appropriate buffer between upper management and staff
   d. Making productivity more important than the quality of the supervisory relationship

5. Several clinicians on your staff are complaining that the new agency forms are too confusing and cumbersome. How would you respond?

6. As a new supervisor you are supervising John, an experienced clinician, who comes to supervision late and shows little interest in engaging with you. How would you handle this?

2

Laying the Foundation—Part 1

Competencies Applied with Practice Behaviors — in This Chapter				
■ Professional Identity	■ Ethical Practice	✖ Critical Thinking	■ Diversity in Practice	■ Human Rights & Justice
■ Research-Based Practice	✖ Human Behavior	■ Policy Practice	✖ Practice Contexts	✖ Engage, Assess, Intervene, Evaluate

Chapters 2 and 3 will introduce and describe several core concepts; subsequent chapters will talk more fully about their application. You'll find that many of these concepts are interrelated and overlap with each other. Think of them as lenses through which you can view various aspects of the supervisory process. Some, like learning and anxiety-coping styles, help you assess a clinician, anticipate her needs and potential challenges within the supervisory relationship, as well as measure developmental change over time. Others, like leadership styles and aspects of the parallel process, offer you a means of both setting your own goals and tracking your own impact upon a clinician and the larger team. Finally, the Relationship Triangle model provides a visual map of the interconnecting and changeable relationship roles of both supervision and clinical work, and points to the place where the supervisor–clinician relationship should ultimately land.

We'll be covering a lot of ground. Don't worry about trying to absorb it all right now, but instead see what concepts resonate with you and which ideas may be most useful to you in your thinking and work.

Let's start with the first concept: anxiety-coping styles.

ANXIETY-COPING STYLES

Whether it's navigating through some new software for the first time, anticipating an upcoming job interview, or getting up the nerve to tell your mother that you won't be coming home for Christmas this year, anxiety is part and parcel of everyday life. We start here because understanding the way a clinician and a supervisor manage anxiety is key to creating a solid supervisory relationship, as well as helping clinicians learn and master new skills and overcome their own emotional stuckpoints.

Everyone has his own way of coping with anxiety, but some ways of coping are better than others. In *Coping With Conflict: Supervising Counselors and Psychotherapists*, Mueller and Kell (1972) describe 3 broad anxiety-coping styles: approaching, avoiding, and binding.

Anxiety Approachers

People who are anxiety approachers, as the name suggests, are able to move ahead in spite of feeling anxious. And they are aware of feeling the anxiety—they are not the nerves of steel, tough-guy characters that we see in movies who never seem to feel much of anything but anger. Approachers feel it, but are not overwhelmed or intimidated by the feeling itself. Even though working with the software, thinking about an interview, or picking up the phone to call their mother can stir the butterflies inside, approachers also have learned that working slowly with an online tutorial they can figure it out, that 5 minutes into an interview they will settle down, and that planning in advance what to say to their mother and having a plan to help her calm down will ensure that the call will go all right.

Anxiety, approachers have learned, comes with learning something new, with working through a problem. Once they get over the peak of the learning curve, once they take action and do something to solve the problem, the anxiety goes away. It's the ability to feel comfortable enough with feeling uncomfortable that allows anxiety approachers to take acceptable risks, move out of their comfort zones, be creative, and grow. Learning to manage anxiety in this way is the key to building self-esteem and confidence.

Anxiety Avoiders

For anxiety avoiders the feeling of anxiety is not a by-product of a problem; it is the problem. They feel overwhelmed by the emotion, and again as the term suggests, their instincts are to avoid it. They get rattled by the software and shut off the computer, or decide to just give up and go back to the older program. Avoiders lie in bed obsessing about the interview and decide to cancel the interview, often rationalizing that they probably won't get the job anyway. Rather than having that difficult conversation with their mother, they skip it, and either go for Christmas after all, drinking heavily while they are there, or call at the last minute and say they have the flu. Anxiety has the ability to stop them in their tracks. They either back away from the situations creating it, or find ways, such as drugs or alcohol, to stomp the feeling down.

Many therapy clients present with anxiety-avoiding way of coping. For example, they get the electric bill and start ruminating about money. Rather than calling the company or looking for ways to pay the bill, they lay the bill on the pile, not wanting to deal with it, and then go into crisis when their lights are turned off. Or, if their boss looks over their shoulder and criticizes them all day long, rather than being able to be assertive and speaking up to their boss, or going to the human resources department and see if HR can help with the problem, they say nothing, but drink a pint of bourbon when they get home from work.

In therapy they talk about their nerves, look for medication to calm themselves down, and cancel the next appointment if they feel you have pushed them too hard to try something different that leaves them feeling overwhelmed. They lack skills, but more so they lack self-confidence. Their anxiety, and their attempts to avoid it, runs their lives.

Anxiety Binders

Unlike approachers, who acknowledge feeling anxious but talk about solutions as well, or avoiders, who feel anxious, always look flustered, and just don't know what to do next, binders don't feel anxiety. Their tools are control, rigidity, and intellectualization, and with these they have learned how to essentially cut anxiety off before it arises. In potentially anxiety-producing conversations they may change the subject, or tune out what is being said. Their lives may follow tight, rigid routines. In relationships they seem gently but persistently controlling—keeping a sharp eye and tight rein on those around them. Binders are described by others as heady or unemotional. They essentially are not anxious because they never stray from their comfort zone and preemptively keep anxiety at bay.

> ### Engage, Assess, Intervene, Evaluate
>
> **Practice Behavior Example:** *Assess client strengths and limitations.*
>
> **Critical Thinking Question:** Think about the clients you are working with. What are their anxiety-coping styles?

ANXIETY AND RELATIONSHIPS

Should these differing anxiety-coping styles come together in relationships, each will influence the other. Here are the possible combinations.

Approach/Approach

Two approachers would in theory at least have the best of relationships. Imagine, for example, Steve Jobs and Steven Wozniak, the 2 founders of Apple Inc. With just a shared vision they were able to feed off of each other's enthusiasm and creativity to together develop something totally new; they were both able to take risks to work together and solve problems as they arose. In everyday relationships—solid marriages, good friendships—2 approachers are able to communicate clearly, be intimate, and solve problems together so that both the individuals and the relationship can continue to grow.

Approach/Avoid

The avoider sees the approacher as trying to make his life miserable. Just as the avoider gets settled into a comfortable pattern, the approacher is likely to try something new or bring up a topic that the avoider would rather not hear. When problems arise, the approacher talks about forging ahead, while the avoider gets nervous and would rather lie low or retreat. For some avoiders, approachers, with their "let's-do-it" attitude, make the relationship feel too overwhelming for them, and avoiders find reasons to leave.

But approachers can help avoiders learn to become approachers. The key for the approacher is pacing—encouraging the avoider to take small risks that are slightly challenging, but not overwhelming. By mastering these babysteps, the avoider can slowly gain courage and break out of old patterns. If the approacher can be a good role model—talking about his own anxiety while demonstrating how approaching does not lead to the deadly consequences that the avoider images—the avoider's perspective can change.

Over time the avoider can learn that anxiety decreases with action, that self-esteem improves with gradual mastery and success. This is what good parents do with their child who is shy or inherently cautious—support and encourage taking small steps to just "try it." This is what good teachers or coaches do when they challenge students to take a risk and attempt something new and different.

Approach/Bind

This is a difficult match. The approacher often feels frustrated by the binder's control, routines, or rationalizations, and always feels held back or dismissed. The binder tends to perceive the approacher as foolhardy or impulsive, and may use control to change or corral the approacher. Sometimes this combination is seen in client families in which a rebellious teenager goes head-to-head with parents who are highly rational and subtly controlling. Such relationships often flounder—the approacher eventually leaves, while the binder shakes his head in pity or amusement.

Avoid/Avoid

These 2 individuals tend to go around in circles as each scrambles to avoid anxiety. Either new relationships may never get off the ground because both are playing defense, or their mutual sense of helplessness and fear may provide a common link. In long-standing relationships stability is achieved by both joining around a "you and me against the world" stance of mutual distrust and hypervigilance against the outside world, or through "protection pacts," where one person protects the other by creating a distraction when sensing that the other is becoming anxious.

This is often seen clinically in marital and family relationships. A husband, for example, in a family session may start complaining about his bad back immediately after the clinician asks his anxious wife about sex, or a child may knock over a picture on a bookcase when his mother begins to cry. A couple may have an unspoken list of anxiety-producing topics that they agree to avoid—money, a past affair, the death of a child, drinking bouts, illnesses—and another more "comfortable" problem—Johnny's poor schoolwork—may be used as a way to decrease tension when these taboo problems threaten to surface. Again the challenge is providing support while moving toward these anxiety-producing topics so that they can be successfully resolved.

Avoid/Bind

It's easy for an avoider to be seduced by a binder's sense of control and calm. Here is someone, thinks the avoider, who can provide the security and relief he has been looking for. The binder, on his side, feels needed and validated in his stance. Although this relationship may function well for a while, eventually it begins to crumble. The binder over time tires of the avoider's emotionality and helplessness, and responds with greater control, which in turn feels like pressure for the avoider that increases his anxiety, increasing more the binder's control. The cycle deepens. The avoider eventually leaves the relationship, often finding a new binder, with whom the relationship patterns are established again.

Bind/Bind

From an outside perspective such relationships lack emotionality, energy, or intimacy. They seem routinized, superficial, and dull. From within they are stable and conflict-free as long as each person's areas of control don't infringe on the other's. Again this can be seen in marriages where each partner has a defined role and domain—for example, one handles work and money, while the other handles kids and social events. Anxiety and conflict are kept at bay as long as boundaries and responsibilities are respected, and routines stay the same.

While this model is useful in helping you think about anxiety management in an organized way, you shouldn't assume that people are one way or another. There are gradations, and the nuances on one's style are shaped by personality. Most people generally identify with one mode over another, but with enough stress may slip toward the second. Carla, for example, may be in the approacher mode both at work and at home—creative and energetic—but when her husband suddenly gets laid off from his job or her boss pressures her to resolve budget problems by next week, she may feel overwhelmed and find herself drinking more at home, or calling in sick to work. Similarly, Tom's style may be one of binding, filled with routine and control, but when his father suddenly is diagnosed with a terminal illness, he emotionally falls apart and seems unable to make any decisions on the job.

ANXIETY AND THE CLINICIAN

How does this model help supervisors? First, good supervisors are anxiety approachers. Through their example and willingness to approach difficult issues, they are able to move the supervisory process and relationships into more challenging areas. This role-modeling supports clinicians in learning new skills, encourages them to clinically think on their feet, and helps them avoid the passivity or control of avoiders or binders.

Applicants who are anxiety approachers are easy to recognize in job interviews. They are able to talk openly about their anxiety and spontaneously about their emotions. Although they may start the interview stiffly or formally, within a few minutes their natural spontaneity takes over and they appear more relaxed. They are likely to acknowledge their own stress—I'm a bit nervous—then productively move on. If asked a difficult question, they may think out loud, rather than give a pat answer. They are able to be in the moment. They are aware of and able to articulate their strengths and weaknesses. In a phrase, they have good self-esteem. The interviewer is likely to feel stimulated by the interview process.

Those who lean toward anxiety-avoiding will, if not completely overwhelmed, vacillate between bursts of self-confidence and anxiety during an interview. On the job they may be easily rattled, frequently coming to you, like Jodi did in Chapter 1, wringing their hands—"You won't believe what Jason just told me." If a crisis erupts, they may avoid returning calls from clients or put off appointments until they can get some advice, hoping secretly that things will blow over. If the supervisor is able to be supportive, help avoiders think through ways to approach the problem, and encourage them to take acceptable risks, they, like Jodi, can gain skills, learn to trust themselves, and become less avoidant, more approaching.

Those who bind their anxiety may initially impress you in interviews with their intelligence and calmness. Ask them about their clinical approach and they'll likely have a clear model and may even cite research and other facts to back up their thinking. If you hire them, their lack of spontaneity over time becomes apparent. Binders may resist new ideas from you, and in supervisory sessions may keep a tight rein on the process. If you ask a question about reactions or feelings, or make any attempt to penetrate their defenses, you may hear the right words but not feel the right emotion. If pressed harder, they may steer the conversation toward a theoretical discussion, or if all else fails, they claim to be confused.

In sessions with clients binders may have a list of questions in their heads or on paper, and nothing short of an earthquake will derail them from their agenda. They don't listen well, and clients will be quietly ignored if their issues aren't linked to what binders want to pursue. Binders may terminate with those clients who don't seem to prescribe to the approach they have in mind, or both clinician and client will settle into a bind/bind relationship where nothing of real substance is discussed. Fortunately, few binders make it through graduate school in social work. They may be weeded out in fieldwork, or decide that they disagree with some aspect of the therapy process and move to another career track.

Identifying a clinician's primary approach to anxiety is an important starting point in the supervisory assessment. You can begin by asking yourself the following basic questions during initial interviews and during the first weeks of supervision:

- Can this person take risks? Does he look forward to new experiences and challenges?
- Is this person aware of and able to acknowledge his anxiety?
- Is this person able to solve problems and apply skills and knowledge in new situations?
- Can this person listen well to others and take the initiative in supervisory and clinical sessions without attempting to control the process?
- Do I feel comfortable with and stimulated by this person, or do I feel overwhelmed, bored, frustrated, or closed?

Answers to these questions can help you know where to focus your attention, how quickly the supervisee can tackle new tasks and move in new directions, and anticipate the dangers and challenges that may lie ahead. Again, these concepts will be discussed further as we move through the developmental stages.

LEARNING STYLES

If you think of anxiety coping as the underpinning that runs the entire length of the supervisory structure, learning styles can be thought of as the next layer up. Understanding the way a clinician learns best obviously is important in the teaching aspects of your supervisory role, and essential for clinician success. Learning styles not only reflect how a clinician takes in and processes new information, but also reflect the way personalities and approaches—the clinician's and your own—combine to create helpful or unhelpful teaching experience. Two models that you may find useful will be briefly discussed.

Dziuban/Long Model

The Dziuban/Long model (Dziuban & Dziuban, 1997; Long, 1985) differentiates learning along 2 axes: aggressive/passive and independent/dependent. Aggressive/passive refers to the energy the individual brings to learning, while independent/dependent refers to the need for approval and control. Here are each of the combinations and their implications for supervision.

Aggressive/Independent

Aggressive and independent learners are energized and self-starting. They are quick to take action and approach anxiety. They are strong leaders. This is how you ideally want to be as a supervisor and leader, and this is what you look for in your clinicians. Aggressive/independent learners take the acceptable risks necessary for their own clinical and personal growth. Their assertiveness and self-confidence translates into their being open and honest with you regarding their needs and complaints. Their ability to embrace change can in turn inspire clients to do the same. It's easy to see the similarity between them and anxiety approachers.

Aggressive/Dependent

These individuals also have high energy and can be leaders. They differ from their counterparts in that they are more apt to seek out and need approval as part of learning process, and are more inclined to be self-critical. This self-criticism—coupled with a tendency toward perfectionism—can make them cautious. Rather than taking acceptable risks, they become concerned about doing what is right.

This need of aggressive/dependent learners for approval and their sensitivity to you as supervisor means that you need to provide lots of positive feedback to both build a safe and nurturing relationship between you, and help them override their internal critic. As you would for an anxiety avoider, you can help them learn to take acceptable risks by titrating challenges and providing praise for their effort rather than the outcome. Your challenge is to help them lower their internal chatter and expand their comfort zone so that they can approach anxiety more readily.

Passive/Independent

The combination of passivity and independence means that these learners are less initiating, more reactive, and have lower energy, yet want control. The result is that they can quickly view authority in a negative way, especially when feeling micromanaged or pushed to do something they don't want to do and feel that their independence is threatened. In such situations they are apt to seem stubborn or resistant. Under stress they can become withdrawn or inactive.

Needless to say, these individuals can be a real challenge for supervisors. It's easy for you to feel that you always are walking on eggshells around them and need to be careful. Don't. You do want to be sensitive to their needs and fears, but not have them dictate the relationship. The key is to view resistance or withdrawal as red flags letting you know that the clinician is feeling threatened, needs more control, or is stressed. Rather than stepping down, step up, and talk about the problem.

If John, for example, dismisses your suggestions for handling a case, ask if he feels you are being too dictatorial or directive. Explain to him your concerns, reasoning, and intentions; reassure him that you are not taking over his case, but trying to help him think about it differently. If he is getting behind in his paperwork, turn the conversation toward whether he is feeling stressed, while still setting your own deadlines. Your goal is to help John see your role as less negative and more neutral. Link your interventions to his stated goals. Appeal to his rational voice, rather than his reactive one, but do not reward his negativity by giving in. Ideally, however, you want to help John define, understand, and develop his own style, and agree to make this development a front-burner issue of your supervisory relationship. For him to be able to say that he is feeling pushed or stressed, rather than acting out around it, makes for a more open and healthy relationship.

Passive/Dependent

Like those who are aggressive and dependent, these learners too thrive on affection and approval. They too are reactive rather than proactive, are sensitive to others, but rather than digging in or withdrawing, are apt to do more than is required, potentially setting themselves up for burnout. We could imagine them doing well where their responsibilities are clear and relatively routine—working, for example, as case manager where more monitoring is called for than a variety of creative options. Your challenge is help them be more proactive. State this as a goal for supervision: You can please me by doing less of what you think I want and more of what you want to do. Anytime they show signs of independence, give them lots of positive feedback. As with anxiety avoiders, your own modeling of self-confidence and independence is powerful with these clinicians. Over time they can learn to be more initiating.

As with anxiety-coping styles, this model of learning styles can be a useful tool that can help you assess the needs of those you supervise. Ask yourself how independent your supervisees are in their own learning, how much they seek approval, how resistant they are to authority, how self-critical they are of themselves. Bring their style of learning to the forefront of the relationship, so you can best anticipate and accommodate their needs.

✗†✗

Human Behavior

Practice Behavior Example: *Utilize conceptual frameworks to guide the processes of assessment, intervention, and evaluation.*

Critical Thinking Question: Applying the Dziuban/Long model to yourself, how would you characterize your own learning style? How does it affect your work?

Neurolinguistic Programming and Learning

Another paradigm of learning is that based on neurolinguistic programming (NLP). Originally developed in the 1970s by Bandler and Grinder (1979), this approach states that people perceive the world visually, auditorily, or kinesthetically. Visual learners think in terms of images and best learn through diagrams and pictures, PowerPoint presentations, and highly descriptive stories that can create images in their minds. They use the language of seeing in their speech—I see what you mean; What I envision is. . . . When asked a question, their eyes move upward as though they are looking at the ceiling. If you have clinicians who have this style of learning, you want to use visual language as they do, and draw pictures and create visual images.

Auditory learners literally think in terms of words rather than images. They appreciate lectures, and they use the language of hearing in their speech—I hear what you are saying; It sounds to me like. . . . When asked a question, their eyes tend to move slightly to the side rather than up or down. If you are working with clinicians who are auditory learners, feel free to use the lecture approach and use "hearing" words and phrases.

Finally, kinesthetic learners are those who respond to feelings and sensory touch. They learn from hands-on experiences, and they use the language of emotions and touch in their speech—This feels like a good idea; I think I can handle this. When asked a question, their eyes move downward as though they are looking at the floor. With these clinicians make learning experiential—role-plays, cotherapy—and talk the language of feelings and touch.

You can often discern someone's learning style with this model right away, even in a job interview by watching their eye movements and use of language. And if you are talking to a group—a staff meeting, for example—or giving a presentation, use all 3 modes—lecture, PowerPoint with diagrams, experiential exercises—as a way of including all types of learners.

Understanding a clinician's learning style not only makes you a more effective teacher, but helps build rapport and strengthens the relationship. Make a clinician's learning style a topic of discussion at the start, asking interviewees, for example, how they learn best, and by checking in with them in those first few months whether your style of teaching and theirs of learning are a good match.

LEADERSHIP STYLES

While anxiety-coping and learning styles help you understand the clinician, leadership styles help you learn about you—the various roles and styles supervisors may take. Think about your past supervisors and managers, as well as your own personality and possible style as we discuss the different types of leadership styles.

Drill Sergeant

Joan exemplifies all the traits of the drill sergeant leadership style. She runs a tight ship; she on top of what is going on among her team members. She wants weekly updates of their caseload status, she checks case records on a regular basis to see that they are up-to-date, and she issues out weekly emails to staff with reminders about productivity requirements and budget updates. Some would call her a micromanager, and she is in control of herself and others. In supervision she is directive, more inclined to suggest what she feels is best in a case, rather than letting clinicians fumble around on their own.

Practice Context

Practice Behavior Example: *Provide leadership in promoting sustainable changes in service delivery and practice to improve the quality of social services.*

Critical Thinking Question: Social workers provide leadership in promoting change. What does leadership mean to you?

Supervisors like her often seem like anxiety binders in their sense of rigidity and rationality. Communication and expectations are clear and detail-oriented. Their stern manner and little nurturance can be intimidating for those whose learning styles are aggressive/dependent or passive/dependent. Those who are passive/independent can become passive/aggressive in the face of such control, while those who are aggressive/independent can feel constrained and eventually leave the job. Morale can clearly suffer under such leaders, and as with all these styles, there is a danger of clinicians either mimicking the supervisor and treating clients in the same way, or overreacting and going to the other extreme—one of permissiveness, passivity, and blurred boundaries.

Mother Hen

Louis' supervisory style could not be more different than Joan's. In place of Joan's stern control, confrontation, and low emotionality, Louis is warm and nurturing with staff. He easily talks about emotions, tries to avoid confrontation, worries when clinicians are struggling with a difficult case, and advocates strongly for them to those higher up. He is well loved by his staff.

The term *mother hen* is not meant to be pejorative of mothers (or hens) and can be found equally among male and female supervisors. Often the boundaries between supervisor and staff are soft—supervisor and staff go out for drinks on Friday after work, and staff know all details of the supervisor's private life. Problems can arise, however, as clinicians become more skilled and independent, and begin to outgrow this type of supervisor. They begin to feel smothered and dramatically pull away or actually leave, but these emotions and changes are never directly dealt with by either side. Neither wants to hurt the other's feelings.

The biggest issue that arises with mother hen supervisors is their difficulty seeing themselves as part of middle management. Because they ally themselves with their line staff, they may portray upper management as insensitive or uncaring at times. Rather than setting firm limits with staff, as the drill sergeant might, they resist, undermining upper management decisions.

Inconsistent

David's staff brace themselves for each staff meeting, awaiting the "hot topic" of the week. One week David is going on about productivity and billing, the next excited about a new clinical approach that he heard about at a state meeting, other times concerned about ways of improving communication among staff. Most staff go along with the latest topic, knowing that it will quickly be replaced by another; others roll their eyes and wait for this storm to pass. Others are frustrated—one week he tells the staff to contact him by email if they have concerns but never answers them, other times suggests leaving phone messages but isn't dependable about responding.

Inconsistent supervisors like David, as the term suggests, tend to be inconsistent in both their approach and their messages to staff. They are reactive, usually to those above them, rather than proactive and deliberate. They may move, for example, from drill sergeant type of micromanagement to mother hen type of support, to almost neglect depending upon the biggest demands on their time. Their staff understandingly become confused and frustrated, and some may push limits as a way of determining boundaries and limits. Anxious learners feel even more anxious because there is no real stability and reliability, while those more assured get tired of dealing with the supervisor's erratic behavior, and go around him, seeking support from coworkers or other supervisors.

Crisis-Oriented

Unlike inconsistent supervisors who seem to be flitting about and anxious, crisis-oriented supervisors are quickly able to focus and take charge when emergencies arise. In fact, they thrive in those environments, and are excellent role models for that type of work. But once the crisis is over, they tend to lapse into boredom. The day-to-day routine lacks enough stimulation, and there may be lack of follow-through on bureaucratic tasks—records aren't checked, supervisory sessions seem undynamic. The biggest danger is that their stance filters down to staff. Clinicians who are crisis-oriented may encourage clients to terminate treatment once their personal crises are over, rather than moving into middle stages of treatment. New, inexperienced staff who lack a strong clinical foundation can easily feel overwhelmed and undersupported by a crisis-oriented supervisor.

Neglectful

John used to be an engaged and supportive supervisor. But in the past few years as he moves closer to retirement, he realizes that he is essentially tired and coasting. In addition, his adult son has been struggling in his own life lately, and John finds himself preoccupied by this. Essentially, he is doing what he needs to get by, and reluctantly at that.

Like a neglectful parent, this type of supervisor provides little supervision, and staff are essentially left on their own. Sometimes such supervisors have serious difficulties with relationships in general, or feel over their heads in terms of job requirements, and rather than asking for help or seeking training, they lie low and try and get by. Others, like John, are burned out and coasting, sometimes they are preoccupied by their own personal issues and emotions. In their own minds they may rationalize that staff are okay, that they don't need more.

Like siblings with a neglectful parent, the staff learn to take care of themselves, internalize their own frustration and anger, and may find others supervisors as supports. Again, clinicians may pass this style down to their clients, or overreact and do too much.

Balanced

Like the anxiety approacher or aggressive/independent learner, this is the ideal type. These supervisors have what the others lack, namely flexibility. They are able to nurture and support yet confront and set limits when needed. They can effectively handle crises yet stay on top of the day-to-day needs. They can advocate for their staff yet are always aware that they are part of middle management. While able to appropriately use self-disclosure, they are conscious of the hierarchy that is in place. Their individual relationships with staff are proactive, rather than reactive, based on and anticipating each clinician's particular and changing needs. They are creative and resist adopting a one-size-fits-all approach. Clinicians learn to do the same with their own clients.

The balanced style of leadership is what we'll be using as our model throughout. As with anxiety styles, there are gradations, and primary and secondary modes depending on stress and time. A primarily balanced supervisor, for example, may, with enough personal or professional stress, become preoccupied and neglectful, burned out and authoritarian, inconsistent and erratic, but then return to her healthier baseline once the stress abates.

Some supervisors are able to change their styles over time. Those who start out as drill sergeants, for example, may over time soften and become more balanced as they gain experience and skills, feel more secure and less anxious, or receive effective and supportive supervision from their own supervisors. Mother hen supervisors may through personal experience, therapy, or good supervision, learn to confront others and come to see themselves as middle managers. Inconsistent managers can through good role models and coaching learn to be more proactive and less scattered, while crisis-oriented supervisors can discover a different type of challenge and stimulation in the more mundane. Again, think about the leadership styles you have experienced and their impact on your own clinical and supervisory work.

PARALLEL WORLDS

Jim knocks on your door and he looks visibly upset. "Can I talk to you for a minute?"

Jim has just finished a session with Ms. Jones and it did not go well. Her son, Thomas, had cut school again; she was worried that she was going to get laid off from her job; and then on top of all this, social services showed up at her door saying that someone had complained that she was leaving the children home unsupervised. The client was overwhelmed and angry.

"And when I tried to support her and just listen to what she was saying, she then turns on me and says, 'And what good is it for me to come here? This isn't helping, things are getting worse, not better!' Then I got angry; I really didn't know what to say."

Jim sounds angry as he says this. How do you respond?

In their classic text, *The Teaching and Learning of Psychotherapy* (1958), Ekstein and Wallerstein first presented the concept of parallel process. They represented it like this:

S _____ T

T _____ C

This represents 2 separate but interlocking relationships: therapist/client relationship and, above it, supervisor/therapist relationship. The 2 relationships run parallel to each other with the therapist representing the common link between them. According to the parallel process model, the way the client presents to the therapist is often how the therapist will present to the supervisor.

This is what Jim is now doing in supervision. Ms. Jones is in crisis feeling overwhelmed and angry, and when Jim talks about it, he too begins to sound like her—overwhelmed and angry. We have all seen this dynamic at some point in our everyday lives—a husband is criticized and berated by his boss, he comes home and yells at his wife, who then begins to yell at the kids. The emotions move down the line of relationships.

What does this tell us about the way the supervisor needs to respond to Jim? She needs to respond to Jim the way Jim ideally needs to respond to Ms. Jones, namely to continue to actively listen and empathize so he can calm down. The supervisor's realization that parallel process is occurring helps the supervisor stop the emotional reactions from going further and distorting the relationships. Good supervision trickles down to become good therapy.

Because of the power of parallel process, a less-alert supervisor could inadvertently fuel the process. Rather than remaining supportive and clearheaded, suppose the supervisor herself gets upset—she panics and worries about Jim's overall performance, or that Ms. Jones might escalate and threaten legal action against the agency. This might create a situation where the supervisor, rather than stopping the emotional buck, passes it upward. She goes to her supervisor in crisis, which then ignites her supervisor, who then passes the emotions up the organizational chain. Instead of calming the emotional waters they intensify, making effective problem-solving difficult. When everyone up and down the line becomes emotionally reactive, the agency system itself becomes crisis-oriented.

But parallel process does not only move from the bottom up—client to therapist to supervisor—but it also moves from the top down. Let's look at this diagram:

SS _____ S

S _____ T

T _____ C

C _____ Family

Suppose, for example, you go to a directors meeting at 9 a.m. and your supervisor starts off the meeting by talking about the budget deficit. He's upset and begins barking at everyone about clients' unpaid bills, and large number of no-shows. He ends the meeting insisting that everyone talk to their staff and ensure that clinicians are following up with clients about fees and appointments. You leave the meeting shaken and upset. You have a scheduled meeting with your staff at 2 p.m. that afternoon, and essentially you replicate your supervisor's behaviors—angrily bringing up the budget and insisting that everyone hold clients more responsible for their bills and appointments. The clinicians leave the meeting upset. What's likely to happen when they meet with their clients that afternoon?

It would be easy for these dynamics to be replicated. Rather than having a calm but assertive discussion with clients about their bills, staff could sound like the supervisor did, and like them leave clients feeling agitated. It's not hard to imagine clients going home and taking out these emotions on their families. Again, it is the power of parallel process that, just as it does for families, can come to shape an agency culture—rather than being proactive and responsible, an organization can tend toward crisis, disorganization, and overreaction. The good supervisor is able to recognize the dynamic at work and stop the emotional buck as it moves up and down the organizational line.

Let's discuss how this more specifically helps with the process of clinical supervision.

Look for Patterns and Parallel Statements

It's all about perception. There is often a gap between one's intention and perceived behavior. What a supervisor believes is being nonjudgmental, the clinician may see as passive or uncaring. What a supervisor hopes is clear and direct, the clinician may see as critical and demanding. Ideally you want to look for and catch these misperceptions as they occur in the supervisory process, but you can also look at a clinician's behavioral patterns with clients, and by listening for possible projections.

Sue, for example, is always quiet and reserved during supervision, but in sessions with clients seemed to be always scolding them for not doing the homework she assigned. She would talk endlessly about their need to take responsibility for their lives, and even when listening to an audiotape, could not hear how critical she sounded.

Clinicians who are aggressive, controlling, or scolding of their clients are obviously a cause for concern. Such behavior may reflect their own personality, their own way of coping with anxiety, and the ignition of some triggers from their own pasts. But it also may reflect a problem in the supervisory relationship, especially in clinicians who are submissive to their supervisor. Again it's about perception. The clinician may, in fact, be identifying with the aggressor, in this case the supervisor. Unable to deal openly with the supervisor's power, the clinician projects her distorted impression of the supervisor onto her relationship with clients. The clients end up feeling battered, similar to the way the clinician feels in her relationship with the supervisor. Similarly, the clinician who seems to be always passive and indecisive with clients may be inadvertently copying their perceptions of you.

Seeing such patterns and differences between your own presentation and the behavior of a clinician is a red flag that there may be distortions in the supervisory relationship. You need to raise the issue in a way that reduces the clinician's anxiety and can be heard: "Sue, when I hear these tapes, you sound to me to be scolding and frustrated. I'm wondering if you sometimes feel that I am that way with you." This has to be said in an absolutely gentle and calm voice. You don't want to sound like you are scolding her for scolding—that only replicates the process.

Sue may have one of several reactions: She may say no, that it's just that she doesn't really know what to do when clients seem to not follow through—a skill issue—or that this particular client reminds her of her father and it emotionally pushes some old triggers of hers—a countertransference issue. Or she may say no, of course not, but you can tell that Sue is anxious and trying to avoid the conversation. That's fine, you've seeded the idea, the subject is on the table, and she and you can come back to it when she feels less anxious and has time to think about it. Or she may say yes, she does feel criticized at times by you. This is great because now not only is the problem out in the open so you can discuss it, but the clinician has taken a big step in being assertive with you.

Similarly, look for what are called *parallel statements*. You could ask Jim, for example, why he thinks Ms. Jones so easily gets upset and angry. He may say that she gets no support from her husband, or though she is doing her best, or she is isolated and has a hard time asking for help. This may be absolutely accurate and true about Jones. But it is useful, as a supervisor, to ask yourself, especially if it seems that many of Jim's clients seem to him to be lacking support, whether he too feels the same. Out of all the things he could say, why is he saying this now? Is he projecting his feelings and needs on his clients? Perhaps. It gives you information about what may need to change in the supervisory relationship.

It's best to focus on clinical issues and parallel statements separately. When Jim is upset about Jones, the focus needs to be on helping him calm down—by responding to him the way he needs to respond to his client—and then help him decide what to do next. But at a separate time, raise your questions: Jim, I was thinking about your last session with Jones again, and I notice that when you talk about many of your clients, you talk about them lacking support or feeling isolated. I'm just wondering—do you ever feel that way with me, that I am not supportive enough, or do you sometimes feel isolated? Again, it's important that this is said in a calm and open manner.

Be Alert to the Parallel Process Coming Down from Above

You are part of middle management, and you need to be the responsible buffer. If there is emotional chaos going on above you, and coming down the organizational line, avoid mimicking the behavior, emotion, and reactiveness of your supervisors. Instead calm yourself, gather the information you need to understand and solve the problem, and then tell your staff the situation and what you require from them in a clear, nondramatic way.

Educate Clinicians About the Parallel Process

Helping them see how these patterns move up and down the line can help clinicians be more sensitive to their clients and themselves. As we'll discuss later, this is often best taught and learned during Stage 2 of the clinicians' development.

Before closing this introduction to parallel process, let's talk about one other variation that will be discussed more later: the supervisor–therapist professional relationship as it moves through the 4 developmental stages.

Critical thinking

Practice Behavior Example: Analyze models of assessment, prevention, intervention, and evaluation.

Critical Thinking Question: What do you see as the relationship between leadership style and parallel process?

Supervisor Personal History

_____1_____2_____3_____4

Professional Relationship

S _____1_____2_____3_____4_____T

Clinician Personal History

_____1_____2_____3_____4

As said in Chapter 1, it is the nature of doing therapy that the professional and personal are always in danger of overlapping and crossing. This is what this diagram represents. As the supervisor–therapist professional relationship moves through the 4 developmental stages, running in the background are also each one's own personal experiences and history. While the personal can be ignited and affect the process at any point, this is particularly a danger when we get to Stage 3. For now just keep in mind that the professional relationship and personal history can run in parallel tracks.

What these concepts—anxiety–coping styles, learning styles, leadership styles, parallel process—offer you as a supervisor are means of assessing the needs of the clinician in terms of support and approach and help you setting initial supervisory goals. They also highlight your pivotal role in the agency as a role model for professionalism and anxiety approaching, as well as a middle manager who advocates, and buffers, yet enforces agency expectations and standards. What underscores all these concepts is a need for flexibility combined with clarity, for leadership combined with support for individuation and growth. Again, the application of these concepts will be discussed as we move through the 4 developmental stages.

In Chapter 3 we will focus more closely on ways of mapping relationship dynamics over time, and give you an opportunity to explore your own personal expectations of relationships.

SUMMARY

- This chapter focuses on several of the core concepts that form the foundation of clinical social work supervision. The first is that of anxiety-coping styles. There are 3 primary styles—approaching, avoiding, and binding. Those who approach their anxiety feel anxious but have learned that the anxiety is part of learning something new or solving a problem. Avoiders see the feeling of anxiety as the problem, often feel overwhelmed by it, and seek ways to dampen the feeling or others who can fix the problem for them. Binders do not feel anxiety and have learned to keep it at bay through control and rigidity. Supervisors want to be able to model anxiety approaching, and help clinicians move toward approaching behaviors. Clinicians' ability to take acceptable risks in turn helps them be a model for clients, and helps them stay creative.

- Understanding how one learns helps you as a supervisor be most effective as a teacher. Discussed in this chapter are the Dziuban/Long model that defines 4 learning styles: aggressive/independent characterized by high energy and self-confidence; aggressive/dependent characterized by high energy but also self-criticism and caution; passive/independent marked by reactivity, lower energy, and desire for control; and passive/dependent marked by lower energy, reactiveness, and a desire to please. Also discussed is the NLP model of learning styles—visual, auditory, and kinesthetic. Understanding which of these 3 systems an individual relies upon helps you know, for example, whether to teach by creating diagrams and other visual images, by lectures, or by hand-on experiential opportunities.

- Six leadership styles are discussed: drill sergeant with a focus on micromanagement and low nurturance; mother hen with focus on high nurturance but weak boundary setting; inconsistent marked by mixed messages and unreliability; crisis-oriented characterized by focus and energy on crisis situations, but low energy and little prevention after the crisis is over; neglectful marked by insufficient support and interaction with staff; and balanced, blending the best qualities of the other 5.

- Finally, this chapter closes with a discussion of parallel process, the way emotions move up the organizational ladder from clients to clinicians to supervisor, and move down from the reactions of managers above. The good supervisor is able to be an appropriate buffer from what comes above and from below. By being aware of parallel process supervisors can help show clinicians how to respond to clients, as well as can identify when clinicians' statements about clients may also reflect clinicians' own emotions and issues about supervision.

The following questions will test your application and analysis of the content found within this chapter. For additional assessment, including licensing-exam-type questions on applying chapter content to practice behaviors, visit **MySearchLab**.

1. People who bind their anxiety tend to
   a. Easily feel overwhelmed
   b. Not feel anxious and are rigid and controlling
   c. Feel anxious but can be creative
   d. Vacillate between periods of anxiety and depression

2. If a clinician's learning style was primarily kinesthetic, you would help her learn best by
   a. Having her sit in a therapy session with you
   b. Using diagrams to explain concepts
   c. Provide mini-lectures in supervisory sessions
   d. Giving her a textbook to read

3. Ellen easily becomes anxious with new situations and worries about making mistakes. As her supervisor you can help her most by
   a. Being firm and letting her know that she needs to change her attitude
   b. Focusing on her mistakes so she knows what to improve
   c. Being supportive while assigning her to gradually more challenging cases
   d. Tailoring her work so that she is not anxious

4. Social workers who work under the supervision of Brian receive little positive feedback and feel they need to make sure Brian approves of their clinical plans before acting. This reflects Brian's
   a. Drill sergeant leadership style
   b. Inconsistent leadership style
   c. Anxiety-avoiding coping style
   d. Crisis-oriented leadership style

5. Holly comes to supervision emotionally upset by her last client who was in crisis and agitated. How as her supervisor would you respond to her in the supervisory session?

6. Hector gets behind on his paperwork because he is always worried that his notes are not complete enough. How would you respond to Hector's problem?

3

Laying the
Foundation—Part 2

Competencies Applied with Practice Behaviors — in This Chapter				
☒ Professional Identity	◼ Ethical Practice	☒ Critical Thinking	☒ Diversity in Practice	◼ Human Rights & Justice
☒ Research-Based Practice	◼ Human Behavior	◼ Policy Practice	◼ Practice Contexts	◼ Engage, Assess, Intervene, Evaluate

THE RELATIONSHIP TRIANGLE

Parallel process is one way of describing the dynamics within a relationship. Another useful depiction is the Relationship Triangle. It is based on what is called the Karpman or Drama Triangle, originally developed by Steven Karpman (1968), and upon game theory. What follows are my own variation and insights into the model as developed over time. While analyzing the model, track the dynamics on the diagram, and think about the ways it may apply to you, not only in your professional role but in your personal relationships as well. The common interactions will be described first, and then their application to supervision.

Personal Relationships and the Triangle

The triangle represents a relationship between 2 people. The P, R, and V represent different roles that people can play; they are not the people themselves, but roles. The roles interlock and there is always someone on top, who seems to have more power, and someone on the bottom. The relationship moves in a circle, as Figure 3.1.

Figure 3.1 • Relationship Triangle

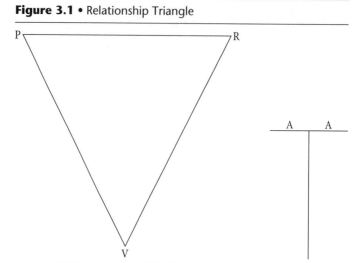

Source: Steven Karpman (1968). Karpman, S. (1968). Fairy tales and script drama analysis. *Transactional Analysis Bulletin, 7(26), 39–43.* Reprinted with permission of Dr. Steven Karpman.

The person in the R position is the rescuer, who essentially has "nice guy" control. He hooks into the V or victim, who feels overwhelmed by problems that seem to be falling down on his head. Often V's anxiety-coping style is one of avoidance. The rescuer steps in and says, "I can help you out. I'll take care of it. Just do what I say, everything will be fine." Oftentimes couples in intimate relationship will begin with some form of this. They psychologically cut a deal: The rescuer agrees to take responsibility for the victim's problems and in return feels needed and has control. The victim agrees to lean on the rescuer and in return has someone to take care of him and avoids having to deal with problems independently. Everyone is seemingly getting his needs met and is happy.

And it works fine, except every once in a while 1 of 2 things happens. Sometimes the rescuer gets tired of doing it all. He feels like he is shouldering all the responsibilities and that the other is not pulling his weight, not giving anything back, not appreciating what the rescuer is doing. Periodically and often without any warning the rescuer gets fed up, angry, resentful. Suddenly he shifts over to P, the persecutor role. He blows up—usually about something minor (for not doing the laundry, for not taking out the trash, etc.)—or acts out—goes out and spends a lot of money, goes on a drinking binge, has an affair. He feels he deserves to do what he does: "Look, after all," he says to himself, "at what I've been putting up with." The message underneath the behavior and anger that usually does not come out very clearly is, "Why don't you grow up! Why don't you take some responsibility! Why do I have to do everything around here! Why don't you appreciate what I am doing for you! This is unfair!" The feeling of unfair is a strong one.

At that point the victim gets scared and moves up to the R position and tries to make up and calm the waters. "I'm sorry," he says. "I didn't realize. I really do appreciate what you do. I'll do better." Then the persecutor feels guilty and remorseful about whatever he did or said and goes down to the victim position and gets depressed. Both then stabilize and go back to their original positions.

Just as the rescuer at times resents being the rescuer, the victim at times resents being the victim. He gets tired of the other one always running the show, always telling him what to do. He gets tired of being looked down on because the rescuer is basically saying, "If it wasn't for me, you wouldn't make it." Every once in a while the victim gets fed up and, like the rescuer, suddenly jumps to the persecutor role. He too blows up and gets angry, usually about something small, or acts out. The message underneath that doesn't usually get clearly said is, "Why don't you get off my back! Leave me alone, stop controlling my life! Back off, I can do things myself!" The rescuer hears this and moves to the victim position. He says to himself, "Poor me, every time I try to help, look what I get." The persecutor then feels bad about whatever he did or said and goes to the rescuer position and says something like, "I was stressed out, off my meds, tired from the kids. I'm sorry." And then they make up and go back to where they originally were.

While everyone gets to move among all the roles, often one will fit more comfortably in one role more than another. This has to do with personality, upbringing, and learned ways of coping. The rescuer as a child was often an only child, was the oldest in the family, or was the one who grew up in a chaotic family; in terms of learning style he tends to be aggressive/passive. He usually did not have many buffers between him and his parents, and learned early on that he could avoid getting in trouble and avoid conflict by being good: "If I can stay on my toes and just do what my parents (and teacher) want me to do all the time, I won't get in any hot water."

This type of person learns to be very sensitive to others as a means of survival. He develops good radar and can pick up the nuances of emotions. He is hyperalert, spends all his energy surveying the environment, stays on his toes, and is ever ready to do what the parents want. Essentially he takes the position of "I'm happy if you're happy, and I need to make sure you are happy." He gets rewarded for being good. His way of coping avoids scary confrontations and provides positive attention.

What works for the child, however, doesn't necessarily work so well for the adult. Now the world is bigger. Rather than just his parents and teacher to pay attention to, the rescuer adult now has many more—his parents, his spouse, his boss, the president of the local Rotary Club, and so on. He now feels pulled in a lot of directions, stretched thin, as he scrambles to accommodate what he thinks others want from him. He can easily feel like a martyr—always sacrificing for others and getting little in return, and is always at risk of burnout.

He also has a hard time knowing what he wants. Because he spent so much of his energy as a child looking outward and doing what others wanted, he knows what he "should" do. In fact his head is always filled with a laundry list of things that should be done. But that is different from wanting, which, unlike lists and rules, is a feeling. Because he was essentially going on autopilot for much of his childhood, he never had the opportunity to sit back and decide what he felt, liked, didn't like, wanted. As an adult if you ask him "But what do you want?" he hesitates and gets stuck. He worries about making the right decision, about not offending anyone in his life, or about upsetting the ever-critical voice in his head.

The adult rescuer is also likely to have a difficult time with anger and conflict (which is why he became good in the first place). Instead of confronting others or being assertive, his tendency is to be nice, to stuff anger down. Essentially he is engaging in magical thinking—"If I do the right things all the time, people will somehow know what I need and give it to me even if I don't tell them." Under stress his first response is to get even nicer. Eventually, however, he begins to gag on his anger and resentment, and blows up. Because he is so uncomfortable with feelings and the drama that often ensues, he feels like his worst dream has come true. Guilt sets in and he shoves it all back down again, only to have it build up again.

The victim, in contrast, as a child was often the youngest in the family, was micromanaged or overprotected by parents, or had older siblings who stepped in and took over whenever he was stuck with a problem. Just as the rescuer missed discovering what he really wanted, the victim in childhood missed opportunities to develop self-confidence that comes from learning to manage problems on his own. He never learned to approach anxiety. Now, as an adult, he easily gets overwhelmed, feels unconfident, and becomes anxious. To handle these feelings he looks to a rescuer who can take over and treat him as his family did.

While the rescuer and victim periodically bounce into the persecutor role, there are certain people who live in that role most of the time. These persecutors can be viewed as the evil twins of the rescuer. Whereas the rescuer controls the relationship by being good and nice, the persecutor controls it by being angry, critical, and blaming. This person, in essence, is the abuser, and obviously some couples start with this persecutor–victim relationship, playing out childhood models and roles. The persecutor learned early on that "when I get scared I get tough. If I can control everything going on around me in an aggressive way, no one can sneak up behind me and get me."

The A stands for *adult* and is similar to Murray Bowen's (1978) concept of differentiated self. This person is not in a role, is more complete, is proactive rather than reactive, is self-responsible rather than blaming, and is outside the triangle. Adults in relationships are peers; they are on the same level in terms of power. The adult says, "I'm responsible for what I think, do, say. If something bothers me, it is *my* problem. If you can do something to help me with *my* problem—the clothes left on the floor—I need to tell you, because you can't read my mind. If you decide not to help me—the clothes don't bother me at all and actually like it that way—I'll need to decide what I'm going to do next to fix my problem. Similarly, if something bothers you, it is *your* problem." The adult is able to remain nonanxious in the presence of the other's anxiety.

This stance doesn't mean that "I don't care about you or that you are completely left to deal with things on your own." Rather it means "if there is something I can do to help you with your problem, tell me what you want me to do. You tell me what you need. What it doesn't mean is that I need to take over and fix it or tell you how to handle it the way I would. And if I decide I can't or won't be able to help you with *your* problem, I trust you can work it out. Again you may not handle it the way I might, but you can do it. I don't need to take over."

Two problems the rescuer and victim have in their relationship are that they do expect a lot of mind reading—"you should know what is going on or how to help without my having to say so"—and then feel frustrated or disappointed or angry when the other does not. They also have distorted sense of responsibility: The rescuer tends to be overresponsible—"your problems are *my* problems, I'm happy if you are happy, and it is my job to make sure you are happy. When I see you are upset, I actually get anxious and want to make it better." In the rescuer's attempt to "make" the victim happy, the victim over time begins to feel pressure and control, which sets up the explosion. Similarly, the victim tends to be underresponsible—"my problems are *your* problems, I expect you to fix them, and I either have to wait for you to do so, or manipulate you into taking over."

Diversity in Practice

Practice Behavior Example: Recognize the extent to which a culture's structures and values may oppress, marginalize, alienate, or create or enhance privilege and power.

Critical Thinking Question: While the "differentiated" self may be seen as an ideal, how might other cultures view this differently?

The adults, in contrast, are clear about who has the problem. This is represented by the vertical line running between them. If you feel it, it's yours. By being aware of who has the problem, the individuals can avoid the defensiveness, anxiety, control, and manipulation of those caught in the triangle. They also can be more intimate.

The problem the rescuer and victim face in their relationship is that the roles, which are not the people themselves but only parts of them, keep them stuck. The rescuer cannot let down his guard, or get too vulnerable because he is afraid that the victim will not be able to handle it. Similarly, the victim cannot ever get too strong because the rescuer will feel threatened and out of a job. The long line in the diagram between the victim and rescuer is true in real life—the emotional distance between them is great. The adults, in contrast, don't have this problem. Both can be responsible, strong, and yet honest and vulnerable. They can take risks, are not locked in roles, and hence can be more open and intimate.

Change Over Time

Two people can obviously be in this pattern for a long time—seemingly getting along, suddenly having some acting out or emotional explosion, making up, returning to their roles, and repeating the pattern over and over again. What can also happen over time, and what often brings couples into therapy, is that one person either is tired of going around the cycle or begins to outgrow the role he is in. Like any other pattern it takes 2 to play the game and as soon as one person begins to move toward the adult position, the other gets scared and tries to pull him back in to keep it going.

If, for example, the rescuer doesn't eventually drop from the weight of it all—gets a heart attack or has some sudden psychological breakdown—he may decide it's time to pull back, define boundaries and problems, and delegate. The classic case of this is the codependent of an alcoholic. The wife, for example, begins to attend Al-Anon meetings and starts to tell her husband, "Jake, I'm not going to call up your boss for you on Monday morning and tell him you are sick. You can call him yourself. I'm not going to pick you up off the front lawn on Saturday night if you get drunk." The wife is stepping out of the triangle and Jake will instinctively try to pull her back in.

If Jake gets drunk on Saturday night, he is going to rip-roaring drunk. If that doesn't work, Jake is likely to switch to one of the other roles: He may shift to the persecutor, get angry, and threaten divorce and custody of the kids or cut off money; or he may get nice, tell her how he is going to start going to AA meetings to appease her and bring her back.

Similarly, if the victim moves to the adult position, the rescuer feels threatened. This is often seen in the empty-nest stage of marriage. The husband has more or less been in charge—making most of the big decisions, financially supporting the family—and the kids begin to leave home. The wife starts to say something like "You know, Bill, I'm thinking of maybe going back to school. I never finished my degree because I stayed home with the kids, and now is a good time to do it. Maybe I'll go back into full-time work. I think I'd like to get my own checking and saving account so I can have my own money and be more independent."

While Bill knows what to do when his wife is in the one-down position, he doesn't know what to do when she shifts. Generally the first thing Bill will instinctively do is be nice but try and talk his wife out of the changes: "Why do you want to go back to school now? You're 50 years old. What are you going to be able to do with a degree? It will cost us 30 grand for tuition, for what? You don't need to get a full-time job. This is a time to take it easy. We don't need another checking account. It will cost $10 a month in fees that we don't need to spend." Stay put is the message. If that doesn't work, Bill may shift to the persecutor role and get angry—"If you want to go to school, you find a way to pay for it. We're not taking it out of our retirement." Or Bill will move to the victim position, get depressed so his wife needs to stay home and take care of him.

Finally, you easily see this dynamic in abusive relationships. If the victim of a persecutor–victim relationship decides to move out of the triangle or out of the relationship and not be a punching bag anymore, the first thing the persecutor will do is more of the same. If he was angry, he is now going to get explosive. He will stalk her, hunt her down, emotionally abuse her, or beat her up. If that doesn't work, he may get nice. He will call up a therapist inquiring about help with anger management, ask the clinician if he could do him a favor and call up his wife or girlfriend and tell her that he called about therapy, and then not follow through. If that doesn't work, he may get depressed, or even threaten to kill himself so she will come back into the relationship.

If all the jockeying around doesn't work, the person left behind has 1 of 2 choices. He may end the relationship and find someone else to play the corresponding role, someone else to control, someone else to take care of him. Or the person left behind can move toward the adult position too.

The challenges of both partners moving to the adult position are several. The natural feeling of the one left behind is that if you care, you'll stay in the triangle. If they both move, the partners need to develop new ways of showing that they care for each other. There will be a period of transition while these new ways are being created, and the new ways will not, at least for a while, feel as good as the old ways. There are also the challenges of learning new skills, especially for the one feeling left behind.

Child Development, Cognitions, and the Triangle

Another way of looking at this model is through a developmental frame. Children are by default in a victim position in that they have little power and skills and are dependent on their parents. The parents usually play a positive rescuer role in that they do feel a responsibility to take care of the child and have her lean on them when she has problems. In some families, however, the parent can be abusive, or even the victim, pushing the young child into taking care of the parent. As children move toward adolescence, they are constantly shifting between victim and emerging adult roles—demanding independence at one moment and collapsing into a heap of dependency the next—all of which keeps parents confused about how to respond. Even as adolescents move toward adulthood, there is often an awkward period during which parents need to give up their rescuing mode and move toward a more peer-like relationship of 2 adults. This can often take years to accomplish.

Finally, think of the model from an individual, internal perspective. For those prone to depression, for example, they often feel like the victim at the mercy of 2 different voices in their heads—the rescuer who is telling them what they should be doing all the time and the persecutor who beats them up when they don't follow through. Cognitive-behavioral therapy or dialectical behavioral therapy tries to help the individual learn to substitute the adult stance and voice for those of the rescuer and persecutor.

Supervision and the Triangle

This model helps with clinical supervision in a couple of ways. Probably from your own experience, as well as those of colleagues, it's no surprise that a great many of those who enter the social work field quite easily fit into the profile of the rescuer. They were often the "good kid" in the family, rarely the rebel. Their sensitivity to the emotions and reactions of others, as well as their often caretaker role, primes them to enter a helping profession.

But they are also prone to the dangers that the Relationship Triangle illustrates, especially those of overresponsibility and difficulty with confrontation. As will be discussed in Chapter 4, this is particularly true during Stage 1, where the power of the supervisor along with the desire to please clients generates those good kid reactions and ways of coping.

The developmental aspect of the triangle also helps to anticipate changes of the course of the supervisory relationship. Following the parenting metaphor, the novice social worker can be seen moving from the dependency that characterizes the victim role to the gradual emergence toward an adult/adult, more peer-like relationship by Stage 4. This process is what will be tracked while exploring supervisory dynamics.

Critical Thinking

Practice Behavior Example: Analyze models of assessment, prevention, intervention, and evaluation.

Critical Thinking Question: What do you see as the relationship between the adult stance and the various leadership styles?

THE BIG 6

Here is one more set of ideas. Unlike the others, these are a group of related miscellaneous concepts, rather than a unified model. Some of these have already been touched on; others will be explored more later. You can think of these as foundational beliefs, what you can always return to when you feel stuck as a supervisor or clinician. As with the other ideas and models, just see what resonates most with your own thinking and needs.

1. How You Do Anything Is How You Do Everything

This concept is actually Buddhist in origin, and it echoes the comments made in Chapter 1 about the importance of process. The emphasis here again is on the *how*, rather than on the *what*. *How* you do things in your life—whether you avoid, are cautious, are confrontive, and whether your style is to jump in, hold back, wait for permission, be reflective—is in essence the template for your relationship with the world. It also implies that if you keep doing the same thing—the how—you will keep winding up in the same spot, keep feeling the same way, even if situation—the content—varies.

We can easily see this playing out, for example, with individuals who are depressed. They are depressed because their everyday lifestyles are often inherently depressing—they lack friends and are socially isolated, they internalize their anger toward others, and they are critical of themselves. Changing what they *do*—going against their own grain and pushing themselves to get out of the house even if they don't feel like, speaking up even though they worry how others may react—can help them change how they *feel*.

The other corollary of this statement is that small changes can grow into large ones: If you change anything—change your fundamental approach, your core *how*—you change everything. This is the essence of therapy, but also the essence of supervision. In addition to the teaching of skills and ideas—the *what*—there is also the challenge of anxiety approaching, proactivity, and flexibility—the *how*, and where you start doesn't really matter.

If Jim, for example, has a difficult time being assertive, or expressing anger, or containing his anger with his wife, he certainly can try to manage these situations head-on, but he can also practice his new response in other, less-challenging situations first—with store clerks who give him the wrong change, with work colleagues who borrow his pen and don't return it, with drivers who cut him off in traffic. Similarly, the rescuing, good kid clinician can practice setting boundaries and be less overresponsible, not just with intimidating clients, but with her teenage son or the committee chair from church. Any change in your process changes you.

2. Look for the Holes

There is a concept in art known as negative space. If an artist, for example, is painting a vase, the negative space is the area around the vase, rather than the vase itself. Similarly, you can apply this to therapy where you, the clinician, are always looking for what is not in the room—the holes (Taibbi, 2007). This is what the family does not talk about—the recent death of grandpa, dad's drinking, positive qualities of 6-year-old Joey, or what the individual never mentions (her anger, her mother, her old boyfriend). This is what you are looking for and this is one of the things you ultimately want the family or individual to talk about. It is not because the content itself is vital—it often is not—but because there is something holding this back. This is often where their fear lies, or where parts of themselves were left. It is often where the solution to their current problem lies as well. To focus upon what they do not is moving them against their grain.

Obviously this concept is related to the one above in that the process of discussing and confronting these topics is more important than the topics themselves. It is also related to the concepts of anxiety coping and learning styles in that supervisors are curious in seeing not only how a clinician responds, but how they can help him move toward where he is not—toward anxiety, toward independence, toward assertiveness and self-support.

As a concept it can help you assess clients and clinicians and develop a preliminary treatment plan. What doesn't the clinician easily talk about, express, do? Look for it, ask about it—to let him know that this can be part of the conversation between you, to possibly open doors to other aspects of his personality and eventually bring them into his professional style.

3. Problems Are Bad Solutions

What you see as a problem—Maria's incomplete paperwork, Felix's passivity in the supervisory relationship—are in the minds of Maria and Felix, not problems but solutions to other problems. Maria may be emotionally overwhelmed by her clients, preoccupied, or distracted, and putting off paperwork is not a problem but a way of keeping one more thing off her plate. Felix has no sense of passivity, but instead feels intimidated when around you; his seeming passivity is his only way of coping with the relationship. Of course, you want to identify the problem as you see it, but that is merely a starting point for discovering the real problem—an emotion, a difficult situation—that lies beneath what you see. Rather than scolding Maria about her paperwork, find out what is getting in the way of her doing it. When Felix falls into his passive state, gently ask about how he is feeling right then and there.

When you do this, you are using your clinical skills to support your supervisory ones. You are not doing therapy, but are also not taking what you see at face value. You are curious about the source of the problem, rather than the problem itself.

Research-Based Practice

Practice Behavior Example: Collect, organize, and interpret client data.

Critical Thinking Question: Think about clients you are currently working with, or friends or family. How is what you see as a problem really for them a bad solution to an underlying problem?

4. Empathize with Emotions, Not Behaviors

Unraveling the emotions that may be contributing to a problem does not mean that you ignore the bottom line. Empathize with clinicians' emotions—that she is overwhelmed, he feels intimidated—yet hold them accountable for behaviors—completing paperwork, showing up and taking an active role in supervision.

As will be explored in Chapter 12, this concept is key for maintaining quality control among your staff. They need to see you as able to empathize with their emotions, and to listen to and appreciate their stories and struggles—the supportive side of supervision. But as a manager and supervisor, you also need to hold them responsible for their professional behavior and performance. If you don't, they fail to learn, and you fail to be a manager.

5. There Are No Mistakes

Mistakes are a hindsight call. People don't set out to make mistakes, but rather they do what they think is best in the moment given what they know. It is what happens next that usually determines whether a decision was a "mistake"—if it turns out well, it was a good idea and choice; if not, it is labeled a mistake.

Another way of looking at this process is to separate it into 2 parts. Part A is assessing the situation and making a decision. Part B is seeing what happens next and if it does not turn out well, seeing this as a new problem that needs to be addressed. Suppose, for example, you as supervisor say to Holly, your supervisee, that you think it would be a good idea that she go to Employee Assistance to help her with the personal stress she is having, which in turn is affecting her work performance. Instead of hearing your statement as a supportive solution, Holly emotionally collapses and interprets your referral as her being one step away from being fired. You could believe you made a mistake by saying what you did, and give yourself a hard time. The other way to look at it is that no, you didn't make a mistake, you made a clear decision, but now you have a new problem—namely, Holly's reaction—which you now have to address. All this applies to supervision in a couple of ways. Clinicians who tend to be rescuers, or aggressive/dependent and self-critical, are often struggling with making the *right* decision. For them the process of making the right decision involves sitting in their chair and thinking about what they should do, then what they want, reconciling the two, then figuring out how to say what they want, then anticipating how the other person will react and how they will respond to that—all before they do anything at all. Making the right decision becomes a huge algorithm of mini-decisions that they can never be certain of. It's not surprising that it is easy for them to feel overwhelmed and incapacitated by the entire process.

Instead clinicians need to hear and learn from you that mistakes are okay, that right decision isn't necessary, or that they need to focus on and act on Part A—what they want to say and do—and then trust that they can handle, with your support, Part B—a new problem based upon what happens next. If they hear this often enough, if you are able to model it, and if they are able to try it, they can learn to be less hard on themselves, less anxious overall.

The other effect of understanding that there are no mistakes is that they also will be better able to take acceptable risks, see that moving forward is taking small steps, and learn to fully utilize the supervisory and clinical process. They will come to trust their own instincts and judgment, which will lead them into their own style. They will come to appreciate the pragmatic nature of therapy, as well as life. And this they can then teach and demonstrate to their clients.

6. Be Honest

If you are stuck with a client, with a clinician, don't bind yourself trying to decode the perfect solution or response. Instead say you are stuck, that you don't know at the moment what to say. Honesty, like being right, can take on the tone of a moral challenge, or connotations of being brutal, or digging down deep into the pit of one's soul. But it is not. It is about being aware, sensitive, present, and open. It is talking about the process, about the elephant in the room, about the holes. What makes honesty difficult is that it does require a self-awareness of what is going on within you at the moment, and can always carry with it an edge of risk and unpredictability. But like being right, it is one baby step of many in the process. It has the power to cut through defenses; it nudges clients and clinicians out of their comfort zone and often into their own honesty. It provides the opportunity for discovering what unfolds within oneself and within the relationship.

A GUIDED IMAGERY EXERCISE

To counterbalance the cognitive exhaustion you might be feeling at this point after marching through all these ideas and models, we are going to close this chapter with an experiential exercise to tap into a different portion of your mind and personality. This exercise will suggest various scenes for you to imagine. Either have someone read the instructions to you, tape-record them and play them back, or read each scene, allow yourself to imagine what you can, and then move on to the next. Take your time; leave enough time for each scene. You will be debriefed after the exercise is over.

Sit quietly and take several deep breaths. Feel yourself settling down. Imagine yourself entering a theater. You walk through the front door and come upon a lobby where there are a lot of people milling around. You walk through the lobby to the auditorium and take the best seat in the house. In front of you is a large stage with a curtain drawn across it. You sit down and make yourself comfortable.

Other people enter now and begin to fill up the seats around you. The house lights go dim and the stage lights go on. A play is about to start.

The curtain rises on the first act of the play. You see yourself on stage, and you are a small child. On stage with you are one or both of your parents. There is something wrong with you. You are upset about something—crying, worrying. Perhaps you hurt yourself, or you are sad. Watch what happens, listen to what is said, see if anyone else is there. . . .

The curtain comes down. The curtain rises on the next act. You again see yourself as a small child, but this time you are with your family, whatever that means to you. It may be you playing with your brothers and sisters, you and your sisters and parents eating dinner, you with grandparents, cousins, aunts, and uncles at Christmas. Watch what happens, listen to what is said. . . .

The curtain comes down. The curtain rises again and now you are older. You are a teenager and on stage with one or both of your parents. They are talking to you about growing up—about school and jobs and careers, about relationships— dating, girls, guys, sex, marriage. Listen to what they say; listen to what you say back. . . .

The curtain comes down. The curtain rises and now you are a bit older. It is that time in your life when you are leaving home for the first time. Perhaps you are going off to college or moving into an apartment with friends, but you are literally packing up your stuff and moving out of the house. One or both of your parents are there with you. Watch what happens, listen to what is said, see if you can tell how you feel at the moment. . . .

The curtain comes down. The curtain rises and you are older again. You are on stage with someone who you see as a mentor to you. It may be your first job supervisor, a coach, college advisor, but it is someone you look up to. Watch what happens, listen to what is said, see if you can be aware of what you most admire about that person. . . .

The curtain comes down. The curtain rises and the time is the present. You are at your job or at school. Watch what happens, see who is there, listen to what is said. . . .

The curtain rises on the final act. The time is sometime in the distant future, a time in your life when people see you as not only someone who is experienced, but someone who is wise. One or two people come to you seeking your advice. They ask you what you most learned over all your years of working and living. Listen to what you say. . . .

The curtain comes down. The house lights go on and the stage lights go off. The audience gets up and begins to leave, and you follow them out. As they are leaving you overhear them talking about the play they have just seen. Listen to what they say about the play. Be aware of how you feel about what they say. When you feel ready, open your eyes.

The question to ask yourself when doing an exercise like this is why are you imagining what you imagined rather than something else? Imagery like this is like dreams; it gives you different information about yourself. It is not prophesy; it indicates where you are now. If you did this same exercise a few weeks from now, it probably would be different.

The first scene was you as a small child who was in trouble. What did you see? You crying and your mother comforting you? You crying and mother telling you to calm down in an emotionless voice? Your mother calming you but your father yelling at you to shut up? You by yourself, upset with no one there?

Why is this important? How is it tied to supervision? We all leave childhood with some black-and-white notion about trust and help. What have you learned about leaning on others? How much can you expect them to comfort you? How much, essentially, can you trust?

This is important because, by definition, supervision is about people coming to you for help. But at some personal level there is a fine line between what you consider to be appropriate helping and people whining and needing to handle things on their own. What are your own standards? What did you see and what did you learn about trust and leaning on others? At what point do you feel people need to just manage on their own?

The next scene was you and family. Again why is this important for supervision? As every television sitcom tells us, workplaces quickly take on family dynamics—the boss as parent, the senior staff as junior parent, and so on. What did you learn about family? What did you see in the scene? How does this shape your own expectations about family relationships? If you were an only child, for example, your experience and tolerance for sibling conflict will likely be different than that of someone with many siblings. Remember that one of the reasons people leave their jobs is because of poor relationships with peers, and often this means that their expectations about the relationships weren't met. How do you react and interact as a leader of a workplace family?

The next scene was you talking with your parents about growing up. Most people don't have such a formal talk with parents, but they do get a lot of messages in adolescence about what makes a good life. What are life's priorities? How important is education? What did you learn about relationships? What is balance between personal happiness and responsibility? Some people hear their parents saying nothing in the scene and the parents contradicting each other. In their adult lives they lack direction or are confused.

Often what you hear your parents say become the "shoulds" that run your life. They are important because of their content, but also their power. How much do these shoulds drive you? How do you balance your shoulds with your wants? How are your priorities different from those you might supervise, and how might that affect your relationships and expectations?

The next scene was you leaving home for the first time. What did you see? The important question here was how did you feel at the moment? Most people talk about being scared and excited. Some are really excited because they are breaking away. Some are overwhelmed with anxiety or feel that their parents are kicking them out.

Why is this important? There is a notion that how you felt when you first left home becomes for you the emotional bottom line for when you leave other things—jobs, relationships—in your life. Even if you were excited, the question is why? What was the undertow to this? Did you feel smothered, perhaps, micromanaged, misunderstood, underappreciated? When you look back over your life, was there some emotional common denominator that became your personal break point for leaving?

This is important to supervision because your bottom lines are likely to be different than others'. When your staff are ready to move on to a different job and you're still staying behind, how do you react? Do you wish them well? Envy them? Resent them and see them as being disloyal? As will be discussed later this often becomes a major issue during Stage 3.

The next scene was with you and your mentor. Who did you see? Some people see supervisors, others parents or grandparents, some no one. The questions asked are: What did you admire about this person? How have these qualities come into you to shape who you are? Do they provide for you a positive role model of how to be? If no one was strongly there in your scene, how have you compensated for this lack?

The scene in the present with you on stage at school or on your job. Out of all that you could have seen what did you see? How does it emotionally reflect your life right now? Were you feeling harried or bored or annoyed or happy? How does this scene mirror or seem different from childhood scenes?

Finally, the last scene, you as an older, wiser person. What did you say to the people who came to you? How was it similar to what your parents or mentor may have said to you? What do you see changing over time?

If you are currently going through a lot of transition—a relationship breakup, moving, starting a new job—you may have had a hard time visualizing this last scene. This is because your unsettled present makes it difficult for you to imagine the future. As your present becomes more settled the future scenes will be easier to see.

While the audience was leaving, what did they say about the play—interesting, boring, happy that the character was able to improve his life as he became older? Most people have some internal voice that wonders how others may see them. The other questions were: How did you feel about what they said? Hurt your feelings, you didn't care? How sensitive are you to what others say and what do you think they think about you? How much does that shape what you do and who you are?

Try not to overanalyze this exercise. Let your mind wander back to you over the next few days and see what settles in, what broad lessons or insights, if any, come to mind. Again, we'll be referring back to this exercise in later chapters.

We've covered a lot of important concepts in Chapters 2 and 3, ideas that we will be returning to and utilizing in our discussion of clinical supervision. Again, see what sifts down, what ideas are most helpful to you, which ones help you make more sense of you, others, your work. Let's begin the exploration of the 4 stages of development.

Professional Identity

Practice Behavior Example: *Practice personal reflection and self-correction to assure continual professional development.*

Critical Thinking Question: When you look back on your own life, is there some emotional bottom line to your leavings? How has this impacted your work in the past?

The following questions will test your application and analysis of the content found within this chapter. For additional assessment, including licensing-exam-type questions on applying chapter content to practice behaviors, visit **MySearchLab**.

1. According to the Relationship Triangle the victim is someone who
   a. Tends to be abusive in relationships
   b. Tends to be overresponsible and highly sensitive to others
   c. Tends to lack self-confidence and is easily overwhelmed
   d. Has a history of trauma

2. One of the dynamics that drives the cycle of the Relationship Triangle is
   a. The power imbalance between rescuers and victims
   b. Both individuals' ability to be intimate and vulnerable
   c. The fact that most people outgrow their role by adolescence
   d. That persecutors have problems with anger

3. When talking about her cases in supervision, Maria most often focuses on the mistakes she feels she has made. If you were to focus on the "holes," you might
   a. Ask her what she feels she did well with a particular client
   b. Talk about mistakes you have made in the past
   c. Say that she seems very self-critical
   d. Say little and let her set the agenda for the supervisory session

4. In his supervisory session Mark asks you a question about narrative therapy that you know little about. It would be best to
   a. Make up some answer so he doesn't lose faith in you as a supervisor
   b. Refer him to another staff person who is familiar with narrative therapy
   c. Tell him that you don't know a lot about narrative therapy, but that you would help him find the answer to his question
   d. Shift the focus and ask him why he is asking that particular question

5. Jennifer is always late for staff meetings. How would you talk to her about this problem?

6. Jack seems anxious and cautious in new situations. Applying the principle of "how you do anything is how you do everything," how could you help Jack be less cautious?

4

Stage 1: Supervisor as Teacher

Competencies Applied with Practice Behaviors — in This Chapter				
☒ Professional Identity	☒ Ethical Practice	☒ Critical Thinking	■ Diversity in Practice	■ Human Rights & Justice
■ Research-Based Practice	■ Human Behavior	■ Policy Practice	■ Practice Contexts	☒ Engage, Assess, Intervene, Evaluate

Do you remember your first days on your first job? Maybe it was a summer job as a lifeguard at a community pool or at McDonald's, or a college job in an office. A bit overwhelming, no doubt—"When you open up in the morning remember, and this is important, that you never.... And when you see a light come on you need to push this button.... These receipts with the red stripe need to go in this drawer.... Fill out the 284 form, not the 287 form whenever...." And you did your best to take it all in, to smile and nod at the right moments, but you felt anxious inside and probably a bit stupid. Making it all the worse was seeing everyone else working there—they seemed so calm, collected, and skilled.

Beginnings stir memories of other beginnings—the start of the new school year, moving to a new neighborhood, the awkwardness of new friendships, marriage, the birth of a child—and emotions—anticipation, optimism, dread, failure, adventure, loss, and certainly anxiety. In this chapter we are going to be talking about the first stage of the supervisory process. Most often this stage is associated with new staff and new clinicians—the latest bachelor of social work or master of social work graduates in their first clinical position. But much of what will be described here applies as well to more experienced staff who may be new to your agency. While they may not have the same clinical challenges, you both will be dealing with the same supervisory process, namely, that of building a solid, supportive, and open relationship.

Stage 1 is about getting off on the right foot and laying the foundation for the other stages to come. Because of this, this is the most important stage in many ways. Falter here and the relationship may never get off the ground—the clinician leaves or seeks out other sources of support—or cracks develop that cause potentially greater problems further down the road.

The beginnings of this stage resonate across all the parallel relationships. As the supervisor works to develop a strong, supportive, and effective relationship with the clinician, the clinician attempts to do the same with the clients. The supervisor's challenges—assessing needs, developing skills, and countering anxiety—parallel those of the clinician. The effects of one relationship—the supervisor's or the clinician's—ripple through the line to shape the others. You as a supervisor have the power and responsibility for shaping both.

Box 4.1 presents a summary of the characteristics, goals, tasks, and challenges of this stage.

Box 4.1 • Overview of Stage 1

Characteristics	Know what you don't know
	Fear/anxiety, performance pressure—pleasing clients and supervisor
	Overwhelmed by content—unable to decide what is important
	Reactive to clients—trying to please, feels like client does
	Struggle with setting structure, establishing trust
	Goals are vague—difficulty defining session goals
Supervisory goals	Create rapport, safety, and support
	Assess clinical skills and knowledge
	Assess anxiety management and learning style
	Provide job orientation
	Create success experiences
	Provide quality control
Supervisory tasks	Raise a range of topics, create variety
	Provide own place, help settle into workplace family
	Provide clear structure and directives regarding expectations
	Provide plenty of positive feedback
	Use self-disclosure to model openness, reduce anxiety
	Develop 3- to 6-month goals—assign readings, tag along with staff
Challenges/dangers	Clinician fear—stop learning, afraid to take acceptable risks and grow
	Clinician rigidity—too narrow a vision, help expand comfort zone
	Clinician overresponsibility—doing too much, help set boundaries
	Supervisory relationship never develops—need to determine underlying problem
	Clinician shows little insight—unable to make changes, understand supervisory concerns
	Spoon-feeding—remote control clinical work, clinician carries out directives of supervisor, both in comfort zone

CHARACTERISTICS OF STAGE 1

Know What You Don't Know

This is probably how you felt after the first day of your first job. You fumbled around, and were clumsy and confused while everyone else was not. For new social workers on the job such feelings are easy to come by. Sure, they may have had some pre-graduate school experience, or some good field placements, but sit them in their first staff meeting or group supervision, or put them with their first clients, and all the theories learned and their pumped-up self-esteem can rapidly turn to mush. Hearing their new colleagues talk about cases, they can feel intimidated; they struggle to keep up with the conversation. While they can diagnose depression, they don't quite know what to say when their client says he's felt depressed for weeks. They are aware of their lack of skills, the holes in their knowledge, and the too many times and places they feel stuck.

Looking Competent While Feeling Incompetent

In spite of all these feelings, there is pressure to not show it. New social workers may not be confident in their skills, but to their clients they need to exude an air of professionalism and skill. They wear suits, take detailed notes, and ask, with empathic facial expressions, how their clients feel.

The pressure, however, comes not only from the expectations of clients, but from the supervisor. In most agencies new staff start out being given 2 seemingly contradictory messages. In the first message the supervisor says, "Welcome to the agency." "I realize that there is a lot to learn and that you may feel overwhelmed by all. If you have any problems, any questions about procedures, feel stuck and unsure about what to do with your clients, come see me. Let me know how I can help, tell me what you need." This means trust me, be vulnerable, confide in me about the ways you feel incompetent.

The second message puts a spin on the first: "According to our agency policy, everyone who is newly hired is automatically on probation for the first 6 months of employment. What this means is that after the 6 months I'll be doing a probationary evaluation. If it seems like this is not a good fit for either of us, the agency can terminate employment without any obligations." This means if you seem to be too incompetent, we'll let you go.

Be open and vulnerable but not too much; it's a difficult bind for new clinicians. If the clinician's personality leans toward that of rescuer—is sensitive to expectations, is eager to please, is happy if you're happy—anxiety and performance pressure rise.

Reactiveness

Therapy clients often live in a reactive mode. The bills they can't pay, the misbehavior in their children that they can't control, the arguments with the spouse that drive them crazy—all these seem to be falling into their laps; they feel constantly under assault. They may blame others or themselves; they feel overwhelmed and uncertain where to begin. They are in crisis and seeking relief.

Unfortunately, new clinicians feeling shaky in their skills, wanting to please both clients and supervisors, are primed to replicate, rather than change, this process of reactiveness and how clients feel. Like their clients they too find it difficult to sort, select, or filter what comes to them. They see a hundred fires burning and are not sure where to start. Because they have trouble shaping the process, they walk out of sessions emotionally flooded by the content, and it is reflected in both their progress notes and their time management. Their notes are detailed, rambling, and extensive: elaborate family information—names, dates, who wore what—and process-type recording of what was said go on and on for pages. Sessions run over time because clinicians are reluctant to cut clients off and do not want to offend them. They don't want clients leaving the session upset because they worry they won't come back.

In supervision new clinicians often replay the session—he said, I said, he said. They have a list of topics and problems they need help with, but walk that fine line of asking for information without giving away how overwhelmed they feel. Your task is to be aware of the parallel process—to respond to clinicians the way the clinicians need to respond to clients. Listen and support to reduce their anxiety; help them partialize problems; model for them a proactive stance.

Critical Thinking

Practice Behavior Example: *Distinguish, appraise, and integrate multiple sources of knowledge, including research-based knowledge, and practice wisdom.*

Critical Thinking Question: What do you see as the relationship between the reactiveness of the first stage and the rescuer role?

SUPERVISORY GOALS AND TASKS OF STAGE 1

What drives this first stage is a confluence of factors: performance pressure and anxiety, the strong pull of the parallel process, limited skills and experience, all within a backdrop of forming a supervisory relationship. You and the clinician are essentially building the train (i.e., the relationship) while it is rolling down the tracks. Here are the goals and tasks that you most need to focus upon.

Create Rapport, Safety, and Support

Just as these are the foundation for therapeutic relationships, so too are they for a strong supervisory relationship. Clinicians who are unable to provide this foundation lose their clients; supervisors lose their ability to supervise.

The keys to building both a good therapeutic and supervisory alliance are leadership, support and sensitivity to the process, and clear expectations and agreement about goals and tasks (Bennett, Mohr, BrintzenhofeSzoc, & Saks, 2008). Leadership means that it is the responsibility of the supervisor to set the pace and define the parameters of the supervisory process. If Teresa, for example, had a terrible weekend with sick kids, had little sleep, and collapses into her chair when you see her in supervision on Monday morning looking worn and tired, is it okay that she mention all this at the start? It depends on whether you ask, or how you respond when she says she is tired and distracted. If she has a client who reminds her a little too much of her critical mother, and finds herself shutting down in sessions with her, is it okay for her to mention her transference reactions to you? Again, it depends on whether you ask, or how you respond when she mentions it.

Engage, Assess, Intervene, Evaluate

Practice Behavior Example: *Use empathy and other interpersonal skills.*

Critical Thinking Question: Social workers need to have strong interpersonal skills to engage clients. What do you see as your strengths in engaging and building rapport with others?

What you choose to talk about and not talk about, how you mix the personal and professional, how much you talk about yourself, your reactions, and your past experiences let Teresa quickly know what is okay and not okay to discuss in supervision. Whatever you decide to do or include, make it your decision—intentional and proactive—rather than being reactive and led by the clinician.

By being intentional and proactive you are taking the lead in clarifying and correcting the expectations that clinicians bring to the relationship. Some of these expectations may have been openly discussed in the job interview or in the first supervisory sessions—What do you need most from supervision? What was most difficult for you in your past supervisory relationships?—but you also will be uncovering and fine-tuning a clinician as you observe him in the first few weeks. You want to be supportive, yet clear about your boundaries and expectations, and you want to build these expectations around what you see as the clinician's needs.

If Mark, for example, is seeking you out 10 times a day to ask questions, it's clear that he needs information, but also needs to learn how to self-regulate and contain his anxiety. Rather than continuing to allow him to set the pace, you may suggest that he write his concerns down and bring them into your supervisory time, rather than constantly calling you, or send you an email with specific questions, rather than merely showing up at your door. If, on the other hand, Mark is more aloof—never sought you out, seems always guarded in supervisory sessions—the time he knocks on your door or calls you up at home in the evening upset about session, you may want to make sure you see him or take the call, rather than put him off; he is taking a risk and moving out of his pattern, and you want to support this first step.

Creating a sense of safety comes from your clarity and compassion. Creating an anxiety-approaching relationship comes from letting clinicians know that they can move outside their comfort zones and receive positive feedback and support from you for doing so.

Here are several concrete things to do as you together frame out the relationship.

Raise a Range of Topics, and Create Variety

Just as clients learn what is safe to talk about based upon the clinician's questions and responses, clinicians are going to know what is safe to talk about only by what you raise and discuss. Making the field of topics wide in the beginning helps clinicians feel that they don't have to be always cautious, that you are open, that there is plenty of room for you both to explore. Again, what's important is that your intention is purposeful, rather than unintentional, and driven by clinicians' supervisory needs, rather than your own personal needs.

In a similar vein, you want to be careful that supervision doesn't get locked into a rigid format. Following a set pattern in supervisory sessions—the client presents cases, the supervisor gives feedback, we then talk about administrative issues—can initially help clinicians emotionally settle. But if this becomes the norm for both of you, if you both stay within a narrow comfort zone in what or how issues are discussed, the relationship and supervisory process have little room for creativity and growth. Instead you want to keep the process always a little off balance. You want to be able to raise new questions and try new ways of approaching issues to desensitize the clinician to change, and through the exploration, discover what works best for both of you.

Provide Clear Structure and Directives

Are clinicians to send you an agenda in advance, can they come with one to a supervisory session, or are they free to come up with one in the moment? If they have a problem, is it okay to call, email, or show up and knock on your door? Is it all right for a clinician to eat her snack during meetings with you? Determine your expectations and standards and be clear about them. If you don't, clinicians will invariably test, and both you and your clinicians will invariably eventually get frustrated.

Follow through on what you say. Have your words and deeds match. This is the foundation for real honesty and trust. If you tell clinicians to email you questions, make sure you answer them quickly. If you want clinicians to prepare an agenda before a meeting, don't let an agenda-less meeting go unnoticed. And if you decide you need to make changes later—have people leave voice messages rather than send emails—feel free to do so, but let everyone know in advance why and how. If you don't, you risk seeming like an inconsistent and unreliable supervisor.

Provide a Place and Tools, Help Settle into the Agency Family

You probably remember those initial days in your field placement or first job where you knew no one and felt so out of place. If the agency didn't seem welcoming—if your supervisor seemed distracted or overly busy, or if you found yourself with no phone, with no computer, or sitting at a desk in the basement away from everyone else—it probably took a toll on your self-esteem and morale.

As a good supervisor you don't want to do this. Give new people a place to work and the tools and equipment they need (and if for some reason you immediately cannot, explain and apologize for the poor introduction); help them feel part of the family by welcoming them and introducing them to everyone (even if they won't remember everyone's name). Let them know who can answer their questions if you are not available. Don't further fuel a new clinician's own sensitivity to being the unwelcomed new kid on the block.

Provide Plenty of Positive Feedback

Know what you don't know means that it's easy for new clinicians to interpret your furrowed brow or nonresponse to their unheard "good morning" as evidence that the critical nonsense swirling in their heads is undoubtedly true. As their supervisor you have to work hard to counter this critical chatter with positive feedback. Let them know what they are doing well—being on time, having agendas, volunteering for tasks, taking things in stride, taking risks by being vulnerable and showing emotion, reaching out, calling you up and asking for help. The rule is to be clear but matter-of-fact about the negative, and enthusiastic about the positive. As long as you're sincere, you can't overdo it.

Acknowledge and Clarify the Double Bind of Probation

Acknowledging that clinicians may be confused or rattled by the mixed messages of supervision and probation goes a long way in letting them know that you are empathic and approachable on such topics. What fuels clinicians' anxieties is their imagination of how the probationary evaluation will be like—undoubtedly something clinically grueling and exacting. Offset such fabrications by showing them what the evaluation actually covers. Assuage their performance anxiety by letting them know that you will be giving them feedback throughout the probationary period; there will be no surprises. If a clinician thinks it would be helpful, plan a 3-month evaluation. This gives you both an opportunity to step back and evaluate the clinical landscape.

Be Honest

This sets the firm foundation for trust and openness. In the early days of relationship building, process—how you say something—is always going to carry more weight than content—what you say. How you present your feelings and ideas will have more impact on the clinician than what those feelings and ideas may actually be.

From the start focus on being in the moment and being clear. Say what you mean. Let the clinician know your intention behind your action, and your worry behind your question. When you don't know what to say, say that you don't know what to say. When clinicians realize that your words can be taken at face value, they no longer need to obsess and worry about what you might have really meant. Using you as a role model, clinicians learn not just what you think, but how to think. They have an opportunity to see how life looks from your side of the desk.

Assess

Simultaneous with relationship building is also the goal of assessing each clinician. Just as clinicians are looking at the strengths and weaknesses that make up their clients, you are looking at the strengths and weaknesses—both personal and clinical—that make up each clinician.

Chapter 3 mentioned the notion of looking for the holes—what it is, in terms of emotions and content, that a clinician doesn't talk about or doesn't show in a session with you. This can lead you to where his anxiety lies. It is a starting point for your own curiosity and your thoughts about where, to be more flexible, he may need to eventually focus and move. At this first stage you can use the idea of holes as a starting point for your assessment—in job interviews, during the first weeks of supervision. Raise these issues and topics to bring them into discussion; explore together how they may influence clinical work and personal style.

Much information about a clinician's self-presentation and clinical knowledge can undoubtedly be discovered in job interviews—for example, when you notice how assertive or unassertive an applicant is, or learn that she worked primarily with elderly clients at her last job, she has never worked with children, or she knows virtually nothing about post-traumatic stress disorder. But as clinicians move through their first cases, you have an opportunity to see the finer points of their skills—how well they can connect with a variety of clients, what types of cases they feel confident with, which pose new challenges.

As the name of this stage suggests, much of what you will be doing is providing training about the agency, the job, and clinical skills. Seeing teaching as one of your primary roles during this stage, as well as setting it as priority of supervision, helps clinicians settle. Clinicians realize that they don't have to know everything after all, and you can help them determine and learn what is most important. But to do this, you need to assess the baseline of skills so you know what gaps need to be most filled.

There are several clinical problems that new clinicians in a wide variety of settings often struggle with. Here are some of the most common ones that you should look for.

Determining Who Has the Problem

While most new clinicians are able to help clients partialize problems, they often get confused about who has the problem. Social services may be worried about a mother's parenting of her children, but the mother is worried only about social services looking over her shoulder or the fact that her children have a "bad attitude." A wife may be worried about her husband's drinking, but the husband is focused only on his wife's depression. While problems are often linked—husband's drinking and wife's depression, for example—taking responsibility and ownership for one's problem defines what one can control and what one cannot. Clinicians who have difficulty sorting out who owns what problems easily wind up feeling like clients do—frustrated, angry, or overresponsible.

Pressure to Have All the Answers

Rather than seeing therapy as a process of helping clients better define their problems and discover their own solutions, new clinicians often feel that they need to already know the answers to all of their clients' problems. Not only is this not possible and prudent, but it only increases clinicians' feelings of knowing what they don't know.

Difficulty Translating Theory and Concepts into Concrete Action

Jim knows that according to structural therapy he needs to support the parental hierarchy, but doesn't know what to actually do in a session to accomplish it. Denise intellectually understands the stages of grief, but feels clinically impotent when a client cries and talks about her guilt and sorrow. How to interact and respond effectively with clients within the session process often seems a mystery to new clinicians, and they are left feeling incompetent and frustrated.

Difficulty Seeing Underlying Issues

Mr. Smith complains about his son who is talking back to him all the time, his supervisor at work who is always critical of him, and his wife who always nags. He is overwhelmed, and within a few minutes of the session, the clinician, seeing all these fires burning, feels much the same.

What the clinician has trouble seeing is what the client has trouble seeing—the underlying issue that runs through each of the problems, namely, Mr. Smith's difficulty with being proactive and assertive, particularly with those who are critical. This ability to discern patterns, to hear common threads, or to uncover core dynamics is often a challenge for new clinicians.

Difficulty Confronting Clients

Part of this comes from a clinician's "good kid" ways of coping—his wanting clients to like him, his fear of conflict—as well as the common countertransference of dealing with clients who are 20 or more years older than him and who remind him of his parents. Rather than holding clients accountable or appropriately confronting them in sessions, new clinicians back away, rationalizing how a more supportive response is best.

Your assessment requires that you differentiate a clinician's learning problems from her problems about learning (Ekstein & Wallerstein, 1958). Learning problems are gaps in knowledge and skills—what needs to be taught and learned. Problems about learning are those situations where clinicians have trouble applying what they know. These are countertransference issues—Teresa's client reminds her of her mother and so she has a difficult time being assertive; Jack does well with most depressed clients, but for some reason seems emotionally dragged down by an elderly gentleman who is grieving the loss of his wife. It's not that Teresa and Jack don't know what to do; it's that their personal reactions are interfering and keeping them from doing what they know. While some clinicians are aware at the start of some of their particular problems about learning, most discover their difficulties, with your help, as they move through cases and reach impasses.

Professional Identity

Practice Behavior Example: *Practice personal reflection and self-correction to assure continual professional development.*

Critical Thinking Question: What do you see as your own learning problems and problems about learning? How do these affect your work with others?

Along with learning problems comes learning style—how best a particular clinician learns new skills and ideas—which was discussed in Chapter 3. Again, this is something you may want to explore as part of the interview process. Some clinicians will say they like to read material ahead of time, or talk about a plan for a session in supervision before the session itself. Some are visual learners; some, more hands-on, learn by demonstration. If you don't know, ask. Try out a variety of modalities and methods—assign readings, have them observe you or other clinicians, do role-plays—and see what seems to them to work the best.

Finally, you want to assess the ways clinicians manage anxiety and how they respond to supervision. Look at how they cope with new situations. How easily are they flustered, and how quickly can they recover? Do they disasterize, shut down, need immediate support, internalize, or intellectualize? How well can they think on their feet, or stay in the moment? You'll want to ask about these issues directly, as well as look for patterns over the first weeks of supervision. Your goal is to reduce anxiety, so clinicians can learn, rather than being distracted by it, and move them toward an anxiety-approaching style. Understanding their coping style and behaviors is the first step.

Supervisory sessions are your primary forum for learning about clinicians' personalities, ways of coping with anxiety, and learning styles. It is also here that you track the development of the supervisor–supervisee relationship. Over time you want to see clinicians focusing more on their cases and less on how well they are doing or what they think you are thinking. If they are struggling—for example, if Kim is remaining closed and cautious, tentatively presenting cases, providing one-word answers to your questions—you want to wonder and ask why. Is she anxious and still feeling unsafe? Does she see you as intimidating or demanding? Does she act in the same way around her colleagues, suggesting that it is more about shyness and less about you?

Similarly, if Joe is trying to control the process through intellectual discussions, and steers away from emotions, you want to see whether his controlling behavior reflects his initial anxiety and whether he is able to relax with you over time, or if in fact his behavior remains entrenched or widespread, making it more of supervisory priority for you.

Look at how hyper- or hyposensitive clinicians may be to your comments and suggestions. Notice if they are able to be assertive and vulnerable with you. When you ask if you are providing what they need in supervision, can they be honest and open, rather than seemingly saying what they think you want to hear.

Orient and Train

Just as clinical assessments form the basis of client treatment plans, your supervisory assessment of the clinician becomes the basis for setting, with the clinician, realistic goals. Some agencies provide formal orientations for new staff, which familiarize them with essential policies and procedures, job benefits, agency structure, and the like. One of your first training responsibilities is to orient new staff to the particulars of your team—the forms you use and how to fill them out, who is seen about what, how to sort priorities, what types of situations and information are essential that you be immediately informed about, and what things can wait. These are the mechanics of the job that usually fluster even an experienced new clinician.

Hopefully, through the interview process you already have a good idea of how much clinical training a new clinician may need, and you are clear in your own mind that you have decided to make the investment. What your training plan needs now is fine-tuning—exactly what, when, and how to teach what is most important that your assessment in the first weeks of supervision provides. Having clinicians tag along with more experienced colleagues is a good way of teaching them simple procedures—sitting in on emergency room crisis assessments, going out to homes to do child abuse investigation, observing an outpatient family session. Working with other staff helps new clinicians build relationships with their colleagues and brings them into the work family. Sitting in on sessions with other staff can, at this stage, be less intimidating than sitting in with you.

While tagging along has its benefits, do this only when you are sure that the supervisory relationship is off the ground and successfully moving forward. The danger here is that in the absence of a positive, if still nascent, supervisory relationship, new clinicians bond to their colleagues rather than you. They may come to rely on their peers for support and information, rather than struggling with a faltering supervisory relationship.

This is worst of all possible worlds for you as a supervisor. Not only does the supervisory relationship fail to develop, but you are effectively out of the loop, diminishing your ability to assure quality control. To avoid this from happening have clinicians team up with a variety of staff, rather than just one. More importantly, however, it's vital that you not be the neglectful supervisor and inadvertently delegate your responsibilities to others. You need to work hard to establish rapport and trust, and tackle the obstacles that arise.

It's a good idea to establish training goals within a 3- to 6-month time frame. Mapping these goals helps reduce clinicians' anxiety about probation, countering the worry that they need to learn about everything. Keep the goals specific—for example, conducting initial intake sessions, applying motivational interviewing with teens—and limited—for example, focusing on 2 or 3 at a time rather than 10, each with clear timelines. If faced with too many goals, clinicians may feel overwhelmed and lose sight of priorities.

As you discuss goals with a clinician and track their implementation, you are looking for a couple of things: Are you both on the same page—that is, is your assessment of a clinician's skills and knowledge similar to his? If not, does this reflect, perhaps, a clinician being overly critical of himself, particularly sensitive to one area of practice, or misinformed about job priorities? Are the clinician's time frames realistic? Is she expecting to do too much because of misjudging what's involved, or her own performance pressure and high expectations? Finally, is the training plan working? Over the next couple of months, is the clinician, in fact, able to learn and master what was laid out? What's important about this is assessing how easy or difficult learning seems to be. Is she easily frustrated? Is she able to follow through without getting scattered? Is she willing and able to apply information to the clinical setting? If the clinician struggles with the process of learning, this serves as red flag for the probationary evaluation.

The way you actually conduct the training depends, of course, upon your resources, your teaching style, the clinician's learning style, and the time you both have to devote to these goals. If a clinician learns best by reading, providing assignments and discussing how to apply reading material to specific cases may be sufficient. If the clinician is an experiential learner, you may want to pair her with staff who have strong skills in certain areas—observing or participating in play-therapy session, an initial assessment, a crisis intervention. One-way mirror observations, video- or audiotaping, role-playing, starting a training group for new clinicians and interns—all become options. The specifics of each of these options will be discussed later, but for now keep in mind that the training plan needs to be collaborative, specific, and realistic.

Create Success Experiences

It's your Thursday staff meeting. "So everyone, just want to let you know that Mike is going to be starting with us on Monday. He doesn't have much of a caseload yet, so if you have some cases you would like to transfer to Mike, please get them to me by tomorrow afternoon."

Poor Mike. What type of cases is he bound to get? Definitely not the easiest. In about 3–4 months, he may come to you saying that he and his wife have been talking. He's thinking he needs to go back to working in schools—summers off, better for childcare. While he may not admit it, he's burned out and feeling that he's not cut out to do this type of work.

Unfortunately, while most situations are not this extreme, it is easy as a supervisor to overlook the new clinician's need for success experiences, especially in those early months. Rather than being deliberate and careful about assignments, supervisors may be tempted, especially if there is a backlog of cases, to simply assign them. New clinicians who are already self-critical now become discouraged.

It's through success that clinicians at any level increase their professional confidence. This positive feedback, in turn, allows them to continue to learn and to approach, rather than avoid, their anxiety. Ideally, you want to be able to match clinical experience to fit your 6-month clinical goals. When this isn't entirely practical—for example, Ellen isn't able to take on a caseload composed entirely of children or couples—you still want to titrate cases so that clinicians don't feel overwhelmed by having to learn too much at once. If more challenging cases need to be assigned—for example, first time work with a child, a more complicated crisis situation, a case involving possible court testimony—map out with the clinician in advance what support is needed for success—pairing up with another clinician for the crisis situation, detailed planning before child sessions, a mini-training on the ins and outs of court work.

Provide Quality Control

All this talk about support, training, and planned success shouldn't distract you from your other primary focus as a supervisor: that of providing quality control. While your expectations need to be flexible enough to adjust for the varying experience of your clinicians, keep sight of the minimum and essential clinical standards that the job requires. Look at emerging patterns—Are clients following through or quickly dropping out? Are clients making progress albeit at a slower pace or in a more scattered way? Is there appropriate case coordination? Look at records—Are they up-to-date? Do they reflect documentation standards? Can you see progress on training goals? Do you have any concerns about boundary or ethical issues, and if you do, can the clinician respond appropriately and immediately to your directives and interventions? If not, why not? Given the clinician's level of experience, is his performance at the level you expect?

CONFRONTING AND MANAGING ANXIETY

All these goals and tasks are part and parcel of the focus of this first stage, that of establishing a sound foundation in terms of the supervisory relationship, the clinician's skills, and the clinician's continued ability to learn and grow. Because the key to the learning is the ability to approach anxiety, let's talk more specifically about ways of helping those who tend to get overwhelmed by anxiety, as well as those tend toward rigidity and control.

Working with the Overly Anxious

Ellen enters her supervisory session visibly upset and emotionally overwhelmed by her recent session with a woman who revealed in detail a history of sexual abuse. Ellen has not worked with any sexual abuse victims before and is distraught both by the content of what she hears and by the sense that the client has laid this enormous problem in her lap.

You have several goals in working with the overly anxious. You want to help them settle their sense of panic, but also help them learn to calm themselves down. You want to help them learn the skills they need to feel more competent, but also help them understand their own emotional triggers of anxiety. You want to help them develop clear plans so they are more proactive, less reactive, and less apt to fall into overresponsibility. Most of all you want to help them increase their tolerance for anxiety and learn to approach so they can take acceptable risks and grow.

Good listening on your part helps to dissipate anxiety, so you want to start by letting the clinician talk and ventilate until she begins to settle down. While it may be tempting to explore her personal reactions—what made her so upset, why did she feel so immobilized—wait. Leading in this direction right away can stir emotional content that would overwhelm the clinician again. Not only might this derail her leaving with a clear clinical plan, but it gives the clinician the impression that she needs to sort through her own personal issues before she can take clinical action.

Instead, it's better to help the clinician step back from her feelings, and into the problem and her clinical role. You might ask Ellen, for example, what she knows about sexual abuse, or what she thinks the client needs most, to help Ellen focus on the larger clinical picture and the knowledge and skills she has. If she lacks information about sexual abuse, you could provide her with some basic information as a way of placing the client and the problem in a larger clinical context. Once she is more settled, you can ask questions about her personal reactions to help her see what triggered her feelings.

This may lead naturally to a discussion of the clinician's ways of coping with strong emotions in others, in handling new situations, her own reactions to abuse and power, and her anxiety about not knowing at the moment what to do. Gently raise these anxiety-producing issues; listen and support as she opens up. Link her personal reactions to her clinical skills—"You seem worried about knowing what to say in the moment, yet when we talk about it now, you seem very clear." Help her develop a clear plan for working with the client—"Let's map out some short- and long-range goals"—and specifically for handling the next session—"What is it you would like to do in the next session? Would it help to do some role-playing?"

By the end of the session the clinician should feel emotionally settled and supported. She should have enough information to know where to focus for the next several sessions, know where to look for further information, and have a clear idea of what she can specifically do. In spite of reactions in the last session, she should now feel confident that she can be proactive and realize that she is not solely responsible for fixing the client's problems. Her job is to work together with the client, just as the supervisor works with the clinician, to explore together the effects of the abuse and ways to overcome them.

Finally, the clinician should know what she did well both with the client and with you—that she was able, in spite of her anxiety, to listen and support the client as the client revealed her secret, that she was open with you, and that she was, contrary to her self-criticism, able to think on her feet within the supervisory session.

You want to be clear and supportive, yet careful that you and clinicians don't get quickly locked into rigid patterns. Because your goal is encouraging clinicians to learn to self-regulate and reduce their own anxiety, you don't want an anxious clinician to always come in flustered and expect you to calm her down, fill her with information, and essentially work harder than she in feeling better and developing a clinical plan.

If you think you are falling into the habit of doing too much, or turning supervision into first aid rather than opportunities for growth, bring this up in supervision, ask the clinician to take the time to evaluate her clinical session before seeing you, or ask her to come up with a plan that you can discuss when you meet. The combination of self-responsibility with support from you will help increase self-confidence and expand the clinician's anxiety threshold.

Working with Controlling and Binding Behaviors

As mentioned earlier, it is rare in clinical work to find true anxiety binders who are completely removed from their anxiety. Many new clinicians, however, will use control as a way of reducing anxiety in specific situations.

Whereas overwhelmed and visibly anxious clinicians tend to draw a supervisor in, and reveal their emotions with little prodding, those who rely upon control—anxiety binders or passive-independent learners—attempt to keep the supervisor away, and withdraw if further stressed. Such a clinician may keep a tight rein on the content of supervisory meetings, just as she does in clinical sessions, only presenting positive aspects of clinical sessions, selective clients, or drawing you into intellectual, but emotionally comfortable, discussions about theory and technique. Your goal is to go beneath these defenses and tap into the clinician's anxiety, in order to bring the clinician into the room and the relationship.

This isn't as difficult as it may sound. The key is being confrontive yet not threatening. If you come on too strong or seem critical and demanding, the clinician will feel invaded, fear that his incompetence will be exposed, and is likely to retreat. A direct but gentle approach is best.

This translates into asking rhetorical questions: "Amy, it seems like you have a lot you want to cover in that session and have a tight agenda. I wonder if tightly planning it helps you feel more comfortable." "Tom, it seems that you are doing a good job with this family, but when I listened to the tape I wondered if the mom didn't follow through with your suggestion because she needed something different." "Tanya, it seems like we can easily drift toward theoretical discussions. I'm wondering why and thinking that it would be more helpful if we could focus more specifically on your questions about cases."

Just as you want to be careful with anxious clinicians of replicating the parallel process of overresponsibility, with controlling clinicians want to be careful of replicating the parallel process of muscling control of the supervisory session and encouraging further distance and resistance. Stating "I wonder . . ." and questions in a neutral tone let the clinician know that you know that more is going on than is being made apparent. By not pressing too hard for an answer or sounding overly critical, you give him time to come back with a more honest response. If he opens up and builds on your statement—"Yes, I guess I do use my agenda kind of like a security blanket; Yes, I actually thought the same thing about the mother after the session; Yes, I think it would be probably help if we focused more on my cases; perhaps I can pull together a list for next time"—you know your statements were on target and accepted.

If, however, the clinician shuts down or becomes defensive—"I'm only coming with an agenda because I thought you said I needed to have one; I'm realizing that it may seem like we are having theoretical discussions, but that is how I learn best"—you know your confrontation was misheard and too strong. If that happens, focus on the problem in the room, namely, the clinician's anxiety or hurt—"I'm not trying to sound critical; I'm just wondering if . . .; I realize that understanding the theory is important, but where it is easy to get stuck, where I got stuck when I first started working, is in translating the theory into specific skills; I'd like to help you do that."

Your goal is to help move the clinician away from his tight script and agenda and toward greater spontaneity and openness. Desensitize him to the give-and-take process by asking about nonclinical topics—kids, graduate school, hobbies—and use self-disclosure to reduce any distorted views of your personality and power. Self-disclosure with such clinician can be a powerful tool, especially when linked with opportunities to see you in action and to hear about your own mistakes. The clinician not only comes to realize that good clinical work is a feedback loop rather than a linear process, he sees through your modeling that everyone can make and survive mistakes.

That being said, you want to make sure that your self-disclosure isn't misconstrued as a breakdown in the hierarchy and accountability. Require that the clinician periodically submit recordings of sessions. If you have clinical questions about a case, matter-of-factly but clearly state your concerns, and make clear recommendations for changes. By staying focused on specific clinical issues, and by delivering them in a neutral tone, your feedback is less likely to feel like a reprimand or personal attack that precipitates withdrawal.

As with anxious clinicians, the process of relaxing defenses and reducing anxiety in controlling clinicians is a gradual one. Your goal at this first stage is to begin the process and be reassured that such changes are possible. As mentioned earlier, anytime a clinician asks a specific question, expresses an emotion, talks about a weakness in a sincere way, or moves off his predetermined course, stay quiet, listen, and give positive feedback. As trust in the relationship builds, anxiety becomes less of roadblock to learning.

Box 4.2 presents a summary of supervisory approaches to these 2 forms of anxiety styles.

Box 4.2 • Managing Anxiety Checklist

Anxiety Avoiding/Overly Anxious Styles	
Goals	Reduce clinician anxiety
	Encourage clinician self-regulation
	Encourage clinician to take acceptable risks and approach anxiety
	Help clinician become more proactive rather than reactive
Tasks	Teach skills, educate on clinical problem
	Develop concrete treatment plans
	Explore emotional triggers of anxiety
	Encourage self-calming; provide opportunities for acceptable risk-taking
Binding/Controlling Styles	
Goals	Increase clinician openness and spontaneity
	Create safety and trust
Tasks	Discuss the supervisory process in neutral, noncritical tone
	Clarify intentions if clinician becomes more closed
	Have clear expectations regarding clinical questions and performance
	Provide positive feedback for any openness/risk-taking

SUPERVISION VERSUS THERAPY

While it's clear that supervision is not therapy, in that its focus is not necessarily on resolving a clinician's personal issues, that doesn't mean that the process at times isn't therapeutic. Again, clinical social work is a profession where the personal and clinical are quickly intertwined. But how therapeutic should supervision be allowed to be? The answer lies largely within your own clinical model and professional values. Psychoanalytic therapy has always used the training analysis as part of its education model; a supervisor oriented toward solution-focused therapy, in contrast, will put greater emphasis on skills. As with other issues that have been discussed, what is important is that you proactively determine your own boundaries and expectations. If you don't, clinicians will test or become confused.

A useful and flexible middle-ground position between extremes of an analytic and purely skill-focused model is one, like the distinction between learning problems and problems about learning, that helps clinicians see how and when their personal reactions are undermining their clinical goals and creating impasses. Suppose, for example, that Cheryl is feeling frustrated and stuck with her client because the client fails to follow through on homework. You can help Cheryl, through questioning, role-playing, or using other experiential techniques (which will be discussed later), to unravel her frustration by identifying the emotional triggers and reactions that are particularly upsetting her with this client.

She may realize, for example, that this client reminds her of her ex-husband, who was critical and passive. You can help her see points at which her countertransference is taking over—where the client triggers her own personal reactions—and prevents her from going any further. Usually, the emotional awareness that her ex-husband is being projected onto her client is enough to help Cheryl move forward. If she still has difficulty following through with clinical recommendations, then something else is going on with this particular client or within the supervisory relationship, and you and Cheryl will need to dig deeper into the problem.

As a clinician's countertransference issues become more clear to you, you'll want to point out such patterns, and help the clinician think through particular cases in advance so she can be alert to potential emotional triggers. Think of yourself as a sideline team trainer who provides first aid if someone is injured in a game. Your job is to help the clinician stay in the game, or if necessary to pull him out, but leave real medical care—therapy itself—to the physician/therapist. If a clinician can't move forward with your help, he needs to be referred to the Employee Assistance Program or outside therapy. Your bottom line is not therapeutic overhaul, but clinical performance and quality work.

You may find clinicians, however, who are all too eager to turn supervision into therapy. The question is why. Is the clinician misunderstanding the role and function of the supervisory relationship? Is this a way of establishing intimacy with you as supervisor? Is it a means of avoiding dealing directly with clinical challenges? You might ask the clinician directly: "John, I notice that you've been talking primarily about yourself and your personal struggles this morning. I appreciate your openness, but we're not talking very much about your case. I'm wondering if it's easier for you to talk about yourself, or whether you are really feeling that these personal concerns are getting in the way of your clinical work."

If John expresses his desire for therapy, or gives the impression that he feels that his personal issues are affecting his work, you can draw clear lines—you'll help him do the clinical work, but that he needs to find someone else to handle the individual therapy. What is again important is that you are clear in your own mind and with him about the boundary line. Supervisors who are lured into becoming a clinician's therapist find it difficult both to back out of the role later and to evaluate performance fairly.

CHALLENGES AND DANGERS OF STAGE 1

Each stage carries with it dangers, and ways that a clinician's professional development can stop or be derailed. The dangers of this first stage are particularly significant because if not identified and overcome, they can undermine the supervisory process and potentially stop clinical growth. These dangers can be divided into those affecting a clinician and his work, and those that impact the supervisory process.

Clinician Challenges and Dangers

Fear

There really is no other word for it—fear of criticism, fear of anger, fear of confrontation, fear of incompetence and failure, fear of the unknown. Clinicians who cannot master their fear and anxiety not only get forever distracted by their own reactions and get clinically stuck with clients, but their inability to take risks leave them ultimately unable to learn and grow. If Jack constantly worries not only about what he said in his last client session, but whether he is even going to be a good therapist, or obsesses about how he thinks you feel about him, quickly or eventually he will leave the job—because he is never feeling that he is doing well enough, because some other position seems less emotionally taxing and, in his mind, more suited to his skill and personality. He is too handicapped by his fear and unable to adapt to the demands of the work.

Your challenge is to lower Jack's anxiety, help him take acceptable risks to increase his anxiety tolerance and feel successful, and help him learn the clinical skills he needs to be and feel more competent.

Rigidity

While those flooded with fear struggle to move forward, those who stay rigid and controlling despite your help are never able to see what is before them. Their clinical vision is narrow. Sophia seizes upon some clinical concept, therapeutic format, and tries to squeeze, unsuccessfully, every client and problem within it. By overly simplifying her world, the complexity that is life and therapy becomes lost. Like Jack, she may leave or be terminated.

Your challenge is to help Sophia see that rigidity is a poor solution and help her expand her repertoire.

Overresponsibility

This is high risk of this stage. The "good kid" clinician is in danger of working too hard to impress both clients and supervisors. Idealism and the desire to make a difference fuel this even more. Because clinicians have trouble seeing the common thread underneath the variety of problems that clients present, they are scrambling to tend to them all and feel overwhelmed. Because, like clients, clinicians see problems as being "out there" in the environment, rather than originating within the psyche of the clients themselves, they are always trying to patch the holes—getting food stamps, seeking psychological testing, organizing messy living rooms. They are in great danger of burning out.

There is an ethical side to this overresponsibility as well. Boundary lines can become easily blurred. Clinicians lend clients money, take clients' kids to McDonald's because they seem hungry, or volunteer to bring clients a couch on Saturday morning that they got for free from their brother-in-law, all in the spirit of being helpful. Clinicians need your help to understand what is and is not appropriate for their job. They need to understand that doing good doesn't mean doing too much.

Ethical Practice

Practice Behavior Example: Recognize and manage personal values in a way that allows professional values to guide practice.

Critical Thinking Question: How would you handle situations in which a clinician is being overresponsible and blurring boundaries?

Supervisory Challenges and Dangers

The Relationship Never Develops

If, after a couple of months, a clinician is still afraid to be open—is unable to use the supervisor for clinical and emotional support—if a clinician remains anxious, or if there is little trust, then the clinician either is getting those needs met somewhere else—through peers—or is isolated and dying clinically. Without the relationship there is no supervision.

The question again is why, and responsibility for answering it and correcting it is always yours. You need to look first at your own behaviors. Have you, like the clinician, been stuck in fear or rigidity—not engaging, not challenging, not reaching out, not self-disclosing—stopping the relationship in its tracks? Or is it a problem of pacing or neglect—moving too fast, expecting too much, not training or orienting enough, not helping the clinician find a place in the agency family, not screening cases carefully enough and building in failure? Or does the problem lie within the clinician—personality issues keep him from connecting to peers, base skills turn out to be below the minimal level that the job requires. If you need help sorting this out, talk to your own supervisor, and get supervision of your supervision.

There is the question whether this relationship may not be a good match. Should you transfer the clinician to another supervisor? In many agencies, this unfortunately is often not an option. There is no one else to transfer to. If there is, then this needs to be discussed with the clinician as option. Before you do that though, you and the clinician should sort out and agree upon where the problem really lies.

Little Self-Awareness

The clinician seems open and trusting, but something seems to be missing. The clinician has too many blind spots—he doesn't see how he contributes to patterns with clients, shows little insight or curiosity into his own behavior, has a hard time identifying his own mistakes. This is where you use your own clinical skills. Is this a problem of knowledge and learning, or something within his personality? Your responsibility is to again sort this out, get the issues on the table, and explore them with the clinician. Be clear that you are expecting a certain level of self-awareness not because of your own personal standards, but because of how it directly impacts clinical practice.

Spoon-Feeding

Spoon-feeding works like this: A clinician comes to you uncertain about how to handle a certain problem or case. You are off and running, giving detailed information and suggestions on what to do in the next session. The clinician writes it all down and reports next week that it went really well. But now she has a new question. Again you jump on it, providing reams of information and specific suggestions on what to do next, and once again it works great. After a few weeks of this, you both are poised and trained to tackle the question of the week.

Spoon-feeding is powerfully seductive on both sides. If you are inside really a frustrated clinician; if you tend toward being a drill sergeant in style, feel easily comfortable in a teaching role; or if you worry excessively about quality control, then for any and all these reasons you can get hooked. Essentially, you are doing remote-control clinical work, sending the clinician out like a drone to handle what de facto becomes your case. Because you stay within your comfortable roles, you never feel anxious, and the clinician seals the process by giving you steady and wonderful feedback about your skill and knowledge. Finally, you never have to worry about quality control again because you know exactly what is going on in clinical sessions.

On the clinicians' side this is a win-win situation. Not only do they get their questions answered, they don't have to worry what to do, nor do they have to fret about making what you might consider a mistake. In sessions, rather than talking about the clinician's work, you both can just talk about the clients. Clinicians' anxiety goes down, and they know if they just do what you say, you'll be happy.

The downside of this, of course, is that you are not being a supervisor but a clinician, and the clinician is staying dependent and not growing. The way to prevent spoon-feeding is to be aware of it. The way to stop it is to simply put down the spoon and help the clinician learn to feed himself.

In all these dangers the interweaving of anxiety management, skill development, and relationship building can be seen. As supervisor it is your responsibility to demonstrate leadership, discernment, and clarity.

STAGE 1 AND THE EXPERIENCED CLINICIAN

While much of what has been discussed seems to apply to new clinicians, or relatively inexperienced clinicians who may be new to your type of practice or population, experienced clinicians who are simply new to the agency are not immune to many of these same characteristics and challenges. You may not have to worry or spend time on training and clinical skills, but you still need to create a solid relationship, assess style and skill, and provide quality control. Such clinicians may have less anxiety about handling cases, but may still have anxiety about performance and be sensitive to your reactions. Like less-experienced clinicians, they too need to feel welcomed, given plenty of positive feedback, and be encouraged to take risks.

Where new clinicians' resistance stems from their anxiety, more-experienced clinicians' resistance may stem from their expectations. You may see this at times in a clinician's "I don't do windows" stance. Clinicians dig in their heels when given tasks that they don't feel are part of their job. Because they are comfortable and competent in their clinical style and are assertive, they may openly balk at the notion of trying out new approaches or models.

Decide how much this stance affects your ability to supervise, and whether it carries over to clinical work. If you feel clinicians are always seeming resistant to your ideas, or feel entitled, they in fact are not allowing you to supervise them. If this same attitude carries over to clients, with whom they are too directive or controlling, this attitude becomes a genuine clinical concern. You need to get your concerns out in the open and state clearly your own expectations. If you are a new supervisor or younger than the clinician, if you feel intimidated, if you question your own clinical or supervisory skills, taking such a strong stand against a strong clinician can be difficult. Talk with your own supervisor about this and, if necessary, get her input and backing.

Even when an experienced clinician sidesteps these problems, and begins the job with a good attitude, you may come to discover that the clinician and the work are, in fact, not a good fit. The clinician's skills may not be as strong as you thought, or he may be struggling to apply them to the new setting—for example, moving to crisis work rather than the long-term supportive therapy he did before. Or perhaps the new population or problems—work with abused children or the terminally ill—are triggering countertransference issues that he can't seem to overcome.

You may be tempted to minimize these problems, to give him the benefit of the doubt because you feel intimidated and distrust your own assessment, or because you simply are delighted to have such an experienced clinician on board. Don't. Again, this stage is about laying the solid foundation. If you overlook these issues and ignore your own reservations, you'll find it more difficult to make changes later.

PUTTING IT ALL TOGETHER

To consolidate and summarize the issues and changes of each of the stages, let's track, through written self-evaluations, the evolution of one clinician over a period of years. This was written late in Stage 1. The clinician had several years of nonclinical, post-MSW, social work experience before beginning work at a community mental health agency. At the time of this evaluation she had been employed about a year and was working primarily with families in both outpatient and home-based settings. The evaluation covers her own assessment of her theoretical orientation, skills and knowledge, use of self, and use of supervision. As you read each section, listen for both the content—what she chooses to talk about—and the choice of language. We'll highlight important points as we go along. She starts with her own theory of therapy.

> *I tend to operate on the assumption that problems stem from difficulties individuals and families have in coping with their feelings. As I begin with a client I look for pain and try to connect with each person by empathizing with those feelings. I realize that I sometimes move too quickly. I'm learning that one needs to tread softly, especially when looking at pain. I believe that individuals with a family probably do not have effective methods of handling each other's feelings.*

What do you hear in all this? First, she is able to be open with her supervisor about her emotions and anxiety—all good signs. Notice that in her language and in her theory she tends to focus on the generic, global issues—a clinical soup of feelings and pain. She is having difficulty applying theory to practice—timing questions—and the writing itself reflects a lack of organization, skipping from one topic to another. The statement about "needing to tread softly" around pain suggests caution and fear. As a supervisor you might wonder if this is a parallel statement about her own sense of pain—whether it's being projected onto clients or whether as a supervisor you should tread more softly in your relationship with her. You'll find out by gently asking her.

> *I begin with the assumption that change is possible but that change is incredibly frightening. I often perceive resistance as simply fear of losing the familiar. I believe I am careful about over- or underidentifying with one member of the family. The other side of this, however, is that I hesitate to be confrontational or to be an expert. An example is my reluctance to question why a parent failed to follow through with a previously agreed-upon plan. My fears are of not being liked.*
>
> *It is difficult for me to consider myself as powerful. I wonder if I let myself become more of a friend with adults. I'm afraid of hurting someone's feelings.*

Change is incredibly frightening—for whom—the client, the clinician? Here she highlights the "good kid" sensitivity to power, the need to be careful, difficulty with confrontation, fear of not being liked by others, and of hurting or being hurt. As is common for this stage, she struggles with her own sense of power, the uncomfortableness of being an expert, and instead opts for being a friend with adults, a role that in some cases can fuel overresponsibility and blurring of boundaries.

As supervisor you may wonder if she worries about not being liked by you and is sensitive to your own power. Supervision offers clinicians the opportunity to learn how to confront others, and to understand that although feelings may get hurt, they can also be healed. Again, what is remarkable and important is that she is aware of all this and can risk honestly saying it to her supervisor. She is able to approach her anxiety.

> *I believe that growth derives from the way relationships are processed and experienced. I feel that connecting with people and attempting to allow them to experience a different kind of relationship is the essence of therapy. I try to impart a sense that I like the other person and he or she is respected and accepted.*

Here again, in the thinking and language is a certain vagueness and simplicity—a watered-down Rogerian approach—where feelings and relationship can cure all. Again, the statement of wanting to like and be liked.

> *I feel that I can be creative in my work. I am able to think of interventions that are unique to a particular client. I realize that I am reluctant to leave responsibility with those who should have it. I often jump in and rescue partly to avoid pain and to avoid my own lack of confidence. I would like to develop a feel for when it is appropriate to be myself in therapy and when it is imperative that I adopt a professional self.*

There are a couple of things going on here. In spite of saying that she lacks confidence, she also is able to see herself as creative, itself a sign of confidence. She is very much being a rescuer and overresponsible, but again she is aware of it and can acknowledge it. As her supervisor you may wonder whose pain is she trying to avoid by rescuing. Finally, she is struggling with the common problem of roles, dividing the self into professional and personal areas.

> *One difficult area is working with adolescents' families when the parents threaten to throw the child out. My own fear in challenging the parents results in my feeling at a loss as to how to handle the situation. . . . Currently I am having considerable difficulty managing stress and have yet to find an effective way to handle the anxiety I feel at times.*

Out of all the issues she might struggle with, why is she so sensitive to parents expelling children? Is this from her past, or is it in any way a parallel statement and she worries about the supervisor doing the same? Again, ask her. Confrontation comes up again as difficulty; her anxiety makes her feel clinically stuck at times, and is creating stress and potential burnout.

> *Because of my past supervisory experience, I learned to muddle my way through alone. As a result I am in a constant dilemma in that I want help but feel unsure as to how to ask for it and use it. . . . I often experience a real sense of vulnerability that stems from my being new. I often feel overwhelmed and unsure how to start. I think the experience of being given direction and feedback in the very moment it is needed would be ideal. Group supervision is difficult because it intensifies my sense of vulnerability.*

Vulnerability, but again awareness and disclosure of it. The effects of past supervision upon the present relationship, and a clear message to help the clinician use supervision more effectively. The comment about being overwhelmed raises a supervisory concern that you take care not to overwhelm the clinician even more. The desire for instant feedback reflects both the anxiety and the concern about doing therapy right. The reaction to group supervision, of feeling vulnerable and knowing what you don't know, is common during this stage.

Overall this clinician is doing well. Themes and feelings are clearly expressed, and she trusts the supervisory relationship. An avoider may not be as articulate, may have difficulty pinning down the sources of anxiety, would convey an overall sense of being overwhelmed, might be more self-deprecating. A more controlling clinician would certainly be less open, be more intellectual, would focus more on clients and less on self or supervision.

I would like to think about what I enjoy doing rather than worrying about how I am doing it.

This last statement is important in that the clinician is beginning to shift away from doing therapy "right" toward doing it the way she feels most comfortable. This is the beginning of defining a therapeutic voice and style. She is moving away from a self-protective stance and settling into the larger work of therapy and the supervisory relationship.

The clinician is moving toward the next stage of development.

The following questions will test your application and analysis of the content found within this chapter. For additional assessment, including licensing-exam-type questions on applying chapter content to practice behaviors, visit **MySearchLab**.

1. Spoon-feeding refers to

   a. Asking a clinician why she is raising a particular question

   b. Consistently handling a clinician's anxiety by telling her what to do with a particular client problem

   c. Limiting the range of topics discussed in supervision

   d. Giving a clinician too much positive feedback

2. The difference between learning problems and problems about learning is that

   a. Learning problems refer to skills, and problems about learning refer to emotional issues

   b. Learning problems refer to emotional issues, and problems about learning refer to skills

   c. Both are interchangeable and depend on the personality of the clinician

   d. Learning problems refer to new clinicians while problems about learning refer to more experienced clinicians

3. Allyson has a few clients who are always late for appointments or are not paying their bills, yet she never talks to them about this. This is an example of Stage 1 common problems with

   a. Confronting clients

   b. Being organized

   c. Setting clear goals

   d. Being reactive

4. Frank comes to supervision overwhelmed by the number of problems his clients present. This is an example of

   a. Being reactive

   b. Anxiety approaching

   c. Learning problems

   d. Being in victim role

5. Christy often comes to supervision late. How would you handle that with her?

6. John seems to always report that things are going well with his cases. What would you do regarding your need for quality assurance?

5

Stage 2: Supervisor as Guide

No clinician stays a beginner forever, and sometime between 3 and 12 months after starting work, things begin to change: the clinician's anxiety begins to wane, the probationary period is over, and with it, much of the performance pressure and the drive to appear competent. If you've accomplished your supervisory goals of the first stage, providing both safety and clarity, the clinician knows that you are aware of the quality of his work and seen through his efforts to look good enough. It's time to drop masks. It's time for the clinician to slow down, look around, and reflect on his own inner process and its impact on others.

Clients too, depending on the setting, are often moving on a parallel course. Some have left therapy, of course, either because they received what they wanted, or because the clinician wasn't able to move quickly enough to uncover their problems or offer the advice they were seeking. But with the clinician's increasing ability to think systemically and act a bit more flexibly, many of the newer clients are getting what they need sooner, and some of the longer-term clients have moved beyond their initial anxiety and distrust. Like the clinician, many clients are now less overwhelmed and able to reflect on the broader themes of their lives.

Box 5.1 gives a quick overview of this second stage.

Box 5.1 • Overview of Stage 2

Characteristics	Don't know what you know
	Anxiety reduced—settling down
	Dependency—supervisor as role model
	More proactive than reactive; better able to set agenda for therapy and supervision
	More aware of process, impasses
	More self-reflective
Supervisory goals	Help develop "third ear"—see how problems replicated in session
	Increase awareness of use of self
	Increase awareness of anxiety, parallel process
Supervisory tasks	Explore patterns in cases
	Help separate personal issues from skills
	Teach experiential techniques
	Increase use of recordings, observation, co-therapy, written exercises
Challenges/dangers	Encouraging dependency in clients
	Pushing away more independent, less-engaging clients
	Supervision becoming therapy

CHARACTERISTICS OF STAGE 2

Don't Know What You Know

Stage 1 was marked by the feelings of incompetence—know what you don't know. By this stage, the social worker has gained knowledge and skills, but she isn't always able to articulate clearly what she is thinking, doesn't feel always confident in her approach, and isn't always consistent and effective. There is a clear gaining of clinical ground, but a ground that doesn't always feel solid. An unexpectedly productive session with Mr. Thomas, for example, is followed by another where he seems again discouraged and says little. The clinician feels stumped and as discouraged as her client, and is not at all certain what accounts for the change.

Settling Down

Ellen is no longer bombarding you with questions 3 times a day; Tom is no longer controlled and sparse in his supervisory sessions with you. Everyone is able to relax, drop defenses, and lean toward the supervisory relationship in a healthy way—clear measures that you and your clinicians have moved through the first stage. If this settling fails to materialize—Ellen is still openly anxious, Tom is clearly reluctant and controlled—despite months of your best efforts to create a safe and trusting supervisory relationship, you have a clear cause for concern. As mentioned in Chapter 4, a clinician's anxiety and inability to engage in the supervisory relationship would undermine her learning and your ability to supervise. But these situations should not be a surprise and should be rare. If you've done your job and laid down that solid foundation of a relationship, both the clinician and clients will move beyond anxiety and crisis.

What you may see in some clinicians with this settling down is burnout. As mentioned earlier, clinicians at Stage 1 are at risk of burnout due to overresponsibility and performance pressure. Some clinicians, however, will slog through until they pass probation and then seem to collapse. You need to look for signs of burnout—apathy, calling in sick, irritability—and raise your concerns. This is important, not only in terms of your relationship and their performance, but in terms of their long-term productivity and survival in the profession. You need to help clinicians evaluate their caseloads, be ready to suggest time away from the job, and help them talk about any performance pressure stirred by particular clients, by you as supervisor, or by their own expectations. You need also to help clinicians learn to recognize their unique signs of stress and understand that you see burnout as a problem not to be ignored.

Dependency

With a decrease in anxiety, crisis, and performance pressure, there is often a shift for many clinicians from the pseudo-dependency of the earlier stage—an anxiety-based accommodation to what they see as your expectations—to a true dependency based upon a real respect for your personal strengths and skills. At this second stage the clinician looks to you as a role model for clinical social work practice, and you have the potential to step into the role of mentor. Clients are often doing the same: that is, leaning toward and becoming dependent on their therapists.

Proactive Rather Than Reactive

Because the clinician expends less energy focusing on himself—looking professional or preventing collapse—because he has gained knowledge and skills, he can better filter and shape what clients present. Rather than being flooded by details of the client's problems, and feeling much like the client does—reactive and overwhelmed—the clinician can instead prioritize and partialize problems. Sessions no longer run over because the clinician is able to help shape the session agenda rather than just absorb what is presented. Progress notes, which before were loaded with volumes of unnecessary facts, now become more clear and concise.

Self-Reflective

Because the clinician is less anxious and more settled, more skilled and more proactive, this greater sense of control, calm, and focus provides her room for turning inward. Rather than constantly putting out fires, she, with your help, can now step back and see the bigger picture. For many clinicians, this new perspective leads to questions about the individual in the context of the family, or of the present in the context of the greater past. A clinician may, in turn, become curious about her own history—her relationships with parents and siblings, her unique ways of coping—in order to make sense of the larger patterns in her own and in clients' lives.

And clients are often curious and willing to move in these directions as well. Ms. Jones, for example, is no longer just complaining about her husband, but is now wondering why she always gets involved with such uncaring, abusive men. Mr. Smith has stopped fretting about his son's insolence and started talking about problems in his marriage. The therapy moves beyond the presenting problems—the surface actions (the getting of food stamps, the learning of more effective parenting skills)—and has the opportunity to go deeper—to exploring Ms. Jones' past relationships with men, to exploring Mr. Smith's underlying fear that he will turn out like his father as a parent or a husband—with at times the clinician or the client taking the lead. All this can make the clinician excited, rather than just overwhelmed, by the clinical work.

Increased Awareness of Process

Part of this excitement comes from the increased awareness of the clinical process itself. With decreased anxiety and performance pressure, increased skills and self-reflection, you can help the clinician, and the clinician the client, begin to look at the process—the how (how problems are approached, how emotions are handled, how problems may be replicated in the session and within the therapeutic relationship)—rather than the what (a myopic focus on content). For example, instead of worrying about getting money to help pay a client's unpaid electric bill, the clinical conversation can now turn on what happens when the electric bill arrives that the client decides to stack it up on the kitchen counter with the rest of the mail and ignore it until the lights are turned off.

This shift from exclusive focus on content to that of the underlying process is a paradigm change for many clinicians, and a healthier one at that. The clinician discovers that he doesn't have to somehow put out all the fires out there in clients' world to please them, or win them and you over, in order to be good at his job. Instead, he now can pay attention to the process unfolding in the session, see that how you do anything is how you do everything, and help clients change the way they approach their problems and emotions. This usually has a startling effect that helps clinicians realize both the limits and the liberation of their power. Rather than trying to impact the client's entire wider world, clinicians can narrow their focus to what happens during the session with the client.

This realization further reduces the anxiety and pressure a clinician feels, and through the parallel process, the clinician can help the client to do the same. Now the therapist can learn to stay step-by-step with the client. For example, when Julie makes an interpretation to her client Mary, and Mary responds with a "Yes, but . . ." or turns away, Julie can catch the disconnection and adjust right then and there, "Mary, it sounds like you aren't agreeing with my idea," rather than anxiously marching ahead and wondering later why Mary canceled her next appointment. Julie can see how Mary's problems are at times replicated in the session— that Mary passively ignoring Julie's suggestions, for example, is exactly what she does when confronted with stressful situations in her everyday life. By focusing on such behavior right there and then, by learning to pay attention to and track the micro-process in the session, the clinician learns to detect resistance and transference–countertransference dynamics, learns to utilize the session process to promote client change.

Managing Impasses

This follows logically from the aforementioned characteristics of this stage. Because both clinicians and clients are often reaching the middle phases of treatment, it becomes easier to see places and patterns where the clinical process bogs down. You notice, for example, that Ellen does not only get clinically stuck with Mr. Jones but also with clients like Mr. Jones who tend to be aggressive and demanding in sessions. Your and Ellen's challenge is to determine how much of the problem comes from learning problems or problems about learning—her lack of skills or countertransference issues where her emotional reactions interfere with her ability to utilize her skills.

SUPERVISORY GOALS OF STAGE 2

During the first stage much of your supervisory focus was on teaching—as an end—in terms of orienting the clinician to the agency and job, training in clinical theory—and as a means—creating an atmosphere of trust and safety. Now that the clinician is less anxious, more proactive, and able to be more responsible for her learning, like self-reflection, there is room for more curiosity and genuine desire for greater clinical depth. Your role now shifts to that of a guide. She, as much as you, is likely to set the pace and supervisory agenda. Rather than helping her develop treatment plans from scratch, you help her fine-tune her thinking and plans. And because the supervisory relationship and the clinician are less fragile, you can now also be more confrontive.

When Ellen came to you during the first stage, anxious and uncertain about how to address her client's sexual abuse, you focused on skills and information as a way to reduce her anxiety; you encouraged her to be more proactive in the next session. Now that her anxiety is lower, and now that she has more skills, the supervisory discussion can turn more toward her own emotional reactions—How did you feel when your client described what had happened to her?—and to the details of the session process that earlier she was unaware of—Why did you say that right then? Where earlier she left the session feeling better because she knew what to do next, now she can leave the session feeling better because she was challenged and now understands more—about herself and the client—and is able to apply this insight and information to treatment.

While helping clinicians identify their specific reactions in specific cases is valuable, so too is helping them see the broader patterns and themes in their own work. Now is a good time, for example, to have conversations about a clinician's management of anxiety: Can you tell when you are getting anxious in a session? How do you tend to react? Can you identify the triggers that set off these reactions? Rather than creating a dust storm of anxiety as they would have earlier, such questions can now be given some careful consideration. By asking these broader questions, you can help the clinician realize what she contributes to the clinical relationship. You can help her begin to detect her patterns and process.

And process is what this stage is about—helping the clinician firmly develop that "third ear"—to be able to be aware of what is happening in the room there and then with a client, rather than ruminating about a solution to the client's latest problem. Point out when you see the parallel process at work—with the clinician feeling the same as the client and replicating the interactions with you—as a way of helping the clinician recognize its power. Look at the micro-process—the crafting of interpretations, the ability to track a story's nuance, and the emotions that come with it—and help the clinician incorporate this information into the goals of the next session with the client. Discuss together the weaving of content and process, and help the clinician know how and when to shift between both.

Through this focus upon action and reaction, clinical planning and emotional re-sponses, the clinician begins to really understand what is meant by use of self. Through your focus on anxiety and countertransference, parallel process and emotional triggers, the clinician begins to understand how to use the clinical relationship as a medium for change, rather than focusing only on fixing the client's problems "out there." Because the clinician now doesn't know what he knows, your role has shifted from "telling him what he needs to know," to helping him discover what he knows. Point out the gaps between session goals—"I wanted to help the client feel safe"—and outcomes—"But did you hear the edge in your voice and notice the look on the client's face?" Ask about reactions and triggers. Identify all the positives to help the clinician see what works and why, while at the same time ask hard questions to make him curious about what doesn't.

Critical Thinking

Practice Behavior Example: Analyze models of assessment, prevention, intervention, and evaluation.

Critical Thinking Question: While the focus on process is important in therapy and supervision, in what social work tasks might the focus on content be the primary focus?

SUPERVISORY TASKS OF STAGE 2

So how do you actually accomplish these goals of increasing awareness of clinical process and use of self? Here are some tasks to focus upon during this stage.

Explore Patterns in Cases

As mentioned earlier, you now have a track record of cases to look at and you can discover patterns: clients who dropped out after 2 sessions; family sessions with teens where there was more overtalking and arguing than productive conversation; being too aggressive or passive in sessions with court-ordered clients. Detecting the thread that runs through cases is all grist for the supervisory mill. From your perspective, it may be easier for you to see such patterns, but you need not feel that this is your responsibility alone. Instead, this is something you and your clinicians can focus on together. Ask the clinician, for example, to look back over his cases for the past 6 months, notice what he considers the successes and the failures, and give his thoughts about the differences.

What you are looking for in the clinician's evaluation is a balanced and relatively complex perspective. You don't want to hear more, for example, than the clinician's simple assessment that the court-ordered clients were simply resistant. You are curious about the clinician's abil-ity to identify the source of a client's resistance, to describe the way it was played out in the session, and to define the way the clinician responded to it. These thoughts, in turn, become the starting point for further exploration: Why this case rather than the other one that was similar? What might you have done differently if these clients were to come back tomorrow? Are there skills you need to develop in handling such cases and problems, or is there some emotional reaction on your part that makes these cases particularly difficult for you?

The purpose of these types of questions is to help the clinician reflect upon and understand what makes for effective clinical process. If the clinician responds defensively—"I tried but they just wouldn't engage with me"—becomes openly anxious and closes up—"I don't know"—the problem is the room. This is where you use your supervisory and clinical skills to explore what just happened—"I hope you aren't feeling criticized, I'm just wondering if . . .," "You seem anxious by my questions—are you feeling put on the spot?" Your goal is to reduce anxiety, get the conversation back on track, and wonder aloud perhaps if what just happened between you and the clinician parallels what possibly happened between the client and clinician.

Again if the supervisory relationship is strong, these sessions can be important learning moments where the clinician can experientially come to understand how to navigate the shifting clinical tides. By being clear, supportive yet challenging, you help the clinician learn to separate personal from professional. Through your modeling, he learns how to change the patterns as they emerge.

Help Separate Personal Issues from Skills/Theory

This is part and parcel of exploring patterns. What are the learning problems, and what are the problems about learning? Help the clinician understand the difference between them and ask her to decide which is which. Obviously you both should be able to come up with the same answer, but you ask the question so the clinician can figure out for herself what she knows and doesn't. Again, if you are not on the same page—you see Tamara, for example, having trouble with a boy with attention deficit disorder (ADD) because she seems to have trouble setting structure with children; while she feels her problem is one of not fully understanding ADD, you want to obviously begin by understanding what she feels she needs. What does she exactly think she needs to know? How will this knowledge help her in working with this boy? What does she need to do to apply it?

But as her supervisor, you don't want to stop the conversation there. You also are curious about why she isn't seeing what you are seeing, namely the larger pattern of being passive and reactive with children. Have you, as supervisor, failed to point this out earlier? Have you pointed it out, but didn't clearly address how Tamara might handle it differently? Did you do all the right things, but she failed to hear what you were saying or follow through, and if so, why? If the observed problem, her difficulty with structure, is a symptom, what is the underlying issue—her anxiety about children, or her own personal experience and reactions to the parenting she received?

Again, you need not have all the answers, but you do need to not replicate the process by being passive and reactive yourself. Ask the questions, raise the topic, take leadership, and guide the supervisory process toward a mutual exploration and understanding.

Increase Use of Recording, Live Observation

This stage is a good time to make ample use of recording and observation. (We'll will discuss the methods of effectively using recording and observation in a later chapter.) In the first stage, not only would the therapist be ultrasensitive to his own work, but he could not adequately grasp the details of what you are trying to focus upon. Now with your focus upon the clinical process, recording and observation provide ideal ways of tracking the micro-interactions. By honing in on the step-by-step interactions between the clinician and client, the clinician has an opportunity to develop his "third ear."

Because the clinician is more proactive and has clinical filters in place to screen out what is not important, this detailed look at the session process can be absorbed and used. Now that the clinician feels safe, those occasions when the camera was directed toward a blank wall, where the microphone was forgotten to be turned on, and all the other things that happen with the first stage and clinician anxiety are less likely.

Teach Experiential Techniques

Role-plays, guided imagery, empty-chair technique, sculpting—experiential techniques such as these can be valuable adjuncts to treatment and learning. (The teaching and use of these specific techniques will be discussed in a later chapter.) As with recording and observation, the clinician's reduced anxiety and increased proactivity make this a good time to teach these techniques. Demonstrating such techniques earlier would have likely left the clinician feeling overwhelmed and vulnerable, unable to process the experience, and due to performance pressure, unable to implement the technique effectively. Now with a more solid core of skills, such techniques enhance the clinician's work with clients and provide opportunities to identify personal issues.

> ### Engage, Assess, Intervene, Evaluate
>
> **Practice Behavior Example:** *Critically analyze, monitor, and evaluate interventions.*
>
> **Critical Thinking Question:** What experiential techniques have you learned or used that you felt were particularly effective? How do you use or might use them in your work?

Assign Written Exercises

Because the clinician doesn't know what he knows, written exercises become a good means of discovering and articulating what is known. If Carlos, for example, seems to be having difficulty translating overall treatment goals into specific session goals, you may want to suggest to him that he think about the last session with the client, decide from that what might be a next step, map out goals and techniques for a next session, and bring them in to you to discuss and sort through his questions.

How one writes often reflects how one thinks. This type of written preparation can help Carlos consolidate and put into words and plans what he feels initially as confusing or overwhelming, and reduces his feeling put on the spot in the treatment session. If you find that even through writing his thinking is muddy, you can help him clarify his thinking by asking specific and concrete questions: "Tell me what your client most needs to do to build up his confidence." "Did you feel that the homework you assigned to your client was helpful? What do you feel would be a good next behavioral step for your client?" "Tell me why you think the client's drinking is more of a problem than you initially thought?" "Tell me why you think the diagnosis should be major depression rather than dysthymia."

Questions like this, just as they do for clients, help the clinician to sort through and focus his thoughts. Written exercises that encourage the same specificity—write up a treatment plan, map out what you would focus on in the first 3 sessions, assess how your clinical approach has changed over the last year—can do the same, helping the clinician discover what he knows and believes, measure how he and his clients have changed.

IMPASSES, INTIMACY, AND DEPENDENCY

One way of bringing together the characteristics, goals, and tasks of this stage is to look at the relationship among impasses, intimacy, and dependency. As mentioned earlier, one of the sources of impasses with clients is the clinician's limitation of skills. For example, John, through his experience over the past months, is solid in his assessment skills and crisis management skills but seems uncertain how to move through the middle stages of treatment now that the fire of the crisis is out. Tamara has a solid core of clinical skills but has little experience working with someone who discloses childhood abuse and is suffering from post-traumatic stress, and she doesn't know how to proceed. These are learning issues, and your role becomes that of teaching information, directing them to resources, and helping them translate book knowledge into clinical goals and tasks.

But the clinician's skills generally form the smaller part of the problem; with the supervisor's help the clinician can plan and apply the needed clinical first aid to get through the next session. Impasses, however, more often result from collusion, the interweaving of countertransference and transference issues whereby clinician and client make an unconscious agreement to reduce anxiety by falling into patterns that meet the emotional needs of each of them.

One of the most common sources of collusion seen in family and couple work is induction into the system. Here the clinician takes on one of the roles within the family system or absorbs the family's emotional stance. Jodi, for example, may find herself joining with the mother and the other kids in bashing the father for his neglect of the family; in couples therapy Jodi may side consistently with the partner who seems most vocal. Something in Jodi's emotional life identifies with something within the client or system, and she becomes dragged into and a part of the problem. Rather than staying outside the system as a change agent and role model for approaching anxiety, she unwittingly avoids anxiety and supports the dysfunctional patterns that are already present. She loses her emotional independence and with it her therapeutic power and leverage on the system. An impasse occurs.

Clinicians are vulnerable to induction at all stages, though over time with experience and support they are better able to see the signs and anticipate potential inductions. During this second stage, however, some clinicians are prone to overidentify with vulnerable clients—for example, children within a family or the frail older person. The clinician is projecting his own increased vulnerability and sensitivity onto these clients. As supervisor you need to be alert to this pattern and help the clinician separate his own feelings and needs from those of the clients so that he can take a more balanced position.

But an even more common form of collusion that you need to be alert to is that of the clinician using the therapeutic relationship as a refuge. In these situations the clinician and client make significant emotional investments in maintaining the relationship as it currently exists, even when it appears to be working and moving forward.

Ms. Jones, for example, comes in every Tuesday and recites a summary of the week's events to Julie, her therapist. She talks about her reactions, her thoughts; she sighs and cries and gets angry. Julie may offer support or advice, even give her a homework assignment to write a letter to her deceased mother or aborted child. The assignment may or may not get done, but it really doesn't matter. Although the therapeutic content may change, the process remains the same week after week.

It's easy to see this pattern as Ms. Jones' dependency on Julie as a support for the chaos in her life. This in itself is not cause for concern; in fact, it is common in the middle stages of therapy. Such dependency can even be therapeutic—Ms. Jones may have never learned to trust another woman, and her relationship with Julie represents a reparenting opportunity. Similarly what appears like an impasse in her ability to continue to make changes in her life could represent a plateau in progress. After an energetic start, it's time for Ms. Jones to consolidate her gains, or at least not return to baseline considering the enormous stress she is facing.

Yes, this all could be clinically true, but Julie isn't making these clinical arguments; the collusion betrays a seduction. The process has ground to a halt as a result of emotional ruts, routine, and repetition. Without some anxiety within the relationship, there is nothing pushing it forward. Ms. Jones is now treading water and Julie is looking the other way.

Rather than approaching anxiety both client and clinician have become avoiders—both bask in the comfort of the relationship as it is. In part this impasse may be fueled by Julie's difficulty with confrontation—the "good kid" inclination to be happy if the client is happy. But the impasse is also fueled by Julie's deeper need for the relationship. Like others who fit the rescuer profile, Julie has been seduced by intimacy. The closeness, dependency, openness, and trust of the client have drawn Julie into the client's world, filling her own unmet needs. She doesn't want to risk losing this intimacy by pushing therapy forward. For clinicians who grew up with self-sufficiency and lack of trust, who haven't had many opportunities to have their needs met through personal relationships, this can be a particularly powerful experience. If the clinician has struggled during the past months with anxiety, distrust, failure, and the sense of faking it, such intimacy can feel like validation for a job well done.

Your job in such situations is to hold a magnifying glass, viewing the clinician's work with her client from a micro-rather than a macro-level. If you suspect that Julie is letting her client coast along because she is afraid of disturbing the intimacy of the relationship, you need to raise the question of Ms. Jones' dependency on Julie and Julie's reactions to it. You might then point out patterns in the process through video or audiotape, highlighting the lack of anxiety and movement within the session, and raise the question of Julie's own reluctance to disturb the relationship, her own needs for intimacy. Finally, you can tie the relationship/intimacy issue to the supervisory relationship: for example, exploring with Julie her possible dependency on you.

By taking an active stance you are using the supervisory process to isolate the source of the impasse. You are demonstrating ways to handle both the impasse and the process with the client. By saying what is not being said, looking at the relationships both in the supervisory session and with the client, linking the relationship to the presenting problems, and highlighting the parallel issues flowing from client to clinician, and clinician to supervisor, you are demonstrating how to move the process forward.

Again, these techniques are not therapy for the clinician, but rather an effort to increase the clinician's awareness of the ways in which the self becomes entangled in professional practice. After the clinician is able to separate personal needs from professional goals and becomes aware of how she avoids anxiety within the session, you can back off and help the clinician decide what action to take next to help the client. Work performance is still the bottom line.

Even though clinicians can handle more intense emotional content during this stage, you must be careful with pacing. Such emotionally intense sessions need to be balanced with more didactic, intellectual, skill-focused sessions. The times when the supervisor takes responsibility for leading the process need to be countered by instances when the clinician initiates and controls the process. If every supervisory session becomes confrontational, the clinician will begin to retreat. Your sensitivity and concern toward the clinician should model the way in which the clinician should approach the client.

CHALLENGES AND DANGERS OF STAGE 2

Just as Stage 1 presented its own particular dangers and challenges, so too does this stage, centering upon the issue of dependency. Here are some of the variations and concerns.

Pushing Away More Independent, Less-Engaging Clients

While Julie may be drawn to working with someone like Ms. Jones who is dependent upon her, she may also discourage those clients who are less needy, more independent, less willing to engage in longer or deeper therapeutic relationships. The problem is not anxiety over how to work with these independent clients as it was in the first stage, but of rising expectations. Sensing the intimacy and power that a therapeutic relationship can create, the clinician may become bored, lack enthusiasm, and be more reactive or passive with such independent clients.

As supervisor this is usually a work-performance issue, as well as a clinical one. You want staff who are willing and able to work with clients across the board. While you'll want to explore with the clinician her different responses to different clients, you'll also need to be clear and firm that the clinician is expected to work a diverse caseload.

Encouraging Dependency in Clients

This is an ethical issue. According to the National Association of Social Workers Code of Ethics (2008), social workers should terminate services to clients when services are no longer needed or no longer serve the client's needs and interests. Dependency can be defined as strong relationship but with no change. In some cases no change is exactly the right clinical goal: that is, helping a client through a supportive relationship to remain stable. But when collusion is the dynamic, this is not a matter of clinical appropriateness but personal comfort.

Obviously you as a supervisor are responsible for confronting such issues. The danger of this stage, however, is you failing to stop the parallel process. You too become seduced by intimacy. Rather than confronting or challenging the clinician, you avoid so as not to disturb the intimacy of the supervisory relationship. You allow the clinician to tread water with his clients just as he treads water with you. You are the source, rather than the solution, to the problem.

Inexperienced supervisors are particularly vulnerable to this danger due to lack of supervisory skill and awareness, and struggles with being confrontive with clinicians. For more experienced supervisors this problem may arise during periods of personal stress—burnout, lack of intimacy in their personal lives—or in supervisory relationships with underlying sexual tensions. As supervisor you must be alert to these dangers. Meeting with your own supervisor, peer supervisors, or a personal therapist, as well as maintaining a healthy personal life, will help you avoid such problems.

Ethical Practice

Practice Behavior Example: *Make ethical decisions by applying standards of the National Association of Social Workers Code of Ethics and, as applicable, of the International Federation of Social Workers/International Association of Schools of Social Work Ethics in Social Work, Statement of Principles.*

Critical Thinking Question: What criteria would you use to decide when termination is appropriate?

Supervision as Therapy

As mentioned earlier, there are some supervisory models, particularly psychodynamic ones, that view the supervisory process as essentially a variation of therapy. Those models begin and end with the framework. The danger of this stage are those situations where the move toward making supervision more therapeutic is actually a reflection of the changing needs of the supervisor and/or clinician.

Again, this is another variation of dependency. As the clinician leans toward the relationship, comes to see the supervisor as a mentor, or as the supervisor works harder to help the clinician separate personal from professional, it is easy for the lines to become blurred. The clinician may actually believe that by you helping her sort through her own issues with her mother you are helping her to ultimately better serve her clients. You too may find reasonable arguments arising within you telling you why discussing these personal issues are appropriate to explore further.

And they may be. What is important here is your clear supervisory intentions and goals in order to avoid stumbling into rationalizations. Some of this will depend on your style, of course, but what you want to avoid is being unclear and reactive, rather than clear and proactive. The clinician may test the boundaries between supervision and therapy simply because he doesn't know what they are. You are the one who needs to decide where they are. Generally it is best to help the clinician become aware of the point where the personal and professional cross so that he can emotionally entangle the threads. Your job is to then help the clinician change the patterns and process with the client.

The seductions here are that you take on the therapist role because you are actually a frustrated clinician and/or this focus is more within your comfort zone, because it increases the intimacy within the supervisory relationship, or because you desire to increase your power or the clinician's dependency on you—all poor supervisory reasons to enter this process. Again, the best defenses against falling into such patterns are the recognition of your own needs and help from your own supervisor or colleagues. They can help you see what you may not be able to see on your own.

Human Behavior

Practice Behavior Example: *Utilize conceptual frameworks to guide the processes of assessment, intervention, and evaluation.*

Critical Thinking Question: At what point for you would you consider suggesting to a clinician that he seek therapy?

Blurred Boundaries

The theme here is the blurring of the personal and professional. Certainly this is what supervision versus therapy is all about, but so too are the blurred lines between personal and professional interactions. There is a danger at this stage for supervisory relationships to become sexual, for work time to cross over to personal time, for work relationships to become friendships. When this happens, your supervisory power and position becomes diluted. Your behavior is potentially unethical and unprofessional.

The boundaries between clinicians and clients can also become blurred. While sexual relationships may occur, they are more likely to happen at the next stage. What happens at this stage are more those awkward situations where clients invite clinicians to their child's play or to a wedding. They border on dual relationships and can be seen as unethical. Again, where earlier the danger of such blurred boundaries arose because clinicians were being overresponsible for clients, now they arise because client and clinician have grown more intimate.

Your job in these situations is to help the clinician clarify his intentions and clinical thinking, and draw clear lines when needed. For example, it may be clinically appropriate for Joe to attend a wedding of a client's family member, but you'll want to coach Joe on how to maintain confidentiality and whether or not he need bring a gift. Once again you set the pace, both in your relationship with the clinician and in helping him do the same with his clients.

MOVING IN AND OUT THE OTHER SIDE

As a way of marking the changes that occur from the first stage to the second, let's look at the self-evaluation of the clinician presented in Chapter 4. Once again she has been asked to assess her theoretical orientation, skills and knowledge, use of self, use of supervision, and goals. It is now 1 year later. Again, her work is primarily with children and families.

> *My theoretical orientation continues to be primarily systemic. I see difficulties arising from the interaction of various elements. The ones I focus on include the developmental stage of the family, the family structure, family and individual histories, the interactional patterns among family members.*

What is remarkable here is not only the clinician's ideas but the clarity of thought and detail. This is the same person who talked vaguely about pain and feelings. Her knowledge base has increased; issues and problems are suddenly more complex.

> *I believe that most presenting problems stem from deficits in the interactions between parents and children. Stemming from the inadequate parenting they received, parents have difficulty meeting their children's needs for unconditional nurturance as well as consistent structure. My intervention usually focus on helping parents better understand their children's and their own needs, and in improving the communication and problem-solving skills within the family.*

Here the clinician identifies with the child, but also appreciates the experience of the parents. She is becoming aware of the issues that lie beneath power and authority.

During the past year I have gained new knowledge of the middle phases of treatment, including ideas about impasses and resistance. I have learned more about my difficult in confronting clients, as well as how my induction into the system can lead to an impasse in treatment. I am learning to use clients' reactions to me to effect change.

This is the heart of this stage. The clinician is aware of process and counter-transference and no longer talks about being good or worrying about having clients like her.

I often present myself as a teammate to the families I work with. Over the past year I have been able to confront clients . . . who know that I am trustworthy and that I care. It would be beneficial to learn when a shift in role is necessary. I would like to work on becoming more directive with clients regarding contracts and follow through on connecting the work of various sessions.

The client's friend has now become the client's teammate. Confrontation is still a problem, but some progress is being made. Confrontation with those who trust probably parallels the supervisory process. The clinician senses when she and the clients are treading water, but in order for her to be more productive, supervision needs to help her isolate the emotional underpinnings.

The negative side to my joining skills is my tendency to feel responsible for the family. I need to develop enough distance to help individuals learn how to take care of themselves, as well as to help prevent my own burnout. I often feel burned out because I allow myself to become isolated, and by not requesting supervision as frequently as I should.

Good insight here. By saying she needs to develop distance means that she has already begun to do so. In late Stage 2 the clinician is moving away from the "good kid" overresponsible approach and even beyond the need for dependency. Burnout is taking its toll, however. Supervision needs to better address this issue.

I have been able to confront my own feelings and learn in supervision by doing more role-plays, live supervision, and recording of sessions. I still struggle with the development of confidence in my professional self.

Again the work confront shows up, different and stronger language from the "feelings and pain" of the year before. The clinician perceives the experiential nature of supervision and the value of self-awareness. Self-confidence is an issue, and she probably needs to have more positive feedback. She is still struggling with the split between professional and personal roles.

I would like to find better ways to handle my anger toward clients. I am beginning to use these feelings as signals of how others might be feeling . . . I realize now how I was more focused on obtaining approval from my supervisor. I would like to use supervision to help me gain a sense of self-approval.

The clinician's first mention of anger, a moving away from the "good kid" stance and her dependency on her supervisor, a desire for self-definition—she has turned the corner toward the next stage.

The following questions will test your application and analysis of the content found within this chapter. For additional assessment, including licensing-exam-type questions on applying chapter content to practice behaviors, visit **MySearchLab**.

1. "Don't know what you know" of Stage 2 of clinical development refers to the fact that the clinician
   a. Has learned a great deal but cannot always articulate or consistently apply it
   b. Feels overwhelmed and incompetent
   c. Still has a lot more to learn
   d. Feels she knows everything and doesn't see her blind spots

2. Recording sessions during the second stage help clinicians
   a. Better organize the data they obtain from clients
   b. See better how the session process unfolds
   c. Learn experiential techniques
   d. Diminish their anxiety by focusing on clients' environmental problems

3. Stephanie is having difficulty setting goals for her next session with Ms. Williams. It would be helpful for you as her supervisor to
   a. Give her suggestions for appropriate goals
   b. Describe for her the overall purpose of goal-setting
   c. Ask her write out a possible plan for the next session and review it with you before she meets with her client
   d. Have her observe a session conducted by another clinician

4. Joe has successfully worked with several clients who are struggling with grief and loss, but seems emotionally overwhelmed when working with Mr. Jones, who has just lost his wife. It would be most helpful in supervision to
   a. Ask Joe what he thinks is particularly bothering him about this case
   b. Have him read some articles on grief in men
   c. Refer Joe to the Employee Assistance Program
   d. Reassign the case to another clinician

5. April has been invited to her client's wedding and asks your permission to attend. How would you respond?

6. Although Mr. Jones seems stable and has accomplished his treatment goals, Mark, his clinician, continues to see him weekly. How would you respond?

6

Stage 3: Supervisor as Gatekeeper

Competencies Applied with Practice Behaviors — in This Chapter				
☒ Professional Identity	☒ Ethical Practice	☒ Critical Thinking	☒ Diversity in Practice	◼ Human Rights & Justice
◼ Research-Based Practice	◼ Human Behavior	◼ Policy Practice	◼ Practice Contexts	◼ Engage, Assess, Intervene, Evaluate

"I get so frustrated with this family. They just don't want to work. They're happy to complain and blame each other, but then they 'forget' to do the homework I assign, they cancel appointments at the last minute. They take no responsibility!"

Ellen has just stomped her foot to underscore her point. She is angry and fed up. A lot of her clients these days have trouble taking responsibility. Rather than *doing* something, they just talk about it. She hasn't noticed that she's complaining as she says all this, or that she has herself been ignoring many of your own suggestions lately.

This is the same Ellen who in the first few months came to supervisory sessions shaking with pages of notes, who knocked on your door seemingly 12 times a day with some question, who 6 months ago clung to your words of wisdom and believed that a close, trusting relationship with clients was the essential ingredient to creating changes in clients' lives. Now she rarely knocks on your door. She comes reeling in, on more than a few occasions, to staff meetings late, and you swear she is doing her progress while you're talking. While her earlier treatment plans were vague goals of increased self-esteem and better communication, now they are filled with energetic action plans, tight time limits, or the latest technique that she just read about in a journal. Not only does she know what she wants, she knows what her clients should want as well. If only they would listen. Welcome to clinician adolescence.

Box 6.1 • **Overview of Stage 3**

Characteristics	Don't know what you don't know
	Increased awareness of anger and power
	Counterdependence—testing of boundaries—beginning individuation
	Exploration, experimentation, desire for change
	Termination/loss/identity issues
Supervisory goals	Maintain boundaries and quality control
	Support exploration and individuation
	Help channel anger appropriately
	Increase awareness of clinician's strengths, style, intuitions
Supervisory tasks	Consider using group supervision or transfer supervision to another
	Teach adjunct approaches, send to training programs
	Help develop career path—increase responsibilities, leadership opportunities
	Use storytelling in place of lecturettes or micro-processing
Challenges/dangers	Move too quickly for clients, too confrontive, terminate poorly
	Truncate relationships—act out anger, impatience, see clients as unmotivated
	Rebellious—act out with supervisor, question policies and procedures, acting too independently

CHARACTERISTICS OF STAGE 3

Like previous stages, this stage too is marked by its own characteristics. We'll discuss them one by one.

Don't Know What You Don't Know

The "know what you don't know" of the first stage—feelings of incompetence and vulnerability—shifted to the "don't know what you know" of the second stage—knowing more but having trouble articulating and applying knowledge and skills consistently. The theme of this stage is the "don't know what you don't know"—an inability to see blind spots and weaknesses. The corollary of this statement is you think you know everything, which gives this stage the adolescent quality of overconfidence, empowerment, entitlement, and even arrogance.

Anger and Power

We had the foreshadowing of this in the clinician's self-evaluation in Chapter 5—her new awareness of anger toward clients. This anger and frustration fuel Ellen's impatience. In contrast to the intimacy and settling in of the second stage, this stage is often one of action and reaction, of wanting clients to do not just talk. Sessions with Ms. Jones are no longer filled with exploration of her own past pain and trauma. Now she is encouraged to quit tolerating the abuse or neglect of others, stop being the victim, and cast aside her powerlessness. Confrontation has replaced supportive listening.

And such goals may be absolutely appropriate. Ms. Jones may need to take action or may benefit by being more assertive in her relationships. That's not the issue. The concern of this stage is that the clinician moves too fast, presses too hard to define emotions and needs that clients may be only intimating, or advocates too strongly for the underdogs at the expense of others in the therapeutic relationship. Rather than changing the process, the clinician may merely replicate it—by becoming the client's new "drill sergeant" and ignoring the important issues of helping the client learn about the inner working of her relationship with authority figures. Again impatience and potentially clinician-driven, rather than client-driven, treatment.

This increased comfort with anger brings with it the clinician's increased comfort with personal power. Rather than imitating the supervisor, the clinician is beginning to define who she is in terms of style and strengths. That being said, the clinician's presentation in supervision is often inconsistent. Just when you think that the clinician has finally knocked you off the pedestal, the clinician goes into an emotional slump and seeks you out for advice, support, and approval. Over the course of this stage this yin and yang inconsistency gradually subsides. The clinician's newly discovered self emerges for longer periods, allowing for an increasing measure of stability in an essentially unstable period of professional development.

> ### Critical Thinking
>
> ***Practice Behavior Example:*** *Analyze models of assessment, prevention, intervention, and evaluation.*
>
> **Critical Thinking Question:** What is your own theory of resistance?

Counterdependence

The feelings of anger and power are new and contribute not only to the impatience but also to the clinical blind spots and the testing of limits. If the dependency of the last stage can be characterized as "You say black, I too say black," the counterdependence of this stage can be characterized as "You say black, I say white," with one saying white being dependent on the other saying black first. The clinicians are back to a reactiveness, a bouncing off of, now you, the supervisor, rather than off of clients.

You see this counterdependence and limit testing behind Ellen's lateness for meetings, her getting behind on paperwork, and her sudden and open complaining about changes in snow policy and mileage reimbursement rates. The anxiety that drove her behavior in the earlier stages—feelings of being overwhelmed, desires to do things perfectly, confusion about what is expected—is now replaced by an alert annoyance—that procedures or policies are outdated, that meetings are boring and irrelevant, that paperwork is the least important aspect of the work. Your clinical suggestions have become to her predictable and tired, and she counters them with other, newer theories that she has recently attached to.

Exploration, Experimentation, Desire for Change

All this spills into a restlessness that is projected onto clients, further fueling the desire for clients do more. This same restlessness also spills into supervision, adding to the feeling of constraint, that supervision has less to offer in terms of new skills and information.

It shows itself in wanting to explore new clinical approaches and techniques. Application of new technology, certification programs in hypnosis, postgraduate programs in object relations, or year-long institutes on working with trauma or autism all may peak interest. In some cases this restlessness leads to a desire to leave the agency or the field altogether—enter private practice, work as a policy analyst at the state capital, become a real estate broker, or get an MBA. Clinicians talk about wanting work that is less emotionally taxing, that doesn't require being on call or weekends, and that has clear outcomes. Some explore, decide to stay, but look for ways to expand their work. Others leave for a time and return. Some leave and never return.

This desire for change makes sense and is a testament to your own effectiveness and success as a supervisor. Thanks to you and your relationship with the clinician, she has grown in skill and style. She has acquired talents and skills that are likely being underutilized. She has outgrown her job, and her sense of self and view of life have grown with it. Your challenge is finding ways to help this more experienced clinician use her growing skills and talents to feel energized and creative, rather than stymied and stale.

GROWING UP AND OUT

Your emotional support, modeling, and opportunities for approaching anxiety have helped the clinician learn that risk-taking need not lead to disaster, and that mistakes don't automatically lead to criticism. With your guidance the clinician realizes that he doesn't need to be overresponsible, that good therapy isn't about pleasing others or being careful not to get others upset. Through the honesty and intimacy in his relationship with you, the clinician has learned to bring such intimacy and honesty into his relationships with clients. This led to the dependency of the second stage and the soaking up of your ideas and style, and now spawns individuation. The clinician is finally moving away from the "good kid" image and is shifting away from the rescuer role. Growing self-confidence enables the clinician to move away and explore.

Events in a clinician's personal life can further fuel this process. Marriage or having a child can underscore the need for separation or the establishment of new rules and routines, respectively. Midlife issues can cause one to feel that she deserves more, that it's time to stop accommodating to everyone else and assert oneself. At the early points of this stage the clinician may not yet always know what he wants, but is much more clear about what he doesn't like. For clinicians who never had the opportunity to shed the "shoulds" in their life, all this waking up to options can be particularly intoxicating.

And once again, clinicians are tempted to bring the dynamics and themes of this stage to their work with clients. Mr. Smith should not have tolerated such a dead-end job; adolescent Shawn should stand up to his parents and tell them what he really thinks. The mix of strong emotions—anger and impatience—together with overidentification with clients and the clinician's inexperience with all of this makes pacing difficult. Like an adolescent learning to drive a car, the clinician may swerve off the road, go too fast or slow, or find it difficult to know when to apply the brakes.

But there is a tension that permeates this stage. As Stoltenberg, McNeill, and Delworth (1998) point out, this stage of transition can be a turbulent one for both clinician and supervisor. The clinician, no longer dependent upon you, no longer hanging onto every word that you speak, is less concerned about being good or making sure you or clients are happy. You feel less comfortable about what the clinician may or may not do in a session, and your raising issues can lead to long philosophical discussions about change and the nature of therapy. The clinician is establishing her own clinical identity. But with this separation can come for you a sense of loss and grief.

The most famous clinical example of the tumult of this stage can be seen in the relationship between Sigmund Freud and Carl Jung. Jung, the longtime student of Freud, reaches a point in his own development where he begins to intellectually and emotionally pull away. Rather than blindly following Freud's model of analysis, Jung begins to develop his own style and thinking based upon his new ideas of archetypes. Rather than supporting his ideas, Freud instead feels threatened and resentful. He is unable to tolerate the separation. Jung is cast out. The relationship between them is ruptured, and never healed.

This is where the professional and personal overlap. The tension arises in your responsibility as supervisor to maintain quality control while encouraging independence and individuation, of reconciling your own priorities and visions of the work with the new ideas that the clinician presents. Some supervisors who felt comfortable in the role of mentor now, like Freud, feel threatened by the clinician's seeming dismissal of their role and ideas. Those who relaxed knowing that the clinician and supervisor were always on the same page now feel anxious with this seeming loose cannon of an employee. Those who felt that the supervisor and clinician were working together as a team toward the same vision now feel betrayed when the clinician's vision has changed. And when the clinician talks about moving on to another job, it's easy for some supervisors to wonder why they too are still there.

Again, the changes and challenges of this stage are signs not of failure, but actually of healthy growth. They are the norm, not the abnormal. Navigating this stage requires you, the supervisor, to balance support with appropriate limit setting.

SUPERVISORY GOALS AND TASKS

The subtitle of this stage—supervisor as gatekeeper—represents this balance: the monitoring of boundaries while opening doors to an expanding clinical self. Here are the essential goals and tasks of this stage.

Maintain Boundaries and Quality Control

When Ellen comes to meetings late, you want to let her know that such lateness is not tolerated. When Tom fails to turn in his paperwork on time, you want to remind him of deadlines and let him know that delays are not acceptable practice. Even if you begin to feel old-fashioned when the clinician begins to talk about the latest therapeutic techniques, you are responsible for making sure that the clinician performs according to agency standards.

You want to use your power and authority around administrative issues judiciously during this stage. While in the first few months of supervision, you approached Ellen and Tom cautiously to make sure that their anxiety didn't overwhelm them, you now use your power to clearly

Professional Identity

Practice Behavior Example: *Practice personal reflection and self-correction to assure continual professional development.*

Critical Thinking Question: How difficult is it for you to set boundaries? What do you need to be able to do this better?

reinforce expectations and priorities, and ensure overall quality control. During this stage, administrative supervision often shifts from less of what the clinician needs to do his or her job to what you need to feel you need to do yours.

How clinicians handle any setting of boundaries by you depends, of course, upon their personalities, yours, and the quality of your relationship. As with the other stages, you set the tone and pace. With a quick mention by you, Ellen may now show up on time for all her meetings, while Tom is still failing to turn in his paperwork on time. Be matter-of-fact in your approach, but persistent. Focus on identifying any underlying issues. If not doing the paperwork is Tom's solution, what is the problem? Is he overworked or burned out? Does he for some reason not see why paperwork is just as much a priority as seeing clients? Does his behavior reflect a shift in the relationship and a testing of limits?

Raise these questions and issues to Tom. Offer to address underlying concerns (he really is overworked), but also stick to the bottom lines and the need for his compliance. If this fails to get results, you need to increase consequences (written warnings rather than verbal, tighter deadlines, corrective action plans). Again, you want to empathize with emotions, provide positive feedback when it is due, but do not tolerate irresponsible behaviors.

While handling such administrative issues can be cognitively clear and straightforward, but emotionally aggravating, clinical issues can be more muddied. The challenge is sorting out what are valid emerging differences in style and approach between you and the clinician from what you may see as ineffective or inept practice. Because this stage is characterized by "don't know what you don't know," you want to stay alert to clinicians' blind spots—to treatment plans that are not well thought out, to assumptions about clients that reflect clinicians' own projections and needs. Just as in the second stage you were sensitive to clinician–client dependency, now you need to be sensitive to clinicians' impatience and control.

You want to be tactful yet clear. If you believe, for example, that Ellen is pushing a teenager too hard to confront his parents, that the parents aren't ready to listen, and that the therapeutic agenda is more Ellen's than the teenager's, you need to point this out gently: "Ellen, even though you did a good job preparing John to talk to his parents, I don't think the parents heard what he was saying. Watch the videotape. Notice the parents' behavior, how dad is staring off in another direction and doesn't seem to be listening."

You want to give the clinician room to shape the session process, but help her also stay clear about clinical bottom lines. Focus on goals rather than micromanaging means; look for concrete measures of effectiveness—watching recordings for effective clinical process, documentation of clear behavioral changes in clients. Confront to clarify the clinician's thinking: Why are you suddenly pushing this client to make so many changes? Tell me how you are thinking about this family and why seeing the teenager instead of working with the parents is best. As you listen to cases over the course of weeks, and as you review case records, look for new clinical patterns—overuse of particular techniques, patterns in no-show rates, a moving toward work with particular clients or problems and not others. Your vantage point and responsibility is to see the bigger picture, to see what the clinician cannot. Use your clinical skills to assess the clinician's own.

If you have clinical concerns—that Ellen is minimizing a client's level of depression or failing to adequately coordinate services with other providers—step up and raise these issues. Assess whether the problem is one of skill, or oversight based upon emotional or personal reactions. If Ellen responds defensively, or fails to hear your concerns, her response becomes the problem in the room that you need to address. Don't let her possible negative response keep you from discussing what you feel is important. To do so means that you are abdicating your authority and responsibility.

And if you find the clinician generally pulling back, providing you with insufficient information to know what is going on within her caseload and leaving you uncomfortable and in the dark, request from her what you need to do your job—periodic updates on client status, copies of treatment plans or progress notes. Help her understand your intentions and needs—that your job is to remain up-to-date about the work and needs of the staff and clients rather than an effort to specifically micromanage her. Be a role model of how to effectively confront and manage relationship changes.

Support Exploration and Individuation

All this accountability and limit setting is the quality control side of supervision that you have been focusing on all along. The other side—the support and nurturing of professional growth—is equally important. To focus only on the first in the early stages—a drill sergeant stance—would have only increased the clinician's anxiety, made the development of a quality supervisory relationship difficult, and likely resulted in the clinician leaving the agency or stopping learning. Taking such one-sided focus now will fuel power struggles, stir feelings of distrust and resentment, possibly create passive/aggressive behavior on the part of the clinician, all decreasing your influence, and like Freud and Jung, potentially rupturing the supervisory relationship.

Given the outward, expanding focus of this stage, one of your challenges, as mentioned earlier, is that of helping the clinician find ways of utilizing her growing repertoire of clinical and leadership skills. This is a good time to get the clinician involved in other activities both inside and outside the agency—for example, serving on an interagency committee addressing runaways or an agency committee reviewing personnel policies. Have her work with you on a grant proposal, or assign her to a team that is doing the preparation for a license review.

This is a good time for group supervision. Where before the clinician felt intimidated in the presence of peers, now she can feel empowered. She has an opportunity to serve as a role model to less-experienced staff, and the group becomes a wonderful forum to showing off skills and talents. Similarly, this may be a good time to consider the clinician taking on supervisory tasks—facilitating a training group for interns, overseeing the work of paraprofessionals, volunteers, students—or considering more formal training in supervision—attendance at workshops on supervision, supervisory sessions, specifically for supervision of supervision.

This is also a good time to consider bringing in other mentors. If Marcus, for example, is now interested in object-relations approaches to treatment, something you know little about, consider having Susan, who is well versed in this theory, supervise him on several cases. If Kim is interested in learning more about managing trauma, and there is an ongoing training program on this in town, consider sending her to it rather than feeling the responsibility of training her on this yourself.

For those clinicians seeking more intensive training, this is a good time to do the 3-year certification programs in hypnosis or family therapy, or the multi-weekend workshops on couples therapy. Because clinicians have a more solid clinical base, new ideas, rather than creating confusion as they would have done earlier, now can be integrated.

It is this move toward integrating, rather than disseminating, information that is the biggest shift in the supervisory process. Help the clinician to see himself more clearly by providing plenty of feedback about what you see as the clinician's unique skills and strengths—John, you do a wonderful job of engaging these reluctant men in these families; Teresa, you are particularly good at quickly assessing the underlying issues with crisis couples. Pointing out what you see as important and valuable differences between you and the clinician in strength and style can go a long way in providing support. It helps keep the supervisory relationship strong even as the clinician moves away.

Rather than lecturettes of the first stage or the diligent focus on the micro-process of sessions in the second stage, this is a good time to use storytelling—your own experiences with certain clients or problems—as a way of making your point without sounding dismissive of clinicians' ideas. Jack, for example, talks with you about enactments that he has been doing with parents who have trouble getting their children to mind them. In clinical sessions, he asks the parents to enforce the limits they have set, for example, making their child sit still and not run around the room. With encouragement and coaching during the session, he tries to help the parents to offer choices, enforce limits, rather than give in.

Jack, you realize, has thought through this intervention clearly and is much more forceful and directive than he was in the past. Before he seemed intimidated by the parents and gravitated toward working individually with the child. Now his own increased sense of power pushes him to empower the parents. But you are concerned that in his impatience for the parents to make changes at home and "shape the kids up," he has not devoted enough time to practicing the techniques with them, or adequately explored underlying dynamics in the couple's relationship. You're worried that he is moving too quickly, expecting too much from the parents, that they could easily get frustrated and overreact trying to implement these tactics at home on their own.

Obviously, if your concerns are great enough, you need to raise all these questions directly with Jack. On the other hand, you can also tell a story about a similar case you had in which the parents did, in fact, have trouble using physical restraint at home and lost control; or about a client who really didn't understand the point of what you as a clinician were doing, went along in the session to accommodate, but then dropped out of treatment. The story becomes a way for you to make your point, and for Jack to listen and learn without feeling criticized or controlled.

We are back to our parenting metaphor—that good supervision, like good parenting, involves being able to adapt your style to the clinician's changing needs. The challenge at this stage is finding ways of communicating and being heard, when the clinician may be feeling that you have less to say; of maintaining clear boundaries when the clinician may feel that none are needed.

Help Channel Anger Appropriately

The quick sense of restlessness, frustration, and impatience with clients, with the agency, and with you needs to be channeled productively, rather than acted out. Parallel process says that you need to respond to the clinician the way she needs to respond to clients. Rather than ignoring or minimizing the clinician's complaints, pulling away or acting punitively, you want to help the clinician learn to use these feelings as information about what she needs or what underlying problems need to be addressed. Talk with Tom about his struggle with time management so that his paperwork can be completed on time. Help

Jack see what supports the parents he is seeing in treatment might need, rather than moving too quickly or assuming that they are resistive. Assign Teresa to the staff personnel committee that is reviewing the inclement weather policy, rather than just getting upset yourself about her rants over having to come to work when it snows.

Again for those clinicians who are moving out of the rescuer role and feeling more and more empowered, these strong emotions are new territory. They need your help in putting them in perspective, in being intentional and clinically clear rather than impulsive, proactive rather than reactive. Model this clarity, calmness. Be proactive yourself. Help them define the needs beneath the anger by once again pointing out what you see, raising the issues, using your clinical skills to shape the process in the supervisory session.

CHALLENGES AND DANGERS OF STAGE 3

"This is a most dangerous stage in your training," says Obi-Wan Kenobi of *Stars Wars*, "when you will be susceptible to the forces of the dark side."

And it is. Though the anxiety and dependency of the previous stages have faded, the enemy of this stage—power—is the most threatening in many ways. Think of any scandal that you have ever heard about. It is not the freshman congressman who falls prey to corruption, but the senior senator who has been in office for decades. It is not the rookie ball player who is involved in sex or drug scandal, but the seasoned veteran. When you feel you are at the top and have figured it all out, that you are invincible and will never get caught, when you get cocky and arrogant, it is power that is blinding you.

While the temptations for social workers may seem less dramatic, they are present all the same. This is the time of dangerous ethical violations—rationalizing having sex with a client, taking on cases that are over your head, or irresponsibly using a new technique because you falsely believe you can handle it all. It is drifting into dual relationships where you ask a client in your therapy group who happens to be a contractor if he could come by and give you a quick estimate on some remodeling of your house. The rationalization and justification come easily. Here are two examples.

Sam was a rising star among the clinical staff of the agency. He split his clinical time providing behavioral coaching to children in school who were having behavioral difficulties, and working with parents in their homes doing much the same. One day his supervisor receives an email from a referral source. Included in the email was a copy of an email that Sam had sent to her. In his note Sam informs the referral source that he has decided to terminate with the Jones family because he felt that they were resistant, not working hard enough to apply the skills he was showing them. As a P.S. on the note he wrote that while he was ending with the parents, he felt he had a good relationship with the young boy and that he would be happy to see him in his private practice if she felt it was a good idea.

Maggie was a longtime case manager who worked hard for her clients. Her clients appreciated her quick response to their questions and her always-helpful direction. Maggie needed to go on medical leave for several weeks following minor surgery. She would be home-bound and unable to come to work because she couldn't drive or walk around much. Her supervisor told her before she left to change her voicemail message, telling callers that she was out and if they had any questions to call the supervisor directly. Maggie left; the supervisor noticed that no client calls were being directed to her. She checked Maggie's voicemail message. It told callers that she was out on medical leave but they should feel free to call her at home if they had any questions.

The situation with Sam shows a few overlapping characteristics of this stage. First, he becomes impatient with this client family, and rather than discussing it with his supervisor, unilaterally decides that termination is appropriate. He takes responsibility for informing the referral source, but again it is all without his supervisor's awareness. Finally, he is arrogant and entitled. In violation of agency policy he did not inform his supervisor that he was starting a private practice, and then, again in violation of agency policy, was trying to transfer agency clients to his private practice. Perhaps in his own mind he thought the policy was irrelevant and assumed that he knew best what the family needed, that he wouldn't get caught, or that bringing it all up with his supervisor wasn't necessary and could be avoided.

Ethical Practice

Practice Behavior Example: *Obligation to conduct themselves ethically and engage in ethical decision-making.*

Critical Thinking Question: How would you handle the situation with Sam?

The situation with Maggie seems less ethically dangerous but is a concern all the same. Unlike Sam whose motives are questionable, Maggie probably saw no reason not to continue to help her clients since much of her work was telephone based anyhow, and she may have been worried about being stuck at home and getting bored. The concern again is that she didn't feel she needed to talk about any of this with her supervisor, that she wouldn't get caught, that it was no big deal. And while seeming innocuous enough, it is a big deal simply because the supervisor is left out of the loop. If something had gone wrong, would Maggie have told the supervisor or held back because she was worried she'd get in trouble? Quality control had broken down and the supervisor's directives were being ignored.

What these examples show are the changing nature of the supervisory relationship. Sam and Maggie feel independent, no longer feel pressure to comply, to get permission, or to always check in with their supervisors. For the supervisor there is the question of unethical, noncomplying behavior, but also of relationship change and breakdown of authority and influence. This is where you as supervisor need to have a dual focus on maintaining boundaries and exploring underlying issues.

If Sam and Maggie's behaviors were in their minds a solution, what were the problems? Why didn't Sam comply with agency policy regarding private practice? What kept him from discussing termination with his supervisor? Was he afraid she wouldn't support him, does he disagree with her style, was he worried that it would be confrontational and he didn't want to deal with it, did he really think that she wouldn't care? What about referring calls to the supervisor rather than Maggie caused Maggie to both disregard it and not talk about it? Was she feeling micromanaged? Did you feel that advocating for her working from home was merely a waste of time? As supervisor you need not have the answers to these questions; your job is to merely raise them and create a productive conversation.

But some supervisors fail to have these conversations, and this is another danger at this stage. Some are simply afraid of any confrontation with staff. This is the mother hen supervisor who is comfortable nurturing staff but struggles to set boundaries. He wants staff to like him or believes, as new clinicians do, that if staff like him enough, they will magically automatically know and do what is needed. This is obviously easier in the first two stages when staff are intimidated and anxious or seeking intimacy and are idealizing, but it collapses at this third stage. The staff run amok, doing what they please, learning how to say the right things to reassure the supervisor, but know that there are few, if any, consequences for their actions. Again, such supervisors have failed to become middle managers.

Some supervisors are able to set limits with some clinicians but not others. Often it is because they feel intimidated by the clinician's new knowledge and assertiveness. They may feel that they are indeed old-fashioned and out-of-date. They may be burned out themselves or neglectful of staff for personal reasons. They may have long-standing lack of confidence in their own clinical skills. Those clinicians who are able to sound good—make a reasonable case for what they are planning, talk about theories or techniques that are unfamiliar and frankly difficult for the supervisor to comprehend—cause the supervisor to go along. Supervisors don't want to appear unknowing of the latest trends and new thinking. They don't want to challenge thinking that on the surface seems to make sense. They back down, and let the clinician do what she wants, rationalizing that she is capable and knows what she is doing.

Finally, there are those supervisors, and perhaps in some ways the most dangerous, who encourage staff to act out their own issues. Tom complains about the snow policy, and rather than listening and taking the middle-manager role of clarifying the policy or channeling his complaints to more constructive outlets (e.g., the staff personnel committee), the supervisor encourages him. "Write an email to me, she says, outlining your grievances and I'll send up the line. You have a good point Tom, she says, and you're right. Talk to other staff and see if they feel the same way." It is not the behavior itself that is suspect here, but the supervisor's underlying motivation. The supervisor is allowing the clinician to voice her own anger and feelings of discontent against the administration.

This struggle to set boundaries—whether it comes from fear of confrontation, intimidation, repressed anger, or more deeply, loss and inability to accept the clinician's individuation and separation from the supervisor—leaves the supervisor relinquishing his authority and power as a supervisor. You, as a good supervisor, need to be aware of your own often strong reactions to the changes in clinicians, sort out your own needs and issues from those of the clinician, and be clear about your own responsibilities and priorities. If uncertain or emotionally confused, seek out support and clarification with your own supervisor or respected colleagues.

> ### Diveristy in Practice
>
> ***Practice Behavior Example:*** *Understand how diversity characterizes and shapes the human experience and is critical to the formation of identity.*
>
> **Critical Thinking Question:** American culture supports individuation. How might clients or clinicians from other cultures think of this concept differently?

While it is important to be aware of dangers and not become over- or underreactive to the potential antics of Sam or Maggie, this stage need not be as perilous or dramatic as it may seem. For most clinicians the healthy side of this stage is one of greater assertiveness, less dependence upon you as an idealized role model, greater ability to set boundaries and priorities with clients, less and less fear in making mistakes, and more willingness to act independently. Utilizing skills and developing a solid career path may be problems that you need to address, but ones that can openly be explored and discussed together. Restlessness may lead to healthy exploration and experimentation, but also may be pushed to the side when a new case and clinical challenge suddenly presents itself.

Again, this is a transitional stage in many ways. Independence is marked by out-of-the-blue dependence, decisiveness by sudden indecisiveness. Your role is still one of keeping the supervisory boat on course, even though the clinician is more and more in charge of handling the rudder.

BREAKING AWAY

I believe that problems within a family stem from dysfunctional patterns either in the interactions of family members or between the family and the environment. I tend to concentrate on helping families change their communication patterns and help parents either to reestablish their authority or to solve their marital difficulties. More often than not, my work with families focuses on the parents.

Almost 2 years has passed since the clinician wrote the comments at the end of Chapter 5. Once again, she starts with her clinical theory. As before, her thinking continues to be clear and specific compared to that of her first stage. What is remarkable about her thoughts now is the shift away from the children to supporting the authority of the once-frightening parents. Because she is no longer intimidated by them, she can make them the center of her focus and help them to become change agents of the family. Because she feels more comfortable with her own authority, she is able to better appreciate and work with theirs. Finally, she is seeing that beneath family issues are often unresolved marital issues. What is important to this is not whether you agree with this theory, but rather that she is continuing to evolve in her thinking. Problems are seen as more layered and complex, a far cry particularly from the more one-dimensional thinking of the first stage.

Because of the anxiety that change arouses, it is not always accepted or attempted by clients. I just remember to help the client take responsibility for his or her choice about change and realize that all clients are not ready to make the changes necessary. I am better able to recognize and help clients move beyond the protective shield of anger and withdrawal and express feelings of hurt, rejection, and sadness underneath.

Remember the statement of the first evaluation—that change is incredibly frightening. No more. Her statement about change and anxiety is matter-of-fact. But according to her, change is not always accepted, clients have choice, and not all clients are ready. The more aggressive, more stern perspective of some clinicians at this stage is that clients are simply resistant and that if they don't want to work, the impatient clinician will terminate and move on to someone else.

Her perspective is more gentle and understanding, but still reflects a firmer setting of boundaries, and a realization of limits of her ability to change others. It is different from the dependency of the previous stage, and comes from her increased self-confidence and sense of power. Finally, as she has done with change and anxiety, she has done with anger—it is less a threat, and it has been emotionally neutralized. It is a form of protection, for clients and likely for herself, for softer, more vulnerable emotions. Her thoughts on this are more complex, less black and white.

I feel I have a greater sense of my own power and greater awareness of my own anger. I still have trouble at times with fathers. I feel a lot of pressure to be the expert, but I have much better at raising my concerns and diffusing a power struggle. I worry less about their reactions.

Power and anger are the hallmarks of this stage. Notice that some of the good-kid struggles and pressures remain—dealing with fathers, being an expert—but they are handled in a more adult way. Power does not have to be fought; it can be diffused. Those past worries about hurt feelings and being liked have diminished. Her ability to see all this shows good insight and counters the blindness and dangerous arrogance that can affect some. For them worrying less about their reactions turns into not caring at all about their reactions. Finally, the fact that she can put her reactions in writing and show them to her supervisor indicates that the supervisory relationship is still strong. She is not pulling away and being closed.

> *My primary focus during supervision has been analyzing the way in which my personal struggles and feelings affect how I work with clients. This has been invaluable and has added to my growing sense of differentiation between myself and clients. I learn best now by doing and experimenting. I no longer feel so threatened about the possibility of making mistakes and taking risks. I am much more open to supervision than I was 2 years ago. I am not as intent on needing to be perfect all the time.*

The work of sorting out the professional and personal has continued. There is a constellation of dynamics at work here, each feeding the others. Awareness, taking of risks, increases the greater taking of acceptable risks and increased awareness. Practice with this makes mistakes less an emotional threat, reducing performance pressure, making it easier to be open to clients and supervision. This in turn fuels differentiation from the dependency with clients and also with the supervisor. It is easier to develop and follow one's style. Ideal supervision is no longer about copying the supervisor, having the supervisor immediately tell you exactly what to do, but about experimenting and discovering oneself, experiences that further increase self-confidence and differentiation.

The good kid is withering away. The language has changed to talk of struggle and confrontation, rather than pleasing, worry, and accommodation. Again, the hard form of this shift is the potential blind arrogance of this stage. Rather than no longer being threatened by mistakes or having to be perfect, the clinician believes he never make mistakes, that what he does is right and perfect. If the supervisor disapproves, it is because he is close-minded or rigid; if clients disapprove, it is because they are resistant. This is the attitude that can lead to overcontrol and potential ethical problems.

> *In some respects I reexperienced the sense of calling I used to have for helping people. The added responsibilities that I have taken on this year have helped me step back, reflect on what I know and do, and conceptualize what I believe and practice. I do not feel the overwhelming sense of burnout of the past 2 years. I try to find a healthier balance between my work and personal life. In the next year I would like to do more behind-the-scenes work.*

The late phases of Stage 3 show that the initial dreams have passed through the fire of experience and have been reshaped and updated. With greater balance, burnout is less of an issue and the clinician does not feel the need to save the world. She is ready to move on to other challenges—for her doing behind-the-scenes work, for others new jobs or new fields. Her professional identity is much more clear.

The clinician has come a long way from those first hesitant anxiety-ridden steps. Many of her professional goals and the primary goals of supervision have been accomplished. Unlike the previous two stages, the boundary line between the third and fourth stages is less clearly defined. The changes that follow are small and more gradual as the clinician steps out of the struggles of adolescence, steps away from the dynamics of the Relationship Triangle toward the Adult, and enters peerhood with the supervisor.

The following questions will test your application and analysis of the content found within this chapter. For additional assessment, including licensing-exam-type questions on applying chapter content to practice behaviors, visit **MySearchLab**.

1. Stage 3 is characterized by
   a. Exploration and restless
   b. Dependency on the supervisor
   c. Overresponsibility for the client's progress
   d. Overidentification with children

2. Counterdependence of Stage 3 arises because
   a. The clinician has a great deal of performance anxiety
   b. The clinician is beginning to individuate from the supervisor
   c. The clinician is being seduced by the intimacy of the therapeutic relationship
   d. The supervisor is burned out and cynical

3. Marcus asks to attend a workshop on a new clinical technique that your agency has never used before. What would be the most appropriate response by you as his supervisor?
   a. Deny the request and explain that the new technique is not appropriate for this agency
   b. Request that he discuss this with your supervisor

   c. Ask Marcus to make a proposal and explain within it how this technique could be useful to clients and their treatment
   d. Grant his request only if he is willing to pay for half of the costs

4. Amanda's billing is late again. She assures she will complete it by the end of the week but then does not. What would be the best way of approaching this problem?
   a. Tell her that she did not meet the deadline and that you are considering taking disciplinary action
   b. Give her another week because you realize that she does solid clinical work
   c. Ignore the issue for now and see what happens next
   d. Talk to your supervisor about the overall billing process

5. Charles complains in his supervisory session that one of the couples he is seeing isn't doing the homework he assigns and that he feels that they are resistant; he wants to move toward termination. How would you respond?

6. One of Nichole's clients is a chef at a local restaurant. She mentions in supervision that she asked the client if he might be able to prepare a special dish for her daughter if her family had dinner at the restaurant to celebrate her daughter's graduation. How would you respond?

7

Stage 4: Supervisor as Consultant

Competencies Applied with Practice Behaviors — in This Chapter				
✘ Professional Identity	■ Ethical Practice	✘ Critical Thinking	■ Diversity in Practice	■ Human Rights & Justice
■ Research-Based Practice	✘ Human Behavior	✘ Policy Practice	■ Practice Contexts	■ Engage, Assess, Intervene, Evaluate

It's 8:30 a.m., and sitting across from Sara are a 180-pound teen, Annie, and her 85-pound mother, Gail. The mother looks frazzled already and wears an anxious, wide-eyed look. Her daughter sulks while picking some mud off the bottom of her sneaker. This is not the best way to start the day.

"How did this week go?" Sara asks.

The girl abruptly stops picking at her shoe and glares at her mother. "She won't let me go to the mall!"

Before the clinician has a chance to swallow her coffee, they're at it—the girl yelling at her mother about all the things that her mother won't let her do, the mother yelling back about her daughter's mess of a room before dissolving into tears.

Sara already knows the pattern that is about to be played out. Mom will turn to jelly, which will fuel her daughter's anger even more. The daughter may walk out; at home she has hit her mother.

"Stop!" Sara yells, putting up her hand like a traffic cop. The girl actually does stop for a second. She catches her breath and is about to start again, but Sara yells "Stop" again. "I can't allow you to continue like this. Gail, tell me why you think Annie is so mad."

For the next 40 minutes Sara tries to unravel their communication and emotions. Several times she has to jump in to slow Annie down; several times she has to push Gail to sound more like a mother and less like a sad little girl. With some prodding, they're actually able to work out an agreement about going to the mall and to build in some one-on-one quality time 2 nights during the week.

But that's not the problem, and Sara knows it. The real problem is the unresolved grief: the lingering sadness and anger over the father's death 6 months ago. The mother is just beginning to come out of the fog, struggling to make the transition not only to widowhood and being a single parent, but more important, from being a confidant and defender of her daughter to being a rule-setter. Annie, sensing the power vacuum, is in danger of replacing and replicating the father's role and becoming abusive toward the mother. But there's no time to tackle these issues now. They will have to wait till next week. Maybe, Sara thinks, she ought to see them separately. She decides to wait and see what they look like next week and maybe bring it up in supervision.

Her next client—a 16-year-old boy who was sexually abused by an older cousin last year (why, she thinks, am I getting all these teenagers all of a sudden!), who himself is becoming sexually active and sexually demanding of his girlfriend. The teen seems to come willingly to counseling but doesn't talk. At best he'll answer yes or no to a question, or sometimes give a 2- or 3-word answer. His IQ seems borderline normal.

In contrast with the previous session, work with this client is slow and painstaking. Sara isn't anxious about dealing with the sexual abuse itself; she is just not sure what her goals are. She asks him a lot of questions about his emotions, his fantasies, and his behavior. He hesitates, stares at the floor, then grunts out a word. He seems so passive and afraid. Finally, she asks him what he is most worried about. Slowly, he tells Sara that because of what his cousin did to him he fears that he will become homosexual. She asks him if that is why he's been trying so much to have sex with his girlfriend and he says yes. Sara takes a deep breath. She is beginning to understand how he is thinking. Gently she talks about sexual identity to clear up some of his distortions and fear. But she isn't really sure what to do next. She wonders to herself if she is possibly replicating in her client's mind an abusive process, considering all her questions and his passivity. She makes a mental note to bring this one to supervision.

Supervisory sessions, you find these days, vary. Sometimes they're all business—administrative and clinical. Other days there's not much to talk about and Sara feels impatient. Lately she's been saying that she doesn't have much of an agenda and would like to quit the session early. You don't mind. You even asked her if she wanted to meet every other week. Sara decided that she wasn't ready to do that.

Sara starts her session with you talking about Gail and Annie. She has a video but decides she doesn't need to play it. What she wants are ideas about strategy and timing. She gives you the background and her thoughts, and you agree with her assessment of the process. Together you both weigh the pros and cons of approaching the family's grief individually or together. But then you turn the corner and ask how she feels about working with this family. Sara had problems in the past with grief issues in families, pushing too hard or ignoring them all together. She says that she herself was actually wondering the same thing. Maybe, she says, that's why she didn't steer the session toward the father's death. She needs to think a bit longer about it.

Sara plays the audio recording from the session with the 16-year-old boy. It sounds as grueling as it felt. What do you think, she asks? You ask her to replay a section and then shake your head. You too are concerned about the boy's passivity and wonder how he expresses his anger. Listening, you pick up on how depressed he sounds. You wonder aloud whether psychological testing may be a helpful way of better understanding what is going on inside him. Sara says she will look into it.

After the supervisory session Sara heads for a lunch meeting across town. She recently became the agency representative for an interagency committee studying the duplication of children's services in the community. A lot of the meeting time seems caught up in turf battles; other times the meeting can seem deadly boring. But today she feels involved, takes an active role, and finds herself using the same basic skills she used with Gail and Annie (minus yelling at everyone to stop) to deflect another political battle and steer the process toward something more productive. Even though she's been on the committee for only a few weeks, she feels that she's taking on a leadership role and others respect her opinion. She actually feels pretty proud of herself.

Sara has come a long way, thanks in part to you. By this fourth stage her world and your own have become increasingly similar. Box 7.1 presents an overview of the last stage.

Box 7.1 • Overview of Stage 4

Characteristics	Know what you know
	Supervisor as peer, consultant
	Individuation of clinician
	Changes in role and focus of clinician's work
Supervisory goals	Problem-solve around specific case problems
	Help clinician develop an integrated therapeutic model
	Continue to develop clinical skills
	Expand professional role and work responsibilities
Supervisory tasks	Provide positive feedback regarding strengths and style
	Raise/explore issues around creativity, priorities/role of work
	Develop plans for further training/specialization, clinical challenges
	Move into clinical supervision, administrative tasks, community activities
Challenges/dangers	Coasting—boredom, going on autopilot clinically and in supervision
	Avoidance/ambivalence—supervisor feels threatened, wounds of previous stage not addressed or healed
	Inefficiency—looser boundaries between personal and professional create inefficiency in the workplace, fail to confront quality control issues

GROWING UP—STAGE 4 CHARACTERISTICS

Know What You Know

Though you and clinicians work on different levels, clinicians like Sara reflect the same independence in thought and action. They are flexible in approach and technique and have a fairly integrated and unique system of clinical work. Gone are the anxiety,

Professional Identity

Practice Behavior Example: *Practice personal reflection and self-correction to assure continual professional development.*

Critical Thinking Question: What do you know that you know about clinical practice?

dependency, anger, stubbornness, and myopia of earlier stages. They know their personal and clinical strengths and can acknowledge their weaker points without self-criticism. The blind spots and attitude of the previous stage have disappeared. This is the stage of know what you know.

Supervisor as Peer, Consultant

The supervisory relationship has changed once again. You are now more a peer, and your role is that of a consultant. You are no longer worried about overall work quality, concerned about integrity, and no longer need to set clear boundaries. The power struggling is over. You and clinicians respect each other's expertise.

Individuation

Clinicians like Sara have also earned the respect of others, and enjoy a reputation in the community, among clients as good clinicians and as solid professionals. They stand within their minds, within the agency, and in the larger community solidly on their own two feet. Their worldview has expanded. They have become an integral member of the extended family that makes up the community.

Changes in the Focus and Role of Work

With the expansion come decisions about the role of the work. Although some clinicians have left the agency to develop other parts of themselves and their lives, many of those who remain feel they are called to do exactly what they are doing. Their work represents more than a career or profession. Others, moving out of the clinical stream, look ahead and intuit the different paths open to them as administrators, planners, and the like. Finally, others have made significant changes, not in their tasks, but in the role that work plays in their lives. Those dreams from graduate school that were nurtured in the early years of clinical work are now altered. While the work still remains important and rewarding, other personal interests have pushed work into a smaller corner of their lives.

SUPERVISORY GOALS AND TASKS

The challenges of this stage are in helping the clinician define the work and its place in his life, and continue to grow rather than stagnate. Your goals focus on 2 related areas—the clinical work itself and the work in the context of the agency and career.

Clinical Focus of This Stage

Problem-Solve Around Specific Case Problems

As you move from gatekeeper of the previous stage to the clinical consultant of this stage, your clinical support comes in providing the clinician with another perspective on cases.

You're no longer the better voice, but the outside voice. From your vantage point you are able to see the client through a different lens. You can step back and see the larger picture that is hard for others to grasp when they are in the middle of a situation and close up. Unlike the last stage you're not looking for the blind spots that the clinician can't acknowledge.

Instead, like Sara, the clinician will be coming to you for ideas and is open to your feedback. And so you brainstorm together, you look and listen to recordings and concur with the clinician's perspective, or you point out small things that might have been overlooked. The clinician comes asking with specific questions and together you both develop possible answers.

Help the Clinician Develop an Integrated Therapeutic Model

As part of this process you are also continuing to give feedback to the clinician about his strengths and style—John, you do such a good job helping clients unravel their past traumas; Tanya, you really have a way of being patient and connecting with these reluctant teens who don't want to open up.

Your continuing feedback about the unique skills that the clinician possesses, along with asking questions that push him to define and articulate his thinking, helps him form a clearer picture of his professional self, as well as continues the individuation process begun in the last stage: These are your strengths and weaknesses, you say, these are mine. We respect each other's own competence and clinical style.

Career and Agency Focus of This Stage

Continue to Expand Clinical Skills

The second goal is the continuing challenge of helping the clinician utilize her expanded skills and continue her own clinical and professional growth. As mentioned at Stage 3, you facilitate this process by periodically raising it. Annual evaluations are an obvious time to do this in a more formal way, but even quick check-ins every few months are valuable—How are you feeling about your work these days? How have you been able to use skills you learned at that last conference you went to? Are you feeling creative? Bored?

As you have been doing with all the hard questions that you ask, you are letting the clinician know what is important, and what she can talk about; job satisfaction and career development are certainly an important part of her work and yours. You encourage the clinician to think about her relationship to her work, and together you both map out concrete training goals; brainstorm new clinical challenges in terms of problems, clients, new programs; and explore creative ways of putting the strength of hard-earned skills and style to use.

Expand Work Responsibilities

All this encouraging and brainstorming is particularly important given the limited career ladder in many agencies. One obvious outlet for talents is community work—serving on committees, task forces, developing interagency grants—that put clinical knowledge to work with community development and personal leadership. Expanding opportunities for providing clinical supervision is also a logical step. Some clinicians immerse themselves in particular clinical areas—trauma, eating disorders, autism—or more deeply into specific schools and skills, and come to see themselves as clinical specialists.

Others are ready to take on more administrative assignments—running a new service or team, playing a larger role in budget development, or developing a strategic plan around a particular agency or community issue. Your job is to encourage, to help these clinicians define who they are, what passions are, and how they can continue to grow.

CHALLENGES AND DANGERS OF STAGE 4

Having moved to this level does not mean that you and clinicians are immune to dangers. Here's what you need to be alert to during this stage.

Coasting

Not growing professionally, coasting, though not nearly as toxic as many of the dangers of other stages, is nonetheless not to be ignored. This presents itself as boredom taking over, settling into a job rut, going on autopilot. During Stage 1 we talked about the danger of the clinician stopping learning, then fueled by too much fear and anxiety. Now the clinician can stop learning once again, this time not from too much but from too little.

When this stance infects the supervisory relationship, it is reminiscent of what is known as a stale marriage—the couple who have been married for a long time, who don't argue and fight, but find they are bored with each other and have little in common. They live parallel lives, spend their evenings watching television together but not talking, or going off to their individual computers to surf the Internet. There is no screaming and yelling, and no one is in the depths of emotional pain, but there is little growth and creativity.

The equivalent of a stale marriage in supervisory relationships has much the same tone. You as supervisor aren't worried about blind spots and reckless practice, ethical violations, or high drama. Paperwork gets done, clients are seen, but supervisory sessions may be filled with chitchat about the weekend, about work gossip, about signing off on forms. You and clinicians are coasting along.

And that is the problem. The danger here is that you as the supervisor are colluding with the clinician. Rather than asking the hard questions, you don't. Neither of you are growing, everything is okay, and okay is more comfortable than pushing for anything more. What is more of concern is that this process spills over to work with clients. Clinician and client drift along. It is not the dependency based on intimacy of the second stage, but rather a falling into routine. Ms. Jones comes every week because she has been coming every week for a long time. What her goals are now and whether the clinical work is making a difference in her life are not asked. She continues to come because she has, and no one questions or confronts it.

That, however, is your job. Rather than becoming lulled, you want to move against inertia, remain proactive and creative to move this creativity both up—toward management—and down—toward clinicians and clients. Continue to ask the hard questions, and make creativity a priority.

Avoidance and Ambivalence

Coasting can be seen as a form of laziness and lack of focus. Avoidance and ambivalence reflect something more serious, namely, damage or weakness in the infrastructure of the supervisory relationship itself.

Sometimes the source for these feelings and behaviors comes from you, the supervisor. Like the other stages, the changes that occur in this stage can be difficult for some supervisors to navigate. For all their trust in the clinician's competence, some supervisors discover that this trust has limits. Their mandate to ensure quality control gives them, they believe, the license to keep the clinician on a short rein. Others fear that if they grant the clinician too much freedom, supervision will become too lax, resulting in a loss of control. Some fear that the clinician will surpass them in clinical skill. They are competitive and jealous and find it hard to let others go beyond the level that they themselves have struggled to reach.

For others it is less a competition and more about needing to be needed. They have difficulty envisioning a relationship in which they are needed simply because they have always been there. They are like parents who long after their children are grown call their children several times a day and always give advice or criticism. They continually try to insert their influence, haven't found new areas to focus on, and haven't made the shift to a more peer-like relationship. For these supervisors, their supervisory role has become the measure of their ego and worth. Whatever the variation, the tension that comes with the supervisor's difficulty in shifting roles leaves the clinician feeling confused and avoidant.

Other times the ambivalence and avoidance arise from the past, from unresolved issues within the supervisory relationships, unfilled cracks from the previous stages. If the third stage was particularly bumpy—if, for example, you felt the need to pull rank on the clinician by vetoing unsound clinical decisions, or stung a clinician with a conduct violation for chronic late paperwork—wariness may linger. If the clinician has chronically felt that the supervisor was too controlling, close-minded, or uninterested, the clinician may hold back to go elsewhere for what she needs. If the communication channels were never fully developed and needs, problems, and changes could not be openly discussed, it can be difficult to confront these issues now. Resentment and loss may settle in and make the relationship rigid and unproductive.

The danger of this fourth stage is that the potential of the supervisory relationship was never fully realized, and now the relationship withers and essentially dies. Only the shell of the relationship remains—the formality of accountability and hierarchy—but with little nurturance and substance. Your means of preventing this is to once again approach the anxiety. Verbalize what's happening in the relationship and the room, talk about old wounds and hurt feelings, look for and label signs of withdrawal or misunderstood criticism. You provide a vision of where you would like the relationship to go next. Only by this moving against the grain of the relationship can the underlying anxiety and hurt be dispelled.

Inefficiency

You're told by your supervisor that you need to review your team budget at the beginning of each month, and that the budgeting office will be giving you updated reports the week before. The budget report doesn't come and you let your supervisor know. The supervisor says she will check into it, and a week later the report arrives in your box. Next month the budget is again late and once again you mention it to your supervisor.

She shakes her head. "I'm sorry," she says. "I talked to John [the budget director] last month and he said he would take care of it. This is a bit awkward for me. He and I are friends, and I know he has a lot on his plate right now—some personal issues, as well as a lot of deadlines from the board regarding the upcoming audit. I'm afraid to push him too hard."

These types of situations obviously lack the drama or potential disaster of the previous stage. No one is going to get hurt; no ethics are going to be violated. But it does nonetheless create an inefficiency and ineffectiveness that comes out of simple human relationships. The supervisor and the budget director are friends, and the personal and professional overlap. The intentions are kind, but they ripple across the agency.

The same can happen between you and your clinician. You've been working together for years, and you've reached this more peer-like fourth stage. The hierarchy has weakened. The clinician invites you and your husband over for Thanksgiving, and you all have a good time, or you and she decide to do some private practice work together a couple of evenings a week. Your personal lives get intertwined and it can spill over into your day jobs at the agency. Her paperwork is behind because her mother has been in and out of the hospital and you cut her some slack. She knows you have meetings at the state capital all week, and rather than bothering you about a case that has been bothering her, she muddles through on her own.

Policy Practice

Practice Behavior Example: Collaborate with colleagues and clients for effective policy action.

Critical Thinking Question: What is an example of an agency policy that would create more administrative efficiency?

Again, the stakes are generally low; the underlying issues seemingly of only mild concern. No one is backing away out of fear of confrontation or being passive/aggressive as in the third stage. The relationship lines are a bit muddy, but very far from any entrenched dependency of the second stage. But that being said, it is still your responsibility as supervisor to stay aware of these potential dynamics—the blending of the professional and personal—in order to avoid potential conflicts of interests and negative impact on the work.

Honest and open communication with your clinicians is once again the key. Clarify the boundary lines, and separate the professional and personal. And because sorting these all out can be difficult, don't hesitate to use your own supervisor or trusted colleague as an outside voice and perspective.

MOVING TOWARD INTEGRATION

Let's return for the last time to our clinician. It's been 5 years since supervision at the agency began, and 9 years since she finished graduate school. Once again she is following the same format for her self-evaluation.

My theoretical orientation continues to be based on a family systems model. I assist the family in developing more open, direct, affirming communication; I help parents to establish a more consistent structure and to depersonalize the child's behavior and recognize its developmental nature.

Her statements reflect a consistency—all along she has made communication a central focus of her clinical work. Her clinical theory also reflects an integration. During the second stage she talked about helping parents to understand their children's needs, and in the third stage to help parents reestablish their authority. Now we hear her combining both—the slight shift from parental authority to structure, while retaining the goal of helping parents understand their children's needs.

I believe that parents need to be motivated to change, but realize that what seems like initial resistance is often just anxiety regarding the unfamiliar process of counseling itself. I believe that there is a need for both authenticity and limit setting within the therapeutic relationship. Many behaviors I believe represent attempts to recreate scenarios from unresolved events or traumas. Generally, I do not return to these emotions through history, but try to change the replication of patterns.

Notice the shift from the previous stage in her language and tone. There is no hint of anger and impatience. Notice the slight shift in her thinking. Where in the last stage she talked about clients seeming resistant, having choices, and not at times being ready for therapy, now she is more open and generous. What seems like resistance, she realizes, is really clients' initial anxiety, and that she needs to be patient. Similarly, the talk of authenticity harks back to Stage 1, but now it finally combined with proactivity and power of limit setting. Finally, while she tended to focus upon trauma in the second stage by tracking back with a client through her history, she now keeps tackling such issues through process.

The clinician is both supportive and strong. Good kid fears of rejection and confrontation, as well as the adolescent's sloppy use of power, have been essentially resolved.

I notice when anxious or stressed that I sometimes still fall back into my saving mode. But I'm much more sensitive to it, and realize that it's a signal that I need to take care of myself.

Like all of us, enough stress can push her back to old ways of coping. Once again, however, she shows self-awareness and there is no self-deprecation.

I find myself now using supervision to help maintain my focus, to step back and receive alternative ideas. Supervision has gone beyond assuring the quality of my work to helping me expand my sense of self and professional growth.

Supervision as consultation, as alternative ideas. Less quality control and checking up on and more enhancement of professional growth. Movement toward peerhood.

I would like to take a greater leadership role in the community regarding mental health and children. I also enjoyed training students and would like to continue to do so. I feel that I have much that I can teach and give.

She's right. She does have much to give to clients, students, staff, and community. Of course, there is more to learn, new challenges to face. The transformation from knowledge to wisdom and from being good at to becoming a master takes time.

But she has been successful at shaking those initial doubts, hesitations, and fears that once held her back. She has learned that she can learn from others and from experience that who she is and what she does are intimately connected. She has learned that the vision and dreams we hold inside can, if nurtured, come true, which perhaps is the most important lesson of all.

MOVING THROUGH THE 4 STAGES— SUMMARY OF THE PROCESS

Before closing our discussion of the characteristics and challenges of the 4 stages of clinical development, it may be useful to take a broad look at the process of moving through the stages themselves. Here are some of common questions that arise about the process itself.

Do Clinicians Always Move Forward in a Linear Way or Can There Be Variation?

Yes, clinicians move forward in a linear way in that they don't start, jump to Stage 3, then to Stage 2. They move from Stage 1 to Stage 2 and so on.

That said, this doesn't mean that all stages are the same length or that clinicians all move at the same pace. Tamara may move through Stage 1 relatively quickly due to past experience, personality, overall level of anxiety, the nature of the work, the type and amount of support she receives from her supervisor, while John is inherently more anxious, has less support, has a bigger learning curve, and hence lingers longer. As mentioned earlier, those with experience still move through the same stages, but generally at a quicker pace. The central issues for them are about building trust and safety in the supervisory relationship, and the supervisor retaining her role and not getting intimidated by the clinician.

Moving through stages also doesn't mean that process and progress constitute a developmental forced march. Like other developmental stages in children and adults, there is no 1-day sudden launch into a new stage. Change comes gradually. There is a moving forward—gaining confidence and skills—followed by regrouping and consolidation—before moving forward again. And if under enough stress, if working with insufficient support, it's easy for a clinician to backslide and regress—to fall back into good kid behaviors, to become anxious, to be overresponsible or dependent.

Once again, as supervisor it is up to you to ask the hard questions, wonder aloud what is causing change, help the clinician sort stress from healthy regrouping. You don't want to pull the clinician along at your pace, but be the steady voice of encouragement and support that allows him to move forward at his own.

Finally, while you cannot choreograph or guarantee a clinician's development, you certainly have the power to stall or stop it. Because each stage builds on the others, cracks in structure of any one stage can affect the other. As discussed earlier, this layering process is what makes Stage 1 so crucial. If trust and safety are not developed early on, if the clinician does not bond to you, he will bond to someone else or no one, and you both will wind up just going through the motions of a relationship. You have little real influence, and quality control is a danger. Yes, the clinician may continue to grow, but in spite of, not because of you.

But the same challenges can occur in the other stages. You and the clinician can get stuck in the dependency of the second stage. The power issues of the third stage can be mishandled, and the clinician marches away feeling entitled, or you both can feel misunderstood and wounded, leaving the relationship severely damaged. Stage 4 can turn into a stale marriage, or the clinician senses your ambivalence over her individuation and withdraws.

All these challenges are largely yours to navigate and address. Your supervisory and clinical skill and style come to the forefront in seeing what lies ahead, being curious about what lies beneath, knowing your own vulnerabilities, and ensuring that the foundation and structure of each stage are as sound as they can be.

Even Though Progress Varies by Personality, Strength of Relationship, and So On, How Long Does It Generally Take to Move from Stage 1 to Stage 4?

The clinician we were following through the self-evaluation moved through the stages in 5 years, and in 9 years from the time she graduated. Five years is probably the minimum, between 5 and 10 years a normal range. Again, the variation depends on learning opportunities; level of support; personality, personal issues, natural abilities and talents; and how good the fit between the work and the clinician. Essentially, the better the work and supervisory environment, the better the clinician is able to relax, learn, and enthusiastically throw herself into the work. If the work itself or the work environment is stressful, unsupportive, or if the clinician does not enjoy the work itself, learning is slower or stalled. The analogy is like the differences between a good school with energetic and supportive teachers, creative and individual curriculums and adequate resources and an overcrowded school with burned out teachers, rote curriculums, little attention to students, and inadequate supplies. While all the children will learn differently and have different talents, those in the better schools will have an easier time learning and growing.

It's also helpful to think not only in terms of time but in terms of upward movement. A BSW, for example, doing case management at an agency, may move through the stages as she gains both self-confidence and skill over a number of years. If she were then to go to graduate school, and begin a more clinical position after graduation, she will be starting over at another first stage due to the new relationship and new skill-set. The same is true when she moves from clinician to supervisor.

Accumulated experience obviously can make progress easier—one is more familiar with the process of moving through the stages—but is no substitute for the actual learning and the reshaping on one's professional identity. It can also impede learning as the cracks and wounds of the past impact the present. A clinician, for example, who had an unsupportive or critical supervisor in the past may have difficulty trusting a new one or ones. Your responsibility is to be aware of the ways the past may shape the present relationship, and to bring that awareness into your supervisory style and focus.

How Do Interns and Students in Field Placements Fit into These Stages?

The focus of internships and field placements is learning, and the time at the agency is limited. By design and purpose, these students are at Stage 1 in that your role is primarily that of a teacher. You want to provide learning opportunities and build realistic goals with them about what and how much they might be able to accomplish in the time frame you have.

Human Behavior

Practice Behavior Example: Know about human behavior across the life course; the range of social systems in which people live; and the ways social systems promote or deter people in maintaining or achieving health and well-being.

Critical Thinking Question: What do you see as the biggest challenge in working with interns and students? How could you overcome that challenge?

That said, some students come with past work experience and training. Some are able to settle more quickly than others. The fit between you and them is a good one, and Stage 1 moves toward Stage 2 in a matter of a few months. While still primarily a teacher, the dependency and curiosity of the second stage takes hold. At the end of placement there is feeling that the experience has been a good one, and both you and the students may wish you had more time together.

If you have students who seem to show the characteristics of Stage 3 early in their field placement—an air of entitlement, a testing of boundaries—you want to see it as a way of coping with anxiety through a certain false arrogance, or suspect that this is not about you but something about the clinician's past or personality. This is likely to be rare, but if it occurs you'll need to sort it out by discussing this with the school's field liaison, and by both exploring anxiety and setting clear boundaries with the student.

The need to create a strong relationship is just as important for students, obviously, as it is for staff. What changes the process is the time restrictions. Knowing when someone is leaving and having them in and out of the workweek can make for an emotional holding back and a firmer staying in role. The opportunities for role-modeling are always there, and these initial impressions of you and how you work are often powerful and, at times, indelible ones for students.

This concludes our trek along the developmental path. We now have a broad framework for both anticipating the changing needs of the clinician and shaping the supervisory process to meet these needs. In Chapter 8 we will look more closely at specific supervisory techniques and skills.

The following questions will test your application and analysis of the content found within this chapter. For additional assessment, including licensing-exam-type questions on applying chapter content to practice behaviors, visit **MySearchLab**.

1. Know what you know of the fourth stage refers to
   a. The clinician's belief that she in essence knows everything
   b. The clinician's realistic assessment of her clinical strengths and weaknesses
   c. The clinician's sense that her colleagues know much more than she does
   d. You as a supervisor feeling empowered and in control

2. One of the challenges of supervision during the fourth stage is
   a. Helping clinicians remain creative
   b. Setting clear boundaries to encourage the clinician's individuation
   c. Continuing to deal with clinician dependency
   d. Retaining and replacing clinical staff

3. Susan has cancelled her last 2 supervisory sessions saying that she has no clinical concerns to present. What, as her supervisor, would be your best response?
   a. Tell her that supervision is not an option and that she absolutely needs to keep her sessions
   b. Discuss with her her view of supervision and her supervisory needs
   c. Tell her that is fine and that she can come as clinical concerns arise
   d. Look at her charts to see what she is doing with her clients

4. You and Harold have been working together for many years and socialize outside of work occasionally. He has lately been behind on his paperwork, but you know how much he has been worried about his mother's recent illness. What would be the best way for you to approach this problem?
   a. Realize that this is temporary, that his clinical work is good, and leave it alone
   b. Ask your supervisor to talk to him about it
   c. Talk to him in supervision about his mother and see if that helps him feel better
   d. Talk to him about the paperwork, acknowledge his current stress, and come up with a plan for completion

5. Allie was placed on probation by you 2 years ago due to inappropriate clinical behavior on her part. Though she has significantly improved her performance and is consistently using professional judgment, she seems distant and removed in her supervisory sessions with you. How would you address this in supervision?

6. Bill recently received your community's Social Worker of the Year award, and you find yourself feeling jealous and competitive. How would you handle this?

8

Supervisory Tools and Techniques

Competencies Applied with Practice Behaviors — in This Chapter				
✖ Professional Identity	■ Ethical Practice	✖ Critical Thinking	■ Diversity in Practice	■ Human Rights & Justice
■ Research-Based Practice	✖ Human Behavior	■ Policy Practice	■ Practice Contexts	■ Engage, Assess, Intervene, Evaluate

In Chapters 2 to 4 we looked at the larger developmental landscape that makes up clinical supervision—forming the relationship, assessing and setting goals, anticipating needs, and tailoring supervision to the clinician's growth. But what exactly do you as a supervisor do when you are supervising? This is what we will focus upon in Chapters 8 and 9. In this chapter we will discuss some of the supervisory tools and techniques that can help you make the most of the supervisory sessions.

RUNNING THE SESSION

Basically there are 2 overlapping agendas that set the focus of any supervisory session: yours—what information you need to do your job—and the clinician's—what information she needs to do her job. Your agenda usually centers around quality control—finding out how Matt handled his last session with his potentially suicidal client, whether Karen's progress notes are up-to-date for the audit—and relationship—whether Juan felt criticized by your suggestions about his report. The clinician's agenda usually focus on some type of clinical, emotional, or administrative support: how to talk with 6-year-old Sally about her parents' divorce, feeling anxious about an upcoming court appearance, or seeking approval to attend an upcoming training.

As with all other aspects of supervision, the way you juggle these 2 agendas will ultimately reflect the demands of the workplace, the clinician's stage of development, and your own personal strengths and style. That being the case, it is important that you make clear to the clinician from the start that supervision is primarily for the clinician. This means that the clinician is responsible for having an agenda for the session. This doesn't mean that every interaction has to be planned in advance. Emergencies arise—Matt's client is suicidal—or the clinician may seek you out after a particularly trying session—Tamara feels devastated after her testimony in court. But in normal week-to-week contact the clinician shouldn't be scribbling down an agenda at the beginning of the session while waiting for you to get back from the restroom. The clinician needs to spend some time thinking about what he needs addressed in the session.

Once the clinician knows what you expect, it's up to you to enforce it. If you don't follow through on what you say is important, especially in those first several weeks—Matt finds that his not having an agenda is something you're willing to work around—you're not only encouraging testing behavior, but sending out a message that what you say may or may not be honest and true. The purpose of being firm is to help the clinician see that your words do match your deeds. This translates into reliability and ultimately safety—the clinician knows that you are dependable. Firmness also helps the clinician learn the importance of taking a proactive rather than a reactive role within supervision and with clients.

To think through and articulate clinical goals and problems, rather than unloading problems on cue from the supervisor, avoids the dangers of being spoon-fed and replicating, through the parallel process, what clients often do. You, of course, can have your own agenda—getting quick rundowns on each of the clients on a clinician's caseload, following up on specific cases, checking over case records, or requesting to hear or watch a recording—varying from week to week depending upon your own administrative needs, but not overriding the clinician's responsibility.

You maintain your supervisory focus by establishing clear supervisory goals with the clinician; these goals set priorities and directions for supervision itself. Goals can come from the clinician's sense of needs—I want to learn more about sexual abuse; I want to be more active in family sessions—or from yours—I'd like you to listen for themes; I'd like you to focus on raising questions with clients, rather than worrying about offering them answers. Goals should be mutually agreed upon, behaviorally clear and specific, and include a time frame for achieving them. Although year-long goals derived from the early evaluation are standard, 3- or 6-month goals, especially in the first stage when clinician anxiety is so high, may help you and the clinician weed through concerns and decide what's most important.

Goals can also help you determine how much and what type of teaching is needed. Teaching within the supervisory session can take the form of a mini-lecture, demonstration or observation, role-play, or discussion of clinical readings. The best training is training that can be immediately applied—an assessment outline that can be used with a new case on Thursday, an experiential exercise that can be used with a couple in the afternoon. Information that isn't quickly turned into practice tends to pile up inside the clinician's head, creating more confusion and ultimately more anxiety. Training, even case discussion, should move, particularly in the early stages, from the specific—Mr. Jones' depression—to the general—ways of approaching depression—and back to the specific—what to do with Mr. Jones on Wednesday.

The clinician needs to cut through the flood of facts and details that clients provide by understanding and thinking in terms of broad principles and basic strategies. Tamara, for example, doesn't need to know how to help Eric, who is hyperactive; she instead needs to have basic information about hyperactivity and see how it applies to her work with Eric. Similarly, Tom doesn't need to get lost in the squabble between Mr. and Ms. Jones about washing the dishes, but he needs to see the patterns of blame that keep the cycle going and understand how to break such cycles within the session process.

This teasing out of themes, patterns, and general problems from the client's details, then discussing treatment solutions and strategies based upon theories and techniques that you and the clinician have chosen, is the basic format for discussing cases. This process helps turn an overwhelming load of 20 cases into a more manageable caseload of 10 because the problems and strategies are similar. The application needs to be fine-tuned only for a particular case. By working through this process in supervision, the clinician learns how to approach and think through particular cases. Even as the clinician continues to develop skills and expand his knowledge base over time, this basic approach remains. What changes with experience is the number of perspectives and strategies that the clinician knows and can choose from.

RECORD-KEEPING AND DOCUMENTATION

Most agency accreditation and licensing reviews require that some record be kept of supervisory sessions. Some workplaces use specific forms for each supervisory session that may include a listing of topics discussed, recommendations or courses of action, and supervisory concerns, sometimes signed by both the clinician and the supervisor. Others leave it to the supervisor to set up her own record system.

The *what* of record-keeping—contents of the record—is determined by the *why*—the need for some information rather than others. Obviously, you want to keep a file on each clinician. Here you document by date each supervisory session. You'll want to write down information on cases discussed, as well as administrative matters. Here you can also include copies of performance evaluations, clinician's self-evaluations, requests—for trainings, for time off, and so on. Like a client's clinical record, your supervisory record should be a compendium of your history with a clinician, a receptacle of all contacts and relevant information.

Professional Identity

Practice Behavior Example: *Practice personal reflection and self-correction to assure continual professional development.*

Critical Thinking Question: How has your own documentation changed over time? What does this change reflect about your clinical growth?

Your notes for each session should include enough information to help you remember and identify the clinical case you and the clinician are discussing. You don't need to know extensive information about Mr. Jones, for example—that is in the clinical record—but rather enough information to help you track what you and the clinician discussed about Mr. Jones. This might be the clinician's request for referral information for the client, or her concern about involving his wife in his treatment.

What's essential that you document is what clinical recommendations and specific actions you made to the clinician—what agency you directed Carla to call for referral information, that she should discuss medication with her client, Ms. Smith, at their next session. This information allows you to know how to specifically follow up—Did you call the agency? What was their response? Is Ms. Smith willing to see the psychiatrist?—but also provides a clear paper trail of your interventions, in case there are liability or ethical concerns. Should Jake, for example, report that Mr. Jones seems possibly suicidal, you want to document in your records that you specifically told Jake to (a) call and check in with Mr. Jones by that afternoon; (b) immediately contact the mental health center about the process of obtaining an emergency commitment order should it be needed; (c) note his actions in the clinical record; (d) report back to you about the outcome before the end of the day. Without this information in your notes, there is no protection for you, should Jake, for some reason, fail to follow through.

Similarly, you want to note specific recommendations regarding administrative issues. If you talked with Ann about her coming late to meetings, or her taking sick time without sufficient approval, you want to note not only the topic and discussion, but the outcome—that she, for example, will be given a written conduct offense if she is late again. You also want to note any collateral contacts you may have also made on this matter—for example, telephone calls to your supervisor or human resources, and their recommendations.

Box 8.1 presents an example of notes of a supervisory session with an experienced clinician named Tom (T); cl stands for client.

The mind-set here is one of using records not only to supplement your memory, but to provide a paper trail of your involvement in case management, clinical quality control, and staff performance. Written documentation is the only way to ensure that your intentions, concerns, and actions are clear, appropriate, and timely. Without such a written record, whatever unfolds is subject to misinterpretation and hearsay. Again, when in doubt, seek consultation and clear instruction—from your supervisor, from human resources, from emergency services supervisor, from agency attorney—and document your contacts. This is not being paranoid or untrusting, but simply acting like a responsible manager.

Box 8.1 • Sample Supervisory Notes

Cases

Ms. K.—T concerned about cl's increasing depression—sees triggered by daughter moving away. Role-played discussing with cl referral for medication eval.
Action: T to discuss med. w/ cl next session.

Mr. S—2nd session, anger management. T suspects underlying unresolved grief over loss of father last year. Raised issue of T's loss of his father. Discussed ways of approaching issue w/ cl.
Action: T. to focus next session on cl experience w/ loss.

Bill W.—new case, referred by mo. 14 y/o wm, failing grades, mild symptoms of depression. Parents separating. Cl seen individually, T developed good rapport, cl motivated, open.
Action: T to talk w/ cl about possible fam session w/ parents.

Admin

T wants to attend 1-day workshop on couples therapy—one of his training goals for yr.
Action: T to submit email with costs/budget by Thurs.

RECORDINGS—LEARNING TO SEE AND HEAR

If clinical work is the primary focus of the supervisory process, recordings, both audio and video, can be one of the primary tools. They allow you, the supervisor, to see and/or hear what the clinician is doing in the room with the client. This record of the clinical session not only helps you see how the process and problem unfold, and better understand where and how the clinician gets stuck, but provides you with detailed material from which you can better assess skills.

Compared to live observation, recordings create less disturbance with the session process. This advantage is also the disadvantage: Feedback is not immediate, and the clinical process can be changed only in the next session. While recordings are less intrusive than live observation, most clinicians, unless desensitized to the process through much experience, feel performance pressure when being recorded.

Some clients will obviously object to any type of recording because of self-consciousness or confidentiality fears. Audio recording seems less intrusive and may raise less anxiety and opposition. Often if the clinician is matter-of-fact about introducing the idea of recording, she explains how it is less about the client and more a tool for enhancing the clinician's skills and services, and this helps the client relax. Clients need to know how the recordings will be used, who will have access to them, and where and how they will be kept to ensure privacy and confidentiality (it's easy for clients to worry that these recordings will somehow show up on the Internet). They, of course, need to sign a form granting their permission, and be assured that it is fine if they decline. Clinicians need to be given specific instructions, or role-played, on how to present and handle these requests.

Despite these drawbacks, recordings as a supervisory tool provide a more thorough understanding of the clinical process than can be reported by the clinician in supervision. Audio recordings present the language, voice, and dialogue, complete with silences and cutoffs, of the clinician and client; video recordings show the physical behavior as well. What neither shows is the internal thoughts and unexpressed emotions of the clinician and client. To make the best use of the recording as a learning tool, both the internal and the external need to be brought together.

A good way to do this is to have clinicians analyze the recording before they present it in supervision. Here is a brief outline that clinicians can use to organize their thoughts.

Human Behavior

Practice Behavior Example: *Utilize conceptual frameworks to guide the processes of assessment, intervention, and evaluation.*

Critical Thinking Question: How would you respond to a client who expressed reservations about recording or observing a session?

- *Overview of the case:* Description of the client/couple/family, presenting problems, initial impressions
- *Assessment:* Underlying problems, dynamics, diagnosis
- *Goals:* Long- and short-range treatment goals and strategies
- *Goals for the session:* What the clinician planned to accomplish in the session and its context within the larger goals
- *Evaluation of the session process:* How well the clinician did what he or she set out to do

At first glance this outline may seem extensive and formal. Generally, it is neither. The first time the case is presented, the outline will obviously be longer; in subsequent sessions only updates are needed. Let's translate this into client material.

- *Overview of the case:* Mr. K is 32 years old and was self-referred for anger management after getting upset at an employee at his workplace. He is married, has a 4-year-old child, has not been in therapy before, but seems motivated. Seen twice.
- *Assessment:* Because he runs his own business and because it is relatively new, he is under considerable work stress. He also seems anxious as he puts a lot of pressure on himself to do well. Work problems with employee have been long-standing. Though they occasionally argue, he sees his wife as a source of support and has contained his anger with her. Other recent stressors include the death of his mother in the past 3 months.
- *Goals:* Explore and increase his emotional range, discuss ways of handling stress, help solve problems with employee, and assess possible depression and unresolved grief.
- *Goals for the session:* Discuss his mother's death and his grief reaction.
- *Evaluation of the session process:* As he is reluctant to talk about his mother's death, I explained to him how it may tie in to his anger. He reported that he never grieved his mother's death because he needed to be strong for his other siblings. He has not returned to cemetery. He seemed open and sad when talking about it. I feel I did a good job being supportive, but feel uncertain what to do next.

The outline helps the clinician to listen to the recording and begin an assessment of the clinical process. The clinician can pick out sections that illustrate the process (where and how the client was supportive) or show where communication begins to break down (the client shuts down, becomes defensive), and thus can avoid plowing through the entire recording. You and the clinician can then talk about ways of helping Mr. K in the next session to process his grief and link it to his anger.

Recordings offer benefits that general case discussion does not—a way of doing microanalysis of the session process, the context in which problems and techniques are played out. If Ellen, for example, decides to make an interpretation about a mother's behavior, you and Ellen can actually hear the words, voice, and body language behind the interpretation. More important, you and Ellen can hear the client's immediate reaction in the response that follows—Ms. Jones says she hadn't thought about it that way and becomes quiet and reflective, or Ms. Jones says "Yes, but . . ."—letting Ellen know that her interpretation was not accepted. This kind of listening and gathering of information from within the process is difficult, but made easier with the aid of such a verbal transcript.

You can further refine the clinician's skills by asking the clinician to listen and look with a specific focus. You might ask Ellen while reviewing a recording of a family session, for example, to pick out themes of the various family members—the father's lament that life is unfair or the daughter's claim that no one listens to her—or to observe patterns in the interactions—the ways the father blames and the child always becomes quiet and turns away. Or she may track her impact upon the process—notice, for example, who echoes the clinician's suggestions or who repeatedly turns away, interrupts, or shakes his or her head.

Finally, you can use recordings to bring together clinical thought and action. The easiest way to do this is to play a section of a recording and ask the clinician for an interpretation of the client's responses—what he thinks the client was thinking at that moment in the session, what he thinks the client was feeling. If the clinician has trouble hearing or seeing the patterns or dynamics, you can point them out. For example:

> "Don't pay attention to the words; listen to the difference in the voice and watch the body posture of the husband and wife."
>
> "Every time the father brings this up notice how the child starts to distract the mother."
>
> "You just made a good interpretation—listen to what the client says next to see if he agrees with it."
>
> "The client is saying that she doesn't know how to talk to her sister. I wonder if that is a parallel statement about you as well, that she doesn't know how to talk to you."
>
> "I notice that you sound very different when talking to the mother than when you talk to the father. Why?"

This type of questioning helps the clinician become sensitive to the process and to the ways broad strategies and principles become translated into concrete actions.

Of course, recordings can be used more informally and spontaneously. If John, for example, comes to you rattled after a particularly difficult session with a client, you may ask him to play his recording of the session to help correct any distorted perceptions he may have and lower his anxiety. As the maturing clinician's listening skills, knowledge, and clinical strategies become better established, he is more likely to use recordings to spot-check, fine-tune, or get a second opinion about the clinical process.

How much does a clinician need to record? It depends upon your agreed-upon clinical goals, the clinician's skill level, your quality-control needs for detailed feedback of clinical performance, and the amount of time you and the clinician have to process material. As mentioned earlier, Stage 2 is an ideal time to focus on recording since this is when the clinician begins to make the shift from a focus on crisis and content to proactivity and process. But some supervisors like to begin this process earlier, to desensitize the clinician to recording itself, to spot-check performance, as a way of highlighting the clinical process. The challenge when working with an anxious new clinician is, once again, that the process may increase anxiety, and if too overwhelming, may inhibit the forming of the supervisory relationship.

Certainly, it is a good idea to record sessions of clients who present a difficult-to-manage process. Often it's useful to track intensively 1 or 2 cases at a time as a way of helping clinicians learn to make and carry out session-to-session goals. Some agencies require some review of recordings on a periodic basis—quarterly or semiannually—for quality control or as a basis for clinical evaluations.

Critical Thinking

Practice Behavior Example: *Analyze models of assessment, prevention, intervention, and evaluation.*

Critical Thinking Question: Under what situations or circumstances might you decide that it would be best not to observe a clinical session? Why?

All this potential learning through recording need not be one-sided. Show clinicians recordings of your own clinical work, or if they are in supervisory training, of your own supervisory sessions with clinicians. This strategy not only helps get you off the pedestal, but also demonstrates to clinicians ways of approaching similar clients in a different way. It is most useful when you can explain what you are thinking during the session and show what worked well and what worked poorly.

CLINICAL OBSERVATION

Observation can be of 2 main types—passive or active. Passive observation is watching what occurs in a session, but making no suggestions or interventions during the process; feedback is given after the session is over. Active observation allows you as supervisor to give feedback and suggestions during the course of the clinical session.

Passive Observation

In many ways passive supervision seems to be very much like video recording, because your feedback is given after the act. There are, however, 2 situations where passive supervision is helpful.

One is as a teaching tool for other clinicians or students. This is usually done through a 1-way mirror. You and other clinicians or students can watch a therapy session together, and you can comment on the process, pointing out patterns or skills—notice how tense the client is holding his body; notice how the clinician is mirroring the client's body language; watch how the client reacts now that the clinician has confronted him about not coming to his last appointment—and the students are free to ask questions or make their own comments as the session unfolds. This type of play-by-play commentary helps students and observing clinicians learn how to think, listen, and see as though they themselves were in the room. It provides a sense of real-time decision making, a clear advantage over recording.

The other use of passive observation is to help you better observe the clinician–client interaction, especially if you don't have video-recording capability. This again can be done through a 1-way mirror if that is available, or can be done by you actually "sitting in"—discretely in the corner of the clinical office as the session is going on. While this seems immensely intrusive and anxiety producing for the clinician and client alike, it is in practice usually much less than you may initially assume. What this type of live observation offers is a way for you to closely observe the unfolding of process. Not only are you usually able to see more of what is actually occurring than you might stationed behind a mirror, but you are more apt to clearly detect any tension and change in mood in the room.

When doing this type of live supervision, you want to be as unobtrusive as possible, the proverbial fly on the wall. Sit in the corner and make no eye contact with clients. What will often happen is that clients will initially try to engage you in the conversation—their eye contact and opening comments will be to you or to both you and the clinician. Look at your writing pad or at the floor, or say gently, "Pretend I'm not here," and clients will immediately understand that you are not part of the discussion. Then you take notes about what you observe and feel as if you were conducting the session— what you might say at various points, your own observations of the clients, your own responses to what the client offers—as well as your own reactions to the clinician's interventions—the fact that John didn't pick up on client's comment about his daughter, or that he said exactly what you would have said in response to the client's comment.

As with video or audio recording, a good part of countering client reluctance to live observation is in the presentation. If you and the clinician have already mapped out your observation 1 or 2 weeks in advance, clients can be told by the clinician at a prior session that she is considering having her supervisor sit in next time. The explanation can go something like this: "I've talked with my supervisor and am wondering if you would be okay with her coming into our session next week. She will just sit in the corner and observe me. This is to give me feedback about what I'm doing—it's like those times when the principal sat in the back of the room during one of your classes in school. Think about it, see how you feel, and you can meet her next week."

Again, some clients will have questions; some may say they are uncomfortable; some will say they will think about it. Some clients actually feel more at ease because live observation doesn't raise their concerns about a permanent record the way video recording does, nor does it raise performance pressure. If you meet the clients, you can reinforce with them that your focus is on the clinician, rather than on them. With any type of observation you want to have the client's written consent, and if you (and students) are behind a 1-way mirror, you want to give the clients the option to actually meet you before the session.

After the session you may want to allot some time to debrief the clinician for a few minutes, or have a clear time scheduled to just do this. Newer clinicians are often anxious about getting feedback quickly, so it is a good idea to plan a debriefing as soon as possible.

The debriefing is similar to that of recording—asking the clinician to think about her own reactions to the sessions and the process, her assessment of what went well and what did not, her specific concerns and questions. Your job is to address her concerns—Did you think my confrontation was effective? I felt the teenager was disengaged and I didn't know how to draw him out—as well as raise discrepancies between your observations and the actions of the clinician—I noticed that the wife became quiet when you started asking questions about the couple's sex life and it seemed to me that you didn't notice her resistance, did you? I felt bored when your client started complaining about his boss yet again, did you feel the same way?

Again, the focus is on process—being able to notice and use what is occurring in the room—and processing—how the clinician is able to link theory and technique, assessment with treatment, overall goals with specific session goals.

Active Observation

The obvious advantage of active observation is that you can intervene and help shape its direction and outcome. How immediately you are able to provide feedback depends on your technology. The most immediate is the bug in the ear, followed by telephoning. With the bug in the ear, you are literally able to coach the clinician about what to say or do in the moment—ask the father about this; notice the wife is looking away. Directives obviously need to be clear and succinct, subtle corrections in steering the process. Telephoning into the session is a bit less immediate and certainly seems to clients more intrusive, but offers an opportunity for more detailed feedback.

Some clinicians like this more micro-level of supervision; knowing they have a copilot ready to step in and make corrections lowers their anxiety. Others feel rattled trying to pay attention to both the client and you. While this type of observation clearly helps clinicians know how to respond in the moment, some supervisors worry that it makes clinicians too dependent on the supervisor or causes them to too closely copy the supervisor's style. Clinicians bypass the learning and development of their individual style that comes by having more room and taking risks. Even if you have these concerns, you can still use these methods. You just need to be careful not to overuse them, gradually wean the clinician from them, or have the clinician be proactive, telling you what specific feedback he wants.

In many settings, however, there is no technology available for bug in the ear or telephoning. In that case active observation takes the form of stopping the session to give feedback and direction. This may include you knocking on the 1-way mirror when you see the session going off in a terribly wrong direction and having the clinician leave the session to come discuss the process with you. Or it may include you and the clinician agreeing to stop in the middle of the session to discuss and regroup, similar to halftime break during a football game. If you are sitting in the room, you both may step out for a few minutes for a consultation. Any of these options are effective ways of helping the clinician receive feedback about what you see going well, and what is being missed, helping her regroup and redirect the session focus.

All this raises the question; of how much observation may undermine the client's confidence in the clinician. Obviously with students or interns who tell clients up front their student status, this isn't an issue. If you are observing staff, the context and frequency of your observations will usually determine client reaction. The more frequent, the more micromanaging your feedback, the more it gives the appearance that the supervisor is the one in charge and that the clinician is either not confident or skilled enough to handle the work on her own. If, on the other hand, you are doing a random one-time observation as part of quality control or staff evaluation, it can be made clear that this is about meeting your supervisory needs rather than anything about the clinician's performance in a particular case.

CLINICAL CONSULTATIONS

There is a fine line between observations that are for your own supervisory needs and overall training of the clinician, and those situations where your observation is actually a clinical consultation. In these situations your focus is changing the dynamics of a particular case and you are offering the clinician or clinician and client a new perspective. This can be handled in several ways.

Suppose, for example, that Teresa is feeling that she is at an impasse with her client, Mike, who is seeking help with depression following his job loss. In spite of her best efforts in the session and her giving him homework to do, Mike is making little or no progress. Teresa might ask you to observe a session just to see what you notice and make suggestions to her about changes she might make. She asks Mike if he minds your observing. He consents; you observe, and later give Teresa feedback about what you noticed and suggestions for other foci or techniques. In these cases you are similar to a physician who takes a second look at a patient's x-rays or lab results.

Another way of approaching this, however, would be to take a more active role in the session and focus on the dynamic between the clinician and client. Teresa, for example, might share her frustration with Mike: "Even though we have been meeting several times, it seems to me that we are getting a bit stuck. We seem to keep having the same conversation, and I find myself making the same suggestions. Are you feeling the same?" If Mike is in fact feeling the same, then she asks Mike if he minds you observing their next session. Your observation offers them both a way of moving through the impasse.

You then can either observe and pass your observations on to Teresa alone, or focus on the dynamic between Teresa and Mike and give feedback to them both, for example: "I noticed that you Teresa are trying to encourage Mike to look for work as a way of helping his depression, but I also noticed, Mike, that you get quiet and withdrawn when she starts talking about this. Watching this I was wondering if you perhaps feel that Teresa is moving too quickly, or doesn't understand how difficult this is for you." Your observations and comments change the conversation between them, and uncover the emotional stumbling block.

The most active form of consultation is where you actually come in as a consultant and interview the client or clients yourself while the clinician observes. Because this is so potentially disempowering of the clinician—rather than fine-tuning what she is already doing, you seem to be essentially overriding her, taking charge of her case, and presenting yourself as a higher authority of clinical expertise—you never want to do this merely as a way for you to gain a better perspective of the assessment and treatment goals. You and the clinician may, however, together decide to do this when the clinician's assessments or interventions are, for some reason, being resisted by the clients. Here you are essentially providing backup—supporting the clinician while offering the same information in a new way.

Sometimes the clients' seeming resistance is driven by their own ambivalence about their problem (others are saying there is a problem but they are not convinced), or because they question the clinician's authority or expertise and hear her perspective as simply one more voice added to the chorus of friends and relatives with whom they are already familiar. What you offer is the "white coat" intervention whereby you, after a short opportunity to understand clients' perspective, essentially echo what the clinicians have already stated—that this is what you see as an underlying problem, that you recommend this particular focus of treatment.

This type of intervention is a strategic move that, in a more intense way than observation provides, can help unblock the clients' emotional logjam and increase the credibility of the clinician. It is important that you and the clinician map this out in advance. You want to be certain that you and the clinician are on the same treatment page, clear about the message you and the clinician most want to present, and that you and the clinician agree that the timing of your intervention best fits with the clients' willingness to hear your perspective. The clinician presents this option to clients as a consultation or second opinion. Having the clinician present together with you in the session while you meet with the client affirms the unified front you are presenting.

CO-THERAPY

Co-therapy, the working together on a case, can be a highly effective learning tool with couples or families. What often makes it difficult is the coordination of schedules or the dedication of your time beyond the 1-session observation or consultation. When and how you and the clinician decide to do this depends upon the clinician's stage of development. For clinicians who are at Stage 1, for example, co-therapy is primarily the clinician observing your work. You are in charge and clients quickly see that you are the primary therapist. As clinicians gain experience, the responsibility for the session can be more equally shared. At later stages, the clinician may take the primary role with you stepping in only to support or refocus when the process seems to be going significantly off course.

What is essential in doing co-therapy is planning and choreographing. You and the clinician want to be clear before the therapy session what the clinical focus will be and who is responsible for what. Without this planning you both can trip over each other, and rather than modeling a unified front and clear communication, you both in essence replicate the dysfunctional patterns that the couple or family are already engaged in. Here are some questions to discuss with the clinician before a co-therapy session.

> What is our major goal and objective for this session? What is it we want the couple or family to most understand, think, feel by the end of the session?
> What is it that we need to be careful that we absolutely don't do, that is, replicate the clients' patterns?
> What is it that we most want to model for the couple or parents?
> Who is taking the lead? When should the other step in?

The purpose here is not to control the content, but to intentionally shape the process. It is not about being rigid about what unfolds, but to be clear at the outset so that patterns aren't replicated, and you and the clinician are working in the same direction. Co-therapy with couples or families means that you both are essentially modeling for the clients through your interactions how to work together as parents or as a couple. Without this planning the danger is that you will struggle between yourselves in the room, or out of frustration one of you will give up and let the other run the session.

What you and the clinician decide will obviously depend on your clinical theory, individual styles, and needs of the clients. If you are a male supervisor, for example, and you both are working with a couple where the husband is more dominant and controlling, you both may decide that it might be helpful for the female clinician to model assertiveness, or to actively support the wife when she speaks so that there is no replication of the male dominance. On the other hand, you as the male co-therapist may deliberately model for the husband how to listen and be receptive to the clinician's ideas. Similarly, with a family, one of you may choose to advocate for the quiet teen, while the other helps the parents listen and not interrupt.

If the clinician is taking the lead, let her also dictate your role. It's her case and you want to support her running it as she sees fit. This is also empowering in that it's an opportunity for role reversal—she gets to be in charge of you for a change. Your job is again to supply support and correction as she needs it.

Learning to work together like this takes time and practice, and the first few sessions are likely to be sloppy as you and the clinician try to blend your styles and personalities. It's important to debrief after a session—to review together what went well, what didn't, to understand what you both were thinking and seeing, to come up with a plan for next time. These types of shared clinical experiences are powerful in increasing the relationship and bond between you both.

ROLE-PLAYING

Clinicians like role-playing. It doesn't usually generate the performance anxiety that comes with recordings or observation because clinicians can always choose to be the client and let you have the hard part. Role-playing within the supervisory session becomes an impromptu way for you to understand what a client is like. It also provides with an opportunity to teach specific skills and techniques that the clinician can use in the next clinical session.

Usually it is best to have the clinician play the client; she knows the client's behavior and speech better than you. However, you can also assume the client role at times. In fact, you may be able to portray client responses accurately because of experience with similar clients, making it more realistic, and challenging, for the clinician.

Practically any role can be role-played—from a 3-year-old hyperactive child in play therapy to a cranky 90-year-old grandmother who resists therapy. Role-play doesn't require theatrical talent or a lot of preparation.

It is important that roles be clearly separated. When you are role-playing, role-play; when someone wants to stop, say "stop." Mixing role-play with explanations or questions—"See how I phrased that statement so that she didn't feel so blamed?" or "Why are you asking the brother that?"—can create confusion and disrupt the flow. Keeping the process moving allows the supervisor and clinician to sense what it may feel like to be the client, as well as see the effects of particular techniques.

After the role-play it is important to debrief: How did it feel to be the client? How did you feel when I was more supportive? What did you think when I didn't get angry at what you said? Did you understand why I said that this is the same problem? Debriefing brings the clinician back into her professional role, elicits important material from the experience, and clarifies concrete steps that the clinician can take in the next session.

Role-play should not last too long. You and the clinician should understand what and why you are role-playing—to determine how to confront Ms. Thomas about her neglect of her son, to initiate a conversation about incest with 16-year-old Maria, to evaluate a new imagery technique in working with Mr. Williams, a grieving widower. Once the roles are assigned and role-play has begun, you must ensure that the interchange doesn't go beyond the agreed-upon focus. If the clinician gets too far into the role, there is a danger that you are no longer talking about the client, but about the clinician. Role-play turns into therapy. Five minutes, 10 at the most, is usually enough.

The first few times that role-play is used you should check with the clinician (perhaps at the next supervisory session) whether the technique was useful for learning. Some clinicians, particularly those at Stage 1 and still anxious, aren't ready for it. That doesn't mean that you shouldn't try it, even at the early stages. You are trying to discover what and what doesn't work well in terms of ways the clinician learns best. If you find that the experiential nature of this approach creates too much anxiety or performance pressure, put it off for a later time.

Finally, more generic role-plays are excellent ways to teach specific techniques. Susan wants to know how to use sculpting or drawings or games or genograms. You can demonstrate the technique by having her act out the part of an imaginary client. You should model not only the doing of the technique itself within a session, but also its introduction to the client. Making the transition to a new technique within the session often creates anxiety for the clinician. As with more specific role-playing, it's important to debrief after the demonstration of the technique.

EMPTY-CHAIR WORK

Empty-chair work comes from the gestalt-therapy repertoire. In many ways it serves the same purpose as role-playing. However, instead of 2 people, you and the clinician, playing different roles, the clinician here plays both roles while you observe and guide. Like role-playing, empty-chair work is experiential learning. By assuming both the clinician and client roles, the clinician can experience what is emotionally happening from both sides. The real value of empty-chair work, however, is helping the clinician sort out countertransference—personal issues—from his professional role. An impasse often occurs in treatment because the clinician's personal and emotional reactions are interfering with his professional role and knowledge.

Suppose, for example, that Dana is having trouble with a particular client. He constantly feels misunderstood and frustrated by Ms. Harris or he gets so angry at the way she reacts to her daughter that he is unable to help her see other ways to respond. You suspect that some countertransference issues—problems about learning—are inhibiting Dana's work with this mother. Rather than defining a particular problem within the process, he instead talks about her resistance, lack of motivation, and termination. You ask Dana if he would like to try to sort out the process and his feelings. You place an empty chair in front of him and ask him to imagine Ms. Harris sitting in front of him.

You begin by asking him to tell her what he has just said to you—that he is angry when she reacts to her daughter in particular ways, that he is feeling frustrated by her seeming inability to understand what it is he is trying to help her to do to help her. If Dana is unfamiliar with the technique, he is likely to feel uncomfortable and will probably try to talk about the client with you rather than getting into the role. Redirect him—"Don't tell me, tell her."

So Dana talks about his frustration and anger. When he seems finished, ask him to switch chairs and pretend he is Ms. Harris. What would she say if he said that to her? If Dana has trouble getting started, summarize what Dana said as the clinician—"Ms. Harris, Dana is feeling angry and frustrated by the way you talk to your daughter and doesn't know how to help you."

The goal is to have Dana assume a different role. The clinician will almost always now shift into a different voice and evoke different emotions. Dana, as Ms. Harris, might find himself saying, "You just don't understand how hard it is for me to handle that child." Or, "This child is good for nothing just like her father, and I've tried everything to straighten her out!" Such a response, although never actually voiced in the clinical session, helps Dana tap into the strong emotions and power, as well as the softer emotions and powerlessness underlying the client's behavior. As Dana articulates the emotions and viewpoints of both roles and experiences, the split is not only within the therapeutic relationship, he is also experiencing the split within himself. Your goal is to close the gap between these conflicting emotions through effective, and expanded, communication. To do so, Dana is asked to switch chairs again and respond and to continue to switch back and forth to keep the dialog going.

If at any time the clinician seems stuck, you can help the process along. "Dana, it seems that Ms. Harris doesn't understand why you've been working so hard with her to get her to change—tell her why, tell her what you are most worried about." Or, "Ms. Harris, it seems that Dana is not seeing something in your daughter that you, as her mother, are able to see. What is it that you feel he is understanding about her?" Or, "Dana is feeling frustrated in helping you with your daughter. What is it that you would like him to do most?" The purpose of these interjections is to move the conversation to a deeper level, to tap into the underlying dynamics and emotions, and to bring new awareness to the relationship and process.

At some point the process will slow down, the roles will become less polarized—Dana will talk more gently about his frustration and Ms. Harris less about her anger and more about her worry—and the projections will diminish. The exercise should continue until the role-play successfully runs its course and the emotional and communication barriers are overcome. The clinician should not only be able to initiate a similar conversation with the client, but have some insight into the client's internal dynamics. You should help the clinician develop a clear outline of what to do in the next session and discuss any anticipated problems.

But you can take the exercise a step further by exploring the countertransference issues: "Dana, you've had clients like this before, but you seem particularly stuck with Ms. Harris. Often impasses are created because personal issues get stirred up and affect the professional. Who else, from your personal life, could you put in that chair? Who else would sound critical, whiny, and demanding like Ms. Harris?"

Usually the clinician will hesitantly mention a parent, an ex-spouse, or a sibling. At that point you can establish the link and stop—"Dana, I wonder if some of your emotions relating to your mother might be affecting your reactions to Ms. Harris"—and let Dana's awareness of the countertransference serve as an experiential counter to it. Once this settles in, you can then turn back and discuss what he can do in his next session with Ms. Harris.

The aim here is not to initiate personal therapy, but rather to increase the clinician's emotional awareness of the crossing of personal and professional issues. Usually the issues become clear rather quickly, and the exercise can be ended. You might suggest that the clinician take some time and continue empty-chair work independently, talk to the family member directly about her feelings, or consult with a therapist. Because empty-chair work can be emotionally intensive, it's important that you repeatedly clarify the process and purpose of the work and return repeatedly to the clinical issues at hand: "Dana, I'm not trying to do individual therapy with you; I'm just trying to help you sort out the problem you're having with Ms. Harris. I appreciate your taking risks. Do you understand what you can do differently in your next session with her?"

You should also debrief with regard to the mechanics of the technique, as well as the clinician's reaction to its usefulness as a learning technique. This may have to be done at a later time—later in the day or during the next supervisory session—to present the clinician from becoming emotionally overloaded. This secondary focus on the technique itself further separates the personal from the clinical, the supervisory from the therapeutic process, and the clinician from the client. You can even teach the clinician how to use the technique with clients.

The empty-chair technique works particularly well during the second stage when the clinician's trust is high and anxiety is low. It should not be used at the start of the supervisory relationship because the clinician will feel that he is being analyzed and may close up. The clinician who feels more comfortable with the technique may begin to use it on his own when feeling stuck, or you, after discussing clinical options, may simply say that some countertransference issues seem to be going on and it may be valuable for the clinician to do some empty-chair work to sort it out. This independence helps the clinician learn to be more sensitive to and responsible for his own supervision.

READINGS AND TRAINING RECORDINGS

Using reading material to supplement learning is self-evident and simple to apply. You might suggest books or articles that cover a current interest or problem areas with which the clinician is having trouble. Materials that include vignettes or case transcripts are particularly helpful.

You want to be careful, however, not to use written material to replace direct teaching. There are supervisors who are quick to reach for a book any time a question is asked.

When supervisors don't use themselves as a resource, it's easy for the clinician to interpret this as the supervisor not knowing much about the topic and delegating the answer to someone else, namely, the author of the book. The end effect is that the clinician learns not to ask questions, the strength of the relationship is diminished, and both you and the clinician miss an opportunity to learn and grow. Obviously, if you know little about the clinician's question—"I'm wondering how to approach this from an object-relations perspective"—be honest and say that—"While I have my own way of approaching this problem, I'm less familiar with that particular approach. Here is a book on this that may be helpful. Let me know if you have questions or want to discuss how to apply it." By doing this you are supporting independent exploration while offering support and consultation.

Training recordings refer to professionally made video recordings of treatment session conducted by master trainers. Such recordings bring the therapist's style and techniques alive in a way that can only be suggested in books. Training recordings can be used in the same way that clinical recordings are used—you can point out various behavioral and verbal dynamics and connect the therapist's interventions with theory. Training recordings can also be used to discuss the need for flexibility in therapy: How would the clinician have handled the same case? How is his style different from that of the therapist's? Do differences in style or personality affect the use of this particular approach? Such questions help the clinician avoid becoming intimidated by an expert, as well as to look beyond the mimicking what she sees on the recording. The goal is to help the clinician integrate and apply new information based upon her own style and values.

TRAINING PROGRAMS AND CONFERENCES

External training programs and conferences can be an important adjunct to supervision. As with other aspects of supervision, you want to avoid being reactive, and instead be planful and deliberate. It's all too easy to find a clinician coming to you saying something like: "I just received this brochure in the mail for the training on play therapy. While we hadn't really talked about this, this is something I've always been interested in, and it's not that expensive and actually my sister lives close by so I wouldn't need to stay in a hotel. I was wondering if I could go." Or your supervisor comes to you and says, "The state office is offering an inexpensive 1-day training on working with disabilities. If anyone on your staff wants to go, feel free to send them."

While you may be doing the math and thinking that the close-by sister seals the deal, or that the state conference is a handy perk to offer staff, this isn't the best way to make such decisions. Instead be planful and proactive. As part of setting clinical goals for the year with the clinician, discuss with him limits and supports on external training opportunities. Rather than a hodgepodge of workshops based on convenience of sisters or time of year, base your decisions on clinical focus and clinical needs. Discuss with your supervisor in advance the training needs of your staff so that decisions are not made arbitrarily.

As mentioned earlier, the best times for extensive training programs or programs that present a totally different theoretical orientation is at the third stage when the clinician has a stable and solid clinical base to build upon. At this stage the clinician is not only motivated but best able to integrate older models with new. More novice clinicians who are still getting their sea legs on their primary models often return from such trainings energized perhaps but confused.

WRITTEN EXERCISES

Written assignments can help the clinician think more clearly and quickly. Asking Jake to write out, for example, a summary of 3 or 4 primary interactional patterns in a family session helps him learn to look for the larger dynamics of the case. Similarly, writing a thumbnail sketch of the major themes in a client's history helps him gather details into a more usable whole. The assignment pushes the clinician's thinking in new directions; the physical act of writing helps ground the thought processes.

The types of written exercises you can devise are without limit. The skill lies in knowing how the clinician's thinking needs to be shaped and developed. Generally, writing exercises that help the clinician consolidate his thoughts and pull larger themes out of myriad details are the most valuable. Some clinicians, however, have more specific problems. If Jake, for example, becomes overwhelmed by his client's emotions, you might ask him to outline his own thoughts as he listens to a recording of a session as a way of understanding the source of his own anxiety. Similarly, if a clinician was having difficulty thinking metaphorically when doing play therapy, writing down the metaphors of a recorded play session will help sensitize the clinician to this type of language.

Although written assignments can be time-consuming for the clinician, a little goes a long way. Asking the clinician to do such an assignment a few times within a week may be enough to help her increase skills. As with other supervisory techniques and tools, you need to experiment and hear from the clinician just how useful they are. Because most writing exercises are analytical rather than experiential, they are emotionally safe, and you can feel free to experiment.

Table 8.1 is a list of the various supervisory tools along with their uses and challenges.

Table 8.1 Supervisory Tools and Techniques

	Uses	Challenges
Recordings	Good way to target session process	Clients are uncomfortable, worry about confidentiality; clinicians feel performance pressure
Observation—passive (1-way mirror, sitting in)	Good training for students/others; observe session without interruption; detect emotional changes better	More invasive; possibly undermine client confidence in clinicians
Observation—active (bug in the ear, intermissions)	Able to change session process	More invasive; possibly undermine clinicians; disrupts session flow; clinicians become dependent on direction
Clinical consultation	Provides new perspective on case; highlights client–clinician concerns; break through impasses; reinforce clinical plan	Needs to be choreographed well so as not to not disempower clinicians
Co-therapy	Opportunities for clinicians to see your clinical style; can increase responsibility as clinicians grow	If not planned well, can create unclear or contradictory focus; can be confusing for client; only used for couples or families

EVALUATIONS

Evaluations are a different form of writing exercise and are unfortunately often overlooked as an important learning tool. Part of the problem is bureaucratic: Many personnel-evaluation forms, with their numbers and rating scales for tardiness, personal appearance, and getting along with other staff, don't lend themselves to a thorough clinical evaluation.

The other part of the problem is the awkwardness of the process itself. Too often, evaluations become the yearly ritual with the supervisor circling numbers on a form the day before it's due. She may attach a note asking the clinician to "Look this over and see me if there are any problems." The clinician isn't much surprised by the results, and it's easier not to talk about it.

The value of a good evaluation, especially when the clinician does a self-evaluation, results from the process of having to gather and compress the details of one's clinical work into a broader, more comprehensive statement—an official State of the Professional Self. These opportunities for self-reflection become important markers on the path of professional development, providing both you and the clinician with a good method for comparing and contrasting change.

> ## Human Behavior
>
> **Practice Behavior Example:** *Utilize conceptual frameworks to guide the processes of assessment, intervention, and evaluation.*
>
> **Critical Thinking Question:** Based upon your own experience with work evaluations, what questions or topics do you think would be especially helpful to include in an evaluation? Why?

The process starts by creating tools that fit the needs. Usually this means pushing aside those general and clinically irrelevant personnel-evaluation forms. A few weeks before an evaluation is due, it's helpful to pass along a copy of previous self-evaluations, if any, to the clinician and ask her to do a current self-evaluation based upon the previous year's work. Here is one possible outline.

I. **Assessment of Skills and Knowledge:** *A statement of the clinician's theoretical approach to therapy; rationale for its use in terms of personal style, values, and application to cases; assessment of specific skills and overall knowledge base, including strengths and weaknesses and changes since the most recent evaluation.*

II. **Use of Self:** *A description of the clinician's therapeutic style, personal strengths in working with clients, types of problems or clients who pose the most problems, countertransference issues, and changes since the most recent evaluation.*

III. **Use of Supervision:** *What helps and doesn't help? A statement of learning style; assessment of the supervisory relationship and its relationship to clinical work; changes in the needs, process, or relationship.*

IV. **Summary and Future Goals:** *A summary statement describing how the clinician has changed over the past year; recommendations for future goals, changes in various areas in the coming year, and suggestions of ways to implement them.*

In addition to these areas, a separate section on administrative matters (tardiness, paperwork, etc.) or any other topic (e.g., supervisory skills, community responsibilities) that you or the clinician feel are relevant can be added. The clinician is expected to write his evaluation out, again for the purpose of grounding ideas through the act of writing, but also to provide you with a permanent record of the self-evaluation. The clinician is asked to turn it in before the next supervisory session so that you have a chance to read it.

The self-evaluation can give you a clear idea of just where the clinician is within the developmental process. In the early stages, the language tends to be vague, intellectual, or idealistic; in the later stages, more concrete and practical. Talk of anxiety may shift to language reflecting increased anger and power. As the clinician matures, clearer statements regarding values, style, and countertransference issues reflect the greater self-awareness and experience. By using the self-evaluation as a developmental assessment of the clinician, you can anticipate upcoming changes.

A separate session should be set aside to discuss the self-evaluation. You should ask questions about areas that seem unclear—"What do you have in mind when you say that you want to learn more about chronic illnesses and their impact?"—or to stimulate further thinking—"You say that you have a hard time confronting resistant fathers. Specifically, what do you have trouble with?" Often what is written and discussed is a recapitulation of what has been talked about in supervisory sessions for some time. Occasionally, though, the self-evaluation process will stimulate new ideas and awareness.

Of course, the self-evaluation is only one part of the evaluation process—you need to provide input as well. The self-evaluation helps make this process easier in that you merely need to highlight the gaps between the clinician's perceptions and your own: "You say that you feel incompetent when working with children who are aggressive. I'm surprised to hear you say that. In the recording we saw just last week you did a wonderful job." Or, "You say that you feel that supervision gives you the support that you need, but sometimes I worry that you feel overwhelmed by some of the suggestions I make or seem hesitant to say what you are really thinking." The goal of the process is to reach a consensus, to close the gap in perceptions, to isolate clinical and supervisory problems, and most important, to arrive at clear suggestions for change.

You can't highlight change too much: "In reading your self-evaluation, I notice how much clearer and stronger you sound compared with last year." "On your last evaluation you focused mainly on your work with children; now I hear you talking about parents." "Last year you had difficulty describing your clinical style; this year you had no trouble." Statements such as these underscore the developmental process itself. Clinicians who are feeling burned out or bogged down are left with a stronger sense that, despite their current feelings, a powerful growth process is at work.

Once again, it is the evaluation process rather than the evaluation itself that is most beneficial. The process offers you and the clinician an opportunity to step back and examine what you both have been doing, and to decide together what works, what doesn't, and what to change.

SUMMARY

Box 8.2 gives tips for guiding the supervisory process.

Box 8.2 • Tips for Guiding the Supervisory Process

Require clinicians to have agenda for supervisory sessions

Set 3- to 6-month clinical goals

Enforce your expectations and requirements—provide reliability and diminish testing

Provide training that can be immediately applied

Define themes/patterns/problems rather than overly focusing on client details

Document clinical/administrative recommendations/actions/collateral contacts

Have clinicians review recordings before supervision

Establish clear goals for observation/co-therapy; choreograph supervisory role and process

Role-playing—have clinicians play client; always debrief

Have clinicians do self-assessments; discuss as part of evaluation process

The tools and techniques discussed here should be used to stimulate your own imagination. Just as no approach is perfect and no technique is sure for all clinicians and clients, no single ironclad method guarantees good supervision. Use these tools and techniques as a point of departure for your own experimentation. Discover for yourself what works, what's interesting, and what keeps the supervisory and clinical process challenging and growing.

The following questions will test your application and analysis of the content found within this chapter. For additional assessment, including licensing-exam-type questions on applying chapter content to practice behaviors, visit **MySearchLab**.

1. Passive observation refers to

    a. Discussing cases in supervisory sessions

    b. Observing a clinical session but not interrupting to provide feedback

    c. Observing a clinical session but stopping the session to provide feedback

    d. Observing a recorded clinical session

2. It is important to document in your supervisory records

    a. Clinical recommendations that you made to the clinician regarding a particular case

    b. Detailed notes about what the clinician discussed with the client in a session

    c. Number of sessions a clinician has had with a particular client

    d. The names and birth dates of those seen in couple and family sessions

3. You are doing an empty-chair exercise with Maya regarding a client she has been seeing, who seems to her to be resistant to therapy. In the process of doing the exercise Maya says that she realizes that part of her difficulty with the client is due to the fact that the client reminds her so much of her mother. At that point it would be most appropriate for you to

    a. Ask Maya to imagine her mother sitting in the empty chair and to talk to her about how she feels

    b. Recommend to Maya that she begin individual therapy to work on these issues

    c. Validate her seeing the connection between the client and her mother, but then focus with her on how she can change the patterns between her and the client

    d. Recommend that she transfer the client to another clinician

4. Jack has lots of ideas about how to proceed with a case, but is unsure which path to take. You suggest that he write out a possible treatment plan to help him

    a. Better clarify through writing his own thinking

    b. To document for your own records his clinical progress

    c. To give him a script for conducting the next session with the client

    d. To share his ideas with the client and increase rapport

5. A clinician asks a client about recording a therapy session but the client refuses. What would you recommend that the clinician do next?

6. You ask a clinician to do a self-evaluation and it becomes clear that her assessment of her work is very different from your own. How would you respond?

9

Supervisory Process

Competencies Applied with Practice Behaviors — in This Chapter				
☒ Professional Identity	☐ Ethical Practice	☒ Critical Thinking	☐ Diversity in Practice	☐ Human Rights & Justice
☐ Research-Based Practice	☐ Human Behavior	☒ Policy Practice	☒ Practice Contexts	☐ Engage, Assess, Intervene, Evaluate

Now that we've discussed stages and techniques—the broad brush of what to expect and what to do—the question arises as to you really do in a supervisory session? We're talking about supervisory process and that's what this chapter is about. While we'll discuss some of what to do, more importantly we'll try to convey how to think as a supervisor. As part of this we'll talk more about assessment—both of the clinician and of the session—so that you can use the themes and outcomes of one supervisory session to help you set your goals for the next.

As we go along, be aware of what you are thinking, and what you might say next. We'll stop periodically for commentary.

SESSION WITH AMY

Hi, Amy. So, what's on your agenda for this morning?

I'd like to talk about the Smith family. I met Ms. Smith for the first time last week. Her family doctor has referred her for anxiety. Boy, do they have problems! Her husband was recently laid off from work, and though he will be getting unemployment benefits, they have little in savings and money is already tight. And then her son, Tim, 8 years old, is having trouble in school, fighting with other kids. Her husband is yelling at him all the time about it, but she thinks that that is just making things worse, and then they start arguing about how to handle him. It sounds like the arguments can get pretty bad. She's not sleeping, waking up in the middle of night worrying. She's overwhelmed! I don't know where to start!

Amy is a new clinician. She's talking quickly, and it's easy to hear the parallel process going on here. Ms. Smith is overwhelmed by all the problems in her life right now, and Amy seems to be feeling the same—anxious and overwhelmed, feeling perhaps that she needs to fix it all and fast.

It's often helpful to be aware of what you don't want to do. Here, you obviously don't want to replicate the process, that is, begin to feel overwhelmed like Amy does and feel pressure to fix everything all at once. The problem right now that you want to focus upon is in the room, namely, Amy's anxiety. Though it's tempting and easy to do, you want to be careful that you don't bypass Amy and relieve your and Amy's anxiety by focusing on Ms. Smith and her problems and telling Amy what to do. The danger is falling into spoon-feeding, essentially running the case yourself from your supervisory chair. This relieves anxiety all around, but disempowers Amy, and eventually Ms. Smith.

We can use the parallel process by responding to Amy the way she needs to respond to her client. We need to find why she is so anxious. Is it a learning problem—she needs information about what to do—or is it a problem about learning—she knows what to do but perhaps is feeling overresponsible or lacking self-confidence.

Wow, it sounds like there is a lot going on. So what did you do in the session?
I didn't really know what to say. I mostly just listened, and let her talk about what was going on.
Did you feel like it helped? Did Ms. Smith calm down by getting these things off her chest?
I guess, but I worry that she thought that I didn't really do much, and she's right. I didn't. She is coming back this week though.
Well, that's good. It sounds like you did a pretty good job. So tell me what you are thinking about her and the family.

Amy sounds like a lot of Stage 1 clinicians. She is being reactive and worrying about her performance, hence the intentional decision to give her some positive feedback. She's also being open right now in the supervisory session. This is good; it says a lot about her sense of trust and safety. You want to know how she is thinking about the case to sort out where she is getting stuck.

Well, like I said, I don't know really where to start. I didn't get a good idea about what is going on with her son—whether his problems are coming from school or whether he is carrying things over from home to school. I could see where the father's reaction is probably making it all worse. I guess I wonder how long-standing or broad the marital problems are—are they reacting to the job stress or do they argue about other things?
It seems like you are asking yourself the right questions—how are the different problems related. It also seems like you are maybe feeling the way Ms. Smith does—overwhelmed and unsure where to start.

Yes, I guess I do.
Are you feeling like you need to figure this all out for her?
Yeah, I do.

Amy is asking the right questions, however, again like many new clinicians, her being overwhelmed is partially being fueled by her feeling that she needs to have all the answers right now. Instead, she needs to slow down and explore the problems with the client, both to obtain more information about Ms. Smith's problems and to understand where Ms. Smith gets stuck in solving them. Again, she is being reactive.

How can I help you most right now?

This is a parallel statement. You want to help her settle by focusing on one problem—partialization—just as she needs to help the client settle by deciding where and how she needs help.

Good question. I guess that's where I'm stuck and that's what I need to ask Ms. Smith—where she wants to start.
I agree, that's great. Partialize the problems so that they are less overwhelming, and let her tell you what she needs help with most.
Yeah, that's makes sense. I can do that.
Given the different problems—the son's behavior, the parenting and marital problems, the job stress—is there anything you need to know? Anything you're not sure how to handle?

Helping the client sort priorities will help them both settle. You want to know if there are skill issues that she is worried about to help her be more proactive.

I realize I can ask more about what is going on at school or even get a release to talk to the school folks. I guess I'm not sure what to do about their arguments about parenting.
Finding out more about what is going on at school is a great idea. Where do you get stuck when thinking about the parenting or marital issues?

You are trying to make her be more specific and clear to understand what she needs.

Hmmm . . . I guess I'm not sure how to help with the arguments themselves.
Say some more. What do you mean?
I guess that's where I'm stuck. I worried, but don't really know what's going on.
If your client wants help with the arguments, I'm thinking you need to find out better exactly what goes on—what triggers the arguments, how they flow, how they stop. Just like you need more information about the son's behavior, it would probably help you to better track exactly what happens between the parents. Does this make sense?
Oh, yeah. I guess I'm getting ahead of myself. Sure I guess I can just ask her to describe it more clearly and see how the arguments evolve. I guess I could even ask her to invite her husband to come—that's scary.
Well, that's a great idea, but like you said, we don't need to get ahead of ourselves. If you decide to invite him in, we can talk about it ahead of time. Do you have a better idea what you want to do in the next session with Ms. Smith?

Yeah, I do. I need to see where she wants to start and then get more details about whatever problem she is most worried about rather than jumping ahead of myself. I can do that.

Good. It seems like you have a better handle on it. Are you feeling less overwhelmed?

Yeah, I am. Thanks.

We'll stop here. Obviously that wasn't a full session and we would move on to other cases, or if you had administrative needs—questions about paperwork, wanting updates on other cases—you would bring these up. But let's do a quick assessment of what we saw as a way of recapping and making additional supervisory plans. Let's look at developmental stage and anxiety coping, skills, supervisory relationship, and goals for our next session.

Stage and Anxiety Coping

Stage 1—reactive and feeling overwhelmed by the client's problems, paralleling what the client is feeling. Like the client, Amy was focusing on content more than process—responding to the details of all the different problems, rather than focusing on the client herself or the possible replication of the problem in the room. Could you have talked about this—yes, but not at this time. The problem in the supervisory session was Amy's anxiety. You needed to reduce that so that she can be more effective with the client and walk out of supervision feeling that it was helpful. To overload her with focus on process when she was focused on the client's problems right then might have caused her to feel even more anxious and insecure.

The safe, effective route to take was to treat Amy how she needed to treat the client. Overall, in spite of her anxiety, she was able to settle, be open, think through, and process what you were saying. If she shut down because she was feeling more overloaded or couldn't settle down in the session, this would be more of a concern and focus. You would gently need to explore with her what she was thinking that was keeping her anxiety up.

Skills

From this short exchange it is difficult to tell, and as her supervisor you would have a clearer baseline. The purpose of asking her specific questions is to model what she needs to do with her client (and to reduce her and the client's anxiety). It seems that her basic skills are fine—in this case, she is able to see patterns and formulate the right questions. A good follow-up might be to inquire further about what she needs to know more about in terms of specific problem areas such as relationship conflicts or aggressive children.

Supervisory Relationship

Though anxious, Amy was open and able to talk about how she was feeling—again, a good sign of trust. If she seemed stilted and asked only intellectual or technical questions—"My client, Ms. Smith, disagrees with her husband about how to best manage their aggressive son; can you tell me something about aggression in children"—this would convey a more binding response or less trust. In that case, to offset the intellectualization, you would ask, in a gentle way, more specific questions about what she is thinking, what are her concerns, and what she is feeling. Worst of all, of course, is that the case is not mentioned at all, suggesting a severe lack of trust and a do-it-all-by-myself stance.

If you suspect that the clinician was being accommodating—looking confused, but says, "Oh, sure, that's a great idea!"—this would be a cause for concern: You're saying it's great, but you're looking confused—"Is this really helpful?"—said in a gentle voice would be needed to reduce the "good kid" reaction.

Goals for Next Sessions

You would obviously want to find out how the session with Ms. Smith went—for both quality control and feedback about the effectiveness of your suggestions and Amy's actions. You also may want to get more specific feedback about the session process and possible deeper concerns: "I could tell you were feeling overwhelmed. I thought it would help you the most by . . . was that helpful?" Or, "You've done a good job with other clients like Ms. Smith. What made this case different?" Or, "I noticed you've had a few other cases like this where clients are overwhelmed by multiple problems—I'm wondering why this case is particularly difficult for you and if there is something we should do to best help you with this client?"

Questions like these shift the focus from "what do I do with this case" to "what do I need from supervision to be more successful with these types of cases."

SESSION WITH MARCUS

Marcus has much more experience than Amy and has been in supervision several years. He is presenting a case that involves a couple ordered into counseling as the result of an incident of domestic violence.

> You haven't talked about the court-ordered couple for a few weeks. I'm wondering how that case is going.
>
> Oh, those folks. You know, I hate these court-ordered cases. These folks don't want to be here. By the time they show up in court, they've made up—all is forgiven—and resent coming here and don't get the point. I understand what the judge is doing, but often these cases seem to go nowhere.
>
> I know these cases can be frustrating. What have you been doing with them?
>
> Well, I've seen them twice. Sessions were a waste of time. Yes, their argument got out of control, but it was because they had too much to drink, and they deny there is any alcohol problem. Of course, they say that they've made up and are fine now. I feel like they are stonewalling me, and I'm ready to let them go.

Marcus sounds annoyed and impatient—all very different from Amy's anxiety. He has skills, and the problem here is his own reaction, especially with more resistant clients. That's what we need to talk about.

> It seems that you've been feeling annoyed and impatient with several of your cases lately where the clients seem resistant. I'm wondering what's going on.
>
> I don't know. . . . I guess I'm a bit burned out, and I'm looking forward to my vacation coming up in 2 weeks—that should help a lot. But that's not all of it. I'm just

Critical Thinking

Practice Behavior Example: *Analyze models of assessment, prevention, intervention, and evaluation.*

Critical Thinking Question: Can you think of another way of responding to Marcus' reaction to court-ordered clients? What might be the advantage of this approach?

feeling that therapy is to help people change what they want to change. If you don't want to make any changes, and if you want to change in a different way rather than therapy, that's fine with me. Let's not waste everybody's time.

Marcus is at Stage 3 of his own development. He is defining his own stance and philosophy in an assertive manner, and his openness is a good sign of a strong supervisory relationship. He is not, for example, being closed or passive/aggressive in this session. You want to support his ideas and individuation. On the other hand, as is characteristic for this stage, he's easily impatient and reductionistic in his thinking—if they don't want to work, they can stop. The supervisory challenge is being supportive—and once again being careful to not replicate the process—rather than dismissive of his idea. You need to balance out his clinical stance with agency/community needs and goals.

I'm glad your vacation is coming at a good time. You know you've had cases like this before where clients are reluctant to do therapy. In the past you've worked hard to connect with them. Now you're not working so hard. This is a change.

This is a stepping back to underscore the developmental changes that are occurring within him.

Yeah, I guess you're right. Before I would feel it was my responsibility to keep them in therapy. I guess now I don't.

I'm not going to argue with you about that. We've talked about it before that often with other clients in the past you were probably working too hard, and were too responsible for what happened. I'm concerned now, however, that you've moved too far in the other direction.

What do you mean?

Sure, these clients probably don't want to be here and are trying to minimize what has happened so that they don't have to come back. I'm wondering 2 things: One, that they don't have any experience doing any type of counseling so that the process itself is new and uncomfortable for them. Two, they are probably not used to talking about emotions and problems in this way. I'm guessing that they need some more time just to become more acclimated to the process itself.

I guess that makes sense.

The other point is that the court is looking to us to help deal with what has now become a community issue. Usually the court's concern is about the entire family—the effects of domestic violence on children in the home. As a community agency, I think we need to make a concerted effort to give therapy a try. No, we don't need to be over-responsible and work harder than the clients, but we do need to be clear about the concerns and the problems. I worry that if you just discharge them quickly, it will feed into their own denial about their problems. Does this make sense?

There are a couple of things going on here. First, you are redefining the client resistance as more complex than the simple, they want to work, or not.

As supervisor you are also defining the bigger community picture and placing this case in that larger context, an aspect that the clinician is not aware of or overlooking in his desire to act on his own emotions. Finally, in terms of supervisory process, you are using the parallel process, that is, responding to Marcus the way he needs to respond to his clients—to make a case for therapy, to help the clients understand the rationale and concern in a clear yet supportive manner, to challenge their resistance rather than colluding with them and perpetuating it.

Yeah, I can understand what you are saying. But I'm not sure that they are going to engage.

You're right, at a certain point, we have to decide whether to continue. But I think you need to give it more time. Your clinical skills are in understanding and working through their resistance, and I know you've been able to do that in the past with other cases. If you get stuck, are unsure what to do, we can talk about it here. But I think you need to commit to seeing them for at least a few more sessions.

Use of parallel process again—being clear, being proactive, supporting his skills, offering support.

It makes sense. I can do it.

This sounds solid. If Marcus said this but sounded ambivalent or accommodating, or disagreed with what was being said, you would need to continue to talk about it to see what the underlying issue or emotion was. He would essentially be replicating what the clients are probably doing, and again you need to stop the clinical buck and respond to him the way he needs to respond to the clients by sorting through the source of his resistance and emotions.

Finally, if his resistance to supervision was part of a larger pattern that had been developing, it would be up to you to raise this—that is, point this out and ask about how he is feeling about supervision these days and if something needs to change in your relationship or the way you do supervision together.

As we did with Amy, let's put this session in context by doing a quick assessment of Marcus.

Stage and Anxiety Coping

Marcus is at Stage 3 and your role is clearly that of gatekeeper, wanting to support the development of his own style yet needing to set boundaries where needed. He is able to approach anxiety, feels competent in his skills, but "doesn't fully know what he doesn't know."

Skills

He has had a lot of experience and his skills are strong. If he does have difficulty engaging with this couple and you see it as a learning problem rather than a problem about learning, then you need to help him fill in the clinical gaps. A role-play or live observation or tape review might be a good way to do this.

Supervisory Relationship

This appears strong. He is open emotionally, as well as open to your suggestions and directives; he is not, for example, terminating with these clients and telling you after the act. Again, if there was an emerging pattern of resistance—resisting your suggestions, showing up late for supervision, coming without an agenda—that would signal a problem in the relationship itself that you need to explore.

Goals for Next Sessions

You want to track his burnout, especially after he returns from vacation. You need to address this as a separate issue—possible sources for his burnout. You want to follow up on this case—Was he able to be more patient and engage the clients? Be more clear about process and concerns? Is he clinically stuck in terms of knowing how and what to do next? You want to follow up on the session process—how did he feel after your last supervisory session? Did he understand your perspective? Though it did seem like he was in agreement and not accommodating, it's often a good idea to raise the issue one more time as a way of letting him know that his reactions and feelings toward you and the supervision process are important and will not be dismissed.

As you were careful to do with Amy, you were careful to do here with Marcus as well—that is, make him your focus, not the clients. Rather than using the session to speculate about the clients, brainstorm ways of handling the therapy, or worse yet, colluding with him that the court is being unreasonable and that you should terminate the case, and instead start with him and his reactions. At some point you could brainstorm about clinical approaches, but you are not going to bypass him and do remote-control therapy. And if you administratively do have concerns with court referrals, that is something that you can take up, not with Marcus, but with your own supervisor.

SESSION WITH MARIA

Maria is a child therapist with several years of experience. She has been working with 8-year-old Robert for over a year in play therapy. He came into treatment because of abuse by his parents. He had been removed from the home and had been in a temporary foster home while Social Services decided whether he could return home or need to go into permanent foster care.

> I'm really upset. Social Services has decided to place Robert with his grandparents.
>   What happened?
>   They had a court hearing last week and we thought that the temporary foster home would be continued for a couple of more months. But then it seems that the grandparents finally decided to take Robert. He had a good relationship with them, a home study had initially been done months ago. Social Services and the judge decided to place him with them rather than having him continue to linger in temporary care.
>   You look sad. What's upsetting you the most?

The problem in the room is Maria's emotions. You need to focus on that.

I'm upset because this is so sudden! He is leaving with them tomorrow and he's moving to the other side of the state. There's no time for any more sessions; they are not able to drive him here for any; there is no closure! This isn't good for him! Another loss.

I agree. It sounds like this isn't good for you either.

No, it's not. I've been seeing him for over a year. Yes, I guess I've gotten really connected to him over that time. I am sad. I realize too that this is stirring up personal stuff for me too. It's the anniversary of my dad's death this week. It's only been 2 years and I can feel it when the anniversary comes around.

Maria is open about her emotions and shows insight into part of the source of her sadness. The issue is one of grief. She wasn't able to get closure with Robert. You need to help her clinically decide what she can do, if anything, to help Robert and better terminate their relationship; but rather than jumping to that, it's better to first help support her and her emotions.

I'm sorry that you are feeling upset and I'm sorry it turned out being handled in this way. I'm wondering if you would be willing to try something right now that might help.

Okay.

I'd like you to imagine Robert sitting in the empty chair over there. Can you see him?

Yeah.

Good. What I'd like you to do is tell him what you wish you could say to him if you did have another session with him.

Okay. Robert, I know you're going to be moving away with your grandparents. I'm wondering how you're feeling about that?

Now switch seats. If Robert heard you say that, what would he say back?

(She switches seats.) Yeah, we're leaving tomorrow. (She is talking in a quiet, little-kid voice.) It's okay, I guess. I like my grandparents. My grandpa does a lot of stuff with me. . . .

Okay, switch back. What would you say back to that?

(She switches again.) Yes, I know you've said a lot of times that you really like your grandparents, especially your grandpa. Are you feeling sad about leaving?

(She moves to Robert's chair.) Yeah. I'm going to miss Sally and Tom (the foster parents). My friends. Am I still going to see you?

(She switches back.) That's what we need to talk about. No, we won't be seeing each other because you are going to be moving too far away. I'm happy that you get to live with your grandparents, but I'm feeling sad that I'm not going to be able to see you.

The goal here is to help her emotionally get some closure with Robert. She is obviously engaged in the process. She and Robert go back and forth for some time, her being professional yet empathic, talking to him about his emotions, his changes over time, and her wishes for him in his new home. As Robert she is able to express his emotions, as well as hear and take in the positive feedback she has given him. At a certain point the process slows down.

I think that is all I need to say right now.

You did a good job. How are you feeling right now?

I'm better. Less angry, less sad. There were moments when I realized that what I was saying to Robert was what I wished I could have said to my dad . . . (she gets teary).

*Yeah, thinking about what you said about the anniversary of your dad's death,
I was wondering the same thing—the overlap of the loss of Robert and your dad.*

*Fortunately, I did get to say to my dad before he died most of what I needed to, but
I realize even just doing this that there are some things I probably didn't get to say.*

Is there some way you could do that, get these things off your chest?

*I'll be going to the cemetery this week and I sometimes talk to him when I'm there.
I can think about it some more and figure out better what I'd like to say to him then.*

Good idea. What do you think could help you and Robert have some closure?

*I'm thinking that maybe I can write him a letter and include some stickers that he
likes, or maybe even arrange to call him and talk on the phone. I obviously don't want
to drag this out and do long-distance therapy. I've already talked to Social Services
about tracking him and seeing if he needs to hook up with a therapist there, and they
are taking care of it. I just don't want this sudden cutoff with no closure.*

I agree. It sounds like a good plan.

I feel better. Thanks so much for helping me with this.

Maria is clinically thinking clearly. This supervisory session is about emotional support, as well as separating the professional from the personal. She had already made the connection between Robert and her father. If her reaction to Robert seemed more unusual—she had this happen several times in the past and had not responded so strongly as she did now—you might have explored that further—why now, what about this situation is causing you to feel particularly upset? She then might have talked about her connection to Robert or brought up her father.

Similarly, if she had been seeming particularly sensitive to terminations lately, you might ask her, after the empty-chair work with Robert winds down, whether there is anyone else from her personal life that she could put in the chair, someone whom she feels sad about losing. Then her father may come up. You would not then start therapy by having her talk to her father, but rather just help her be experientially aware that the professional and personal have crossed, and that maybe it would be helpful for her to do some empty-chair work with her father on her own, or write him a letter, just to get things off her chest.

But as you did here, the focus is going to return to the client. After you have helped her sort through and relieve some of her emotions, you want to move toward clinical action—what she can do to provide closure with Robert in a concrete way. This brings the session back into the professional world, provides grounding, and closure in a way to the supervisory session itself. If she doesn't know what to do because of lack of skill—how to contact Social Services, for example, for follow-up—or is unsure how to best phrase things for Robert's understanding, you would help by providing clear instructions and suggestions. This obviously wasn't needed with Maria. Finally, if this case spiked for you any administrative/broader clinical concerns—for example, how Social Services or the courts may be handling foster care placements in general—this would be something you would discuss with your supervisor and come up with a planned response.

As we did with Amy and Marcus, let's do an assessment and plan for Maria.

Stage and Anxiety Coping

Maria is skilled and insightful, open, not anxious, impatient, or unaccommodating to you. She is willing to do the experiential exercise and it works well for her—no red flags, no quality-control concerns. Probably later Stage 2.

Skills

While not the focus of this session, she has good skills—is able to think clearly, anticipate dangers, such as unwittingly encouraging the relationship with Robert continue for too long. If there was a supervisory concern, however, that she had a pattern of getting overly attached to her clients, or was holding onto them too long, this dependency would need to be addressed. You would explore where it is coming from and question whether you are in some way contributing to this pattern through your own relationship with the clinician.

Supervisory Relationship

Strong, as it was with Amy and Marcus. The tone, however, is different. With Amy her anxiety was easily present; with Marcus his frustration and annoyance. This session with Maria has a softer tone, partly due to the issues being explored, but also partly due to the stage of the supervisory relationship—that Stage 2 dependency and leaning more easily on the supervisor.

What you would be concerned about would be a holding of all these emotions in and not bringing them up, or a panic about what to do next, or a worry about what you are thinking about her performance—all Stage 1 characteristics. You would worry if she were not empathic and matter-of-fact, signaling some binding behavior or emotional cutoffs, or if she were angry at the system, and focused mostly on that, overlooking the client's needs—something that you potentially might see with someone at Stage 3.

Goals for Next Sessions

You would want to follow up regarding outreach to Robert, as well as inquiring about Maria's emotional state—Is she feeling better about the termination, about how Robert is? What's behind this is making sure that this didn't leave some emotional wound that might affect her clinical work in the future, for example, that this was so emotionally upsetting that she is afraid to fully engage with children or is too protective of them. You can raise these issues in the next session and then look for signs in future cases.

Should you ask about her father? This is a matter of style and clear supervisory intention. If your overall style is to be more personal, if Maria had talked about her father in the past, or if you feel that asking would help open the relationship up, remove some emotional barriers, then yes, you might. Otherwise, you may wait to see whether she brings it up. It's a decision about context and relationship. What you don't want to do is start asking about her father because it is in some way a more comfortable topic or distraction from more difficult subjects.

SESSION PROCESS REDUX

What these 3 scenarios show is the varied landscape of supervisory sessions. Just as with clinical work, one supervisory stance does clearly not fit all, and each session will have its own tone and focus. As mentioned earlier, the content of a supervisory session will be determined by the clinician's needs—for support, information, consultation—your needs based upon maintaining quality control—update on cases, paperwork—and relationship needs—repairing misunderstandings, discussing and monitoring how well the supervisory process meets the clinician's needs. Your leadership and supervisory skills come in successfully addressing and balancing these 3 different foci.

Box 9.1 is a checklist that may be helpful to you in planning and evaluating specific supervisory sessions.

What underlies these questions are the primary goals and objectives of any supervisory session. Let's highlight now, and as we do, think about their parallels to clinical work, as well as your own past supervisory experiences.

Be Proactive

This has been a mantra we have been chanting from the start. Being proactive in supervisory sessions means both you and the clinician having agendas with decisions

---

Box 9.1 • Supervisory Session Checklist

Goals for the Session

What are your goals for the session?

What specific information do you need to ensure quality control—e.g., status on cases, paperwork questions?

How do your session goals fit into the clinician's overall 3-month goals?

Session's Emotional Tone/Parallel Process

What are the emotions in the room—anxiety, depression, anger, boredom? What is the cause?

Is parallel process being replicated in the session? How do you need to treat the clinician the way the clinician needs to treat the client?

Are you hearing any potential parallel statements—comments about clients that may also apply to supervision?

Skill Assessment

What skills does the clinician need to currently focus upon most? What is your plan for helping the clinician develop these skills?

What new challenges, if any, does the clinician need at this time to continue clinically growing?

Supervisory Relationship

How strong is the current supervisory relationship? How open and trusting is the clinician? How anxious is he around you?

How compliant is the clinician with policies/procedures?

Plans for the Next Session

How is this session different from or similar to others recently? What patterns or themes, if any, do you hear emerging?

What is your agenda for the next session? Is there a need to change the process or focus of the next session to make it more open, more productive?

made about time for each determined at the start. It is about having an objective for the session, again from each side.

Amy's agenda, for example, was to figure out how to sort through all of Ms. Smith's presenting problems; your agenda was to reduce her anxiety, help her not to be overresponsible, help her begin to partialize and prioritize the problems. Marcus' agenda was to express his frustration over his court-ordered case and possibly terminate it; your agenda was to help him see the case in a larger community context, to reframe the clients' resistance, to have him give the case more time, and to be more clear with the clients. Maria's agenda was to get support for her sense of loss; your agenda was to support her, help her separate the personal and professional, as well as develop a plan for therapeutic closure with her client.

Later on in these sessions there may have been time for you to touch on topics important to you—following up on a specific case, inquiring about a deadline. What you did not want to do or see in these sessions was passivity, resistance, unpreparedness, a lapsing into distractions as a way of filling time and avoiding anxiety.

Set Priorities for Sessions

You can't do everything in any one session—be it a clinical or supervisory one—so setting priorities is important. Priorities can be thought of in terms of topics—Amy absolutely wants to know who to contact about getting a psychological evaluation for Ms. Smith's son; you absolutely need to know if she has completed pulling together the stats that you requested from her last week—and you both will need to make sure you cover both these topics in the session.

You can also think of session priorities in terms of process. Think about how you want Maria to feel about Robert by the time she leaves the session—more calm, more clear, more accepting, more proactive. Help Marcus think about his case in a different way so he is less reactive, more patient, less frustrated. Use your skills to help move them toward these goals. Use your knowledge of their developmental stages to titrate the process.

You realize, for example, that while doing empty-chair work with Robert may be highly effective given Maria's experience, insight, and long relationship, suggesting that Amy do the same around Ms. Smith is likely to only increase her anxiety and potentially leave her more confused, not less. Understanding that, you make a clear decision to hold off on such experiential techniques with Amy until her skills are higher, your relationship with her is more grounded, and her overall anxiety is reduced.

Sort Out Skills from Personal Reactions

Or as we have been saying all along, determine what is a learning problem, and what is a problem about learning. Amy's anxiety and feeling pressure to fix all of Ms. Smith's problems was about her emotions and responses. Difficulties she may have in knowing how to partialize problems or clinically approach any one problem may be related to skills. Marcus' reactions to his clients were clearly about him—a problem about learning—not one of skill. Maria's difficulties too were very much about her reactions, not her skills, though she may have needed your ideas to think of other ways of creating closure with her client.

Your supervisory skill comes in exploring, determining, and keeping in mind where each of your clinicians stand on both sides of these issues at any given time, and noting how it changes as they clinically grow.

Look for Patterns

Seeing patterns is your way of sorting out skills from reactions and marking changes over time. Marcus' growing impatience and frustration with court-ordered clients was a change from the way he used to approach them in the past. If this impatience is seen in a range of cases, it tells you about his own evolution and possible personal issues or supervisory issues as the source. If his frustration is isolated to this particular couple and out of the norm for him, this suggests some countertransference that needs to be specifically explored.

Stepping back and surveying the larger landscape of a clinician's work helps you determine goals and objectives. You, from your vantage point and with your own unique perspective, have the opportunity to see the stuckpoints, the themes, the gaps, and the changes over time that clinicians, because they are too close and involved, are unable to see. Clinicians are doing the same for their clients.

Professional Identity

Practice Behavior Example: *Practice personal reflection and self-correction to assure continual professional development.*

Critical Thinking Question: How has your own ability to connect the work of sessions changed over time? What do you need to do this even better?

Connect the Work of Sessions

Part of surveying the larger clinical landscape and part of thinking in terms of longer-term goals and objectives mean placing each supervisory session within a larger context. What often overwhelms clients, and can overwhelm clinicians, particularly those like Amy who are less experienced, is this sense that each problem is new and independent of any others. This lends itself to the "problem of the week" mentality, and the feeling buried under the heap. Clinically you want to help clients and clinicians like Amy see the common process and themes running through them all, and you want to do the same in supervision.

At the end of each supervisory session take a minute to decide what you want to focus on next. What was the moral of the story of the session, and what next step do you and both you and the clinician together need to take to move toward the larger goals that you both have determined? Would it be helpful to work with Amy on having a clearer agenda for her initial client sessions? Does she need help in breaking problems down and setting priorities with clients? Do you need to more vigorously explore with Marcus the source of his burnout, or discuss with him whether he feels that supervision has lately not met his needs and been more a waste of time?

What are the next steps that move the clinician clinically forward, that move your supervisory relationship forward, that are an acceptable risk that approaches anxiety without being overwhelming? Again, this is where your skill and sensitivity come into play. You don't need to get it right the first time—Amy may feel more overwhelmed by the prospect of having a more defined agenda; Marcus may resist talking about the state of supervision—that's fine. You just need to be aware that Amy is overwhelmed and that Marcus is resisting and be able and willing to clarify with them your concerns and intentions, and adjust your focus when you see the session process going off course.

Be Alert to Parallel Process

Think hierarchically. Problems and emotions move up and down the line. Amy feels overwhelmed like her client and you're aware in the session that you need to treat her the way she needs to treat her clients. You need to respond to Marcus the way he needs to respond to his clients with both acknowledgment of his emotions and clarity about the problems and concerns. Awareness of parallel process helps you and the clinician know how to respond in the moment and helps you understand the source of the clinician's reactions.

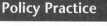

Policy Practice

Practice Behavior Example: Understand that policy affects service delivery and they actively engage in policy practice.

Critical Thinking Question: If you were to make one policy change to ensure quality control within a workplace, what would it be?

But, you are a person in the middle and you need to stay alert to problems and emotions coming from above you or through you. Is Marcus feeling burned out because everyone is feeling burned out, including you and your boss? Is Amy feeling overwhelmed because you are feeling overwhelmed and so she feels sandwiched on both sides? When you look at the larger patterns, how may the supervisory process be replicated in the clinical process? How does the work culture and environment help breed the reactions and issues that your clinicians are struggling with?

The emotional buck stops with you; it certainly should not start with you, and if you are being swept up in what comes down from above, take action. Talk to your boss, talk in the language of his concerns—effectiveness, efficiency, cost—and be an agent for change.

Make Quality Control a Priority

Along with staff support and development, this is the other half of your job. This is the bottom line of performance. Are clinicians able to take acceptable risks and grow *and* provide quality services to clients? Are they able to do good clinical work and be responsible for all the administrative aspects of their jobs, such as record-keeping and report-writing? Do you know the strengths and skills of each of your clinicians well enough to know what type of case is appropriate and what is not appropriate, and what type of supports they may need in order to be successful?

The quality-control aspects of supervision can seem boring or like drudgery—looking through records, tracking completion of assignments—not the stuff that you envisioned doing back in school. But these are essential tasks, and your attitude filters down to your clinicians. If quality-control aspects of the work are pushed to the bottom of your to-do list, they will be pushed to the bottom of theirs. Think of quality control in terms of setting and maintaining standards. Just as you look to concrete behavioral markers to tell you how well clients are doing in their lives, quality-control standards tell you how well clinicians and you are doing in your jobs.

Practice Contexts

Practice Behavior Example: Keep informed, resourceful, and proactive in responding to evolving organizational, community, and societal contexts at all levels of practice.

Critical Thinking Question: What trends do you see evolving in your own workplace and/or your wider community? How might they impact clinical services and practice?

Be Alert to Larger Administrative, Macro-Level Issues

Your vantage point as a supervisor is higher than that of the clinician. The clinician is stepping back to view the wider expanse of a client's world that the client may be able to take in. You are able to see the wide community expanse that the clinician cannot see. So when Marcus talks about the process of court referrals and his frustration, you ask yourself whether this is an isolated or more systemic problem. When Maria describes her disappointment about foster home decisions, you note that as an issue you may need to address from your level as well.

You have the opportunity to see how macro-processes affect not just a family but the families in your community. You can step back and decide whether the outcome of a particular case reflects the skill level of a particular clinician, or represents a breakdown in communication within the agency or between agencies in the community. Is Amy not completing her paperwork because she can't manage her time well and set priorities, or are several of the staff struggling and the problem is one of cumbersome requirements or too large caseloads? You, not the clinician, are the person to lead the charge of these issues. Call up the supervisor at the other agency to discuss coordination. Talk to your supervisor about paperwork concerns and needs to evaluate caseloads. Be alert to the macro-issues, and use your unique perspective for system change.

These are some guidelines to keep in mind as you shape and sort through the supervisory process. You may think of others to add. What you actually do, like clinical work, will reflect your supervisory models, your culture and priorities of the workplace, your own personality and style. With experience your approach will consolidate into one that is uniquely your own. The challenge is to keep it fresh, and to keep it flexible to meet the needs of those whom you supervise. The challenge is to be clear and intentional, and to keep the growing edge of creativity ever in the forefront.

The following questions will test your application and analysis of the content found within this chapter. For additional assessment, including licensing-exam-type questions on applying chapter content to practice behaviors, visit **MySearchLab**.

1. Being proactive in a supervisory session means
   a. Letting the clinician set the pace and agenda of the session
   b. Both you and the clinician having clear agendas for that particular session
   c. Helping clinicians separate skills from emotions
   d. Focusing on the clients and their diagnoses

2. Being aware of the parallel process in a supervisory session helps you as a supervisor
   a. Know how to effectively respond to the clinician in the moment
   b. Formulate a treatment plan for the client
   c. Focus on the influence of the clinician's past personal experiences
   d. Assess agency procedures and policies

3. Ellen seems to present in supervision the "problem of the week" that her clients talk about with her. It would be most useful to help Ellen
   a. Learn the skills and information she needs to address this wide array of problems
   b. Narrow the focus of her therapy sessions to 1 or 2 problems only
   c. See the underlying issues and patterns that the different problems have in common
   d. Organize her time better

4. Every time you make a suggestion to Steve in supervision about ways of approaching a case he answers with a "yes, but." The best way to respond to this would be to
   a. Point out in the session when it happens how he seems to be constantly negating your ideas
   b. Ask him to stop being so resistant and request that he simply do what you suggest
   c. Assume he is feeling anxious and say nothing so that he can calm down
   d. Review with him his clinical goals

5. Sally tends to begin her supervisory sessions by talking about what she did on the weekend. How you respond to this pattern?

6. Ted becomes easily overwhelmed—sad and teary—when talking about some of the children with whom he is working. How would you respond to this?

10

Supervision and Groups

Competencies Applied with Practice Behaviors — in This Chapter				
Professional Identity	Ethical Practice	✘ Critical Thinking	Diversity in Practice	Human Rights & Justice
Research-Based Practice	Human Behavior	Policy Practice	Practice Contexts	✘ Engage, Assess, Intervene, Evaluate

Various types of groups can be an important adjunct to individual supervision. In this chapter we will discuss some of the dos and don'ts of setting up groups, different types to consider, the setting of the structure, and the running of the process. Once again, as we move through these topics, think about any of your own experiences in group supervision— what was helpful, what was not helpful, what you might have done differently.

GROUP THINK

Suppose you have to start the time-consuming budget evaluation process this week, you've been asked to chair that new interagency committee on runaway teens, and you are helping out with clinical assessments while one of your clinicians is out on paternity leave. All this on top of 8 hours a week of individual supervision. Wait, a minute! You just got a great idea! Why not put all of your supervisees together into a group! That will save you 6 hours a week!

In the same way it's tempting to start a therapy group when the client waiting list gets out of control, you may consider group supervision when you are overloaded with responsibilities. Why work your magic on only 1 clinician at a time when you can do 6 in one fell swoop? In addition to saving time and energy, group supervision, you tell yourself, will allow clinicians to learn from one another, develop leadership skills and learn about group process, find role models other than yourself, learn about different clients and new approaches, break down feelings of isolation, and provide an opportunity for emotional support. Actually, now that you think about it, why would you want to do it any other way?

For the same reason you don't place every client who walks through the door in a group. You have to consider the needs of the individuals involved, as well as your own. Group supervision may make it difficult to gauge a clinician's performance. Quality control may be compromised. Most importantly, perhaps, the supervisory relationship may be significantly changed as the intensity and intimacy of individual supervisory relationships are diminished in the presence of others. All this doesn't mean that group supervision isn't a good idea. It can be, but once again it is about being clear and intentional.

Box 10.1 provides a checklist of questions you'll want to ask yourself to help you decide whether and what type of group you want to create. We'll discuss these questions one by one.

Critical Thinking

Practice Behavior Example: *Analyze models of assessment, prevention, intervention, and evaluation.*

Critical Thinking Question: When you consider your own experience with group process, what role do you see group supervision playing in clinical development?

Box 10.1 • **Supervision Group Checklist**

What is the main purpose of the group?

Is the group to be the primary or secondary source of supervision for the members?

Will you be the primary supervisor for both individual and group supervision?

What is the composition of the group?

How large a group do you want?

Is the group time-limited or ongoing, open or closed?

What logistical problems do you need to consider?

What Is the Main Purpose of the Group?

Before you start a supervision group think about what it is you would most like the participants to know, feel, and think when they walk out of the room 2 hours later—ideas on how to treat their cases, better connected to the team and feeling less isolated, opportunities to learn a particular method or techniques in greater detail, increased self-awareness? Something else?

Your first reaction may be to say "all of the above." Don't. Such creative combinations can get muddy fast. Pick one goal or one purpose, and that will help you decide whether you need a group and who would be in it.

Is the Group to Be the Primary or Secondary Source of Supervision for the Members?

Most supervisors would prefer to use groups to supplement individual supervision so that the supervisory relationship doesn't become diluted. But it's conceivable, say, to have a group of experienced clinicians who use a weekly or biweekly supervision group to discuss their work, and use individual supervision primarily for administrative work or support. If the members are expected to get all or most of their clinical needs met through the group, the focus and process will obviously be different.

Will You Be the Primary Supervisor for Both Individual and Group Supervision?

Having someone else lead the group while you do individual supervision provides an additional role model for staff, gives experienced staff a chance for leadership and teaching, and provides an added perspective to the clinician's developing style. If you decide to have someone else facilitate the group, it is important that you both coordinate your foci and goals to avoid unnecessary duplication—the clinician discussing a case twice and feeling oversupervised—as well as avoiding possible confusion from gathering too many perspectives.

If you will be doing both individual and group supervision, be clear about the purpose of each. Are there particular cases you might have staff reserve for group presentation—ones that center around a particular theme, ones that are easier to videotape, ones that demonstrate the use of a particular clinical model? How will you be able to gather the information you need to assure quality control—Is checking case records sufficient? Should clinicians verbally give you an update on all their cases on a regular basis? Should they submit recordings of their work periodically?

How might individual clinicians handle the transition from the intimacy of individual supervision to the public arena of the group—Stage 1 clinicians, for example, are likely to be most anxious and self-conscious. Whether you leave them out of the group or offer them more support about the process may depend on your own style and the personality of the clinicians. Again, think these questions through in advance to avoid both you and clinicians from getting confused or bogged down in the process.

What Is the Composition of the Group?

Obviously, if you have only 3 people on your team, your options for developing a group are few. A few more people than that, however, and you are faced with the question of who to include. Should the group be heterogeneous or homogeneous? Is it better to have all home-based staff, for example, together in one group or should they be mixed with outpatient and case management staff? Is it better to put all the students and beginning staff together for training, or should they be mixed with experienced staff so they can learn through others' case presentations?

The answer lies in determining what combinations are possible and what the main purpose of the group is. Is your primary purpose to create support for the home-based workers who are feeling isolated and burned out—leading toward a homogenous group—or do you want to reduce the division among jobs and develop a large sense of staff cohesiveness—leading toward a heterogeneous group. Would students and new clinicians, by their sheer numbers, quickly dominate a group and reduce the learning opportunities for more experienced staff? Would a mixed group overwhelm the students and beginners? Could the experienced staff serve as models for beginners and still get what they need?

You want to consider the developmental stages of the various clinicians. Because Stage 1 clinicians can easily feel intimidated by the more experienced staff, your primary supervisory needs are to use individual supervision as a way of building your relationship and ensuring quality control. Stage 3 clinicians can often take leadership roles in a group, and it provides them with an opportunity to use and highlight their growing experience. But that said, you also need to think in terms of individual personalities and backgrounds.

> ### Critical Thinking
>
> **Practice Behavior Example:** *Analyze models of assessment, prevention, intervention, and evaluation.*
>
> **Critical Thinking Question:** Who would you consider to be inappropriate for group supervision?

Who, for example, could be a good role model for Susan? Whom could Susan be a good role model for? Would Tom's fly-by-the-seat-of-your-pants approach help a particular student feel less obsessed with doing everything right? Could Teresa's gentle way with resistant parents be a useful counterpoint to your own more direct approach? These more subtle factors can be overlooked when you are considering larges issues of overall purpose and available staff. Nevertheless, such issues can make an important difference in the effectiveness of the group.

How Large a Group Do You Want?

Generally 5 to 8 members is a workable number for group supervision. Other factors can create exceptions to this rule. If the group will be focusing on group process and countertransference issues, you, and the members, may prefer to have a smaller group to facilitate intimacy. Similarly, if the group is a primary source of supervision for the members, and a potentially large number of cases will be presented, small groups work better. If, on the other hand, the group is primarily for training, the number of members may be restricted only by the size of the room.

Is the Group Time-Limited or Ongoing, Open or Closed?

Ongoing and closed groups allow members to develop an appreciation of one another's styles and strengths, as well as provide greater opportunities for developing a deeper level of trust and intimacy. Open-ended groups where new members may come in as someone leaves may disrupt the intimacy or introduce new energy and ideas, but you need to anticipate a period of transition until the new person is acclimated and accepted into the process. Some situations may require a time-limited group, such as a student group that runs through the academic year, or a time-limited supplemental group to support staff while a supervisor is away on leave for a few months.

What Logistical Problems Do You Need to Consider?

A large room isn't available in the mornings, and no one wants to tie up the after-school hours that are needed for clients. You have a standing administrative meeting at 3 p.m. every second and fourth Tuesday of the month. Emergency staff are rotating weekends on call, and are often off on Mondays. The same logistical problems that can interfere with the scheduling of a therapy group can also derail supervision groups. Think through the details, and decide how much a priority the group needs to be in terms of availability of staff and time.

The purpose of these questions is to help you to be clear, to be proactive, and able to best meet the group objective. If you are unsure about the answers to any of these questions, consult with your own supervisor to get a broader perspective.

TYPES OF GROUPS

Most group supervision sessions, like typical individual supervisory sessions, focus on case presentations. But as we've alluded to earlier, this is obviously not the only type of group you may want to consider. Here is a rundown on different types of groups based upon their varying functions.

Heterogeneous Case-Focused Groups

The primary goal of these groups is to discuss cases. The person presenting the case should leave with questions answered and a clear treatment plan. Others learn from the discussion, applying what is said about one case to a similar one of their own. If you have staff with a range of experience and perspectives, it becomes an energetic forum for learning new skills and ways of thinking, and gives more experienced staff an opportunity for leadership.

For new staff, such heterogeneous groups can help them bond with the larger team family. Again, however, keep in mind that these new, less-experienced clinicians can feel intimidated; they may have difficulty processing all the different perspectives, fueling their anxiety and sense of incompetence. They will need your support through individual supervision to gain traction and adequately have their concerns and questions answered. Training can easily be incorporated into case-focused groups: for example, role-plays can be expanded to replicate a family or group therapy sessions; demonstrations of techniques can be realistically portrayed; viewing video recordings can lead to a thorough discussion of process and other clinical options.

Training Groups

Some groups, however, focus primarily on training, generally as a supplement to individual supervision. Training groups usually lack the intensity of standard case-focused groups, and quality control is less of a focus. For example, student groups or a supervision group for newly hired or newly graduated clinicians essentially become training groups. Case presentations serve as launch pads for lectures, demonstrations, and rhetorical questions. The focus is on disseminating information, applying theory to practice, and filling in the gaps in knowledge. Even though students or clinicians may support one another, or have a safe place to lower their own performance expectations and reduce their anxiety, you are clearly the expert and they will turn to you for information about ways to approach specific problems or clients.

A different type of training group is the specialized group that comes together to learn about a specific approach or skill. If several staff, for example, attend a conference on hypnosis or play therapy, they may decide to meet together to help each other apply the newly acquired skills to cases. Or a group may form to read and discuss object-relations theories, or come together to do live observation of certain types of cases. In these types of groups you may bring in a consultant or be an active member learning the skills along with them. Your focus becomes that of facilitating and supporting the process.

Finally, there are training groups that are actually more like training events or meetings. A monthly staff meeting, for example, with a guest presenter, is less about group dynamics or supervision and more about staff enrichment. These events or meetings become opportunities for the staff to be together and share a joint experience.

Staffing Groups

In some settings groups are used to staff new cases as they come in. The purpose may be to decide on diagnosis, to carve out an initial treatment plan, or to decide what services or clinicians need to be assigned. While there is an administrative quality to these groups, they once again provide opportunities for learning, and for you as a supervisor to see how particular clinicians are learning and growing over time. Issues and questions raised in these groups can be brought into individual supervision for further discussion.

Staff Support Groups

While cases may be discussed, the purpose of these groups is less about clinical treatment and more about staff support. They are invaluable for staff who work off-site and are more isolated. Home-based staff, emergency staff who travel to or are based at hospitals, and case managers who may move between client homes and other agencies are all likely candidates. The goal is to get everyone together in the same room, to have them connect with their peers, to feel part of a team rather than a lone individual, to share their experiences, to learn, and to find out that others are dealing with the same issues and problems. Individual supervision becomes the place for more thorough case discussion and for assuring quality control.

These types of staff support groups where you are present and taking a leadership role are obviously different from peer-support groups where there is no supervisor present. They too help reduce isolation among team members and build connections; they provide a place for staff to vent about the work without worrying about what a supervisor is thinking. They can be helpful in maintaining staff morale and preventing burnout, but should not be a substitute—in time or in staff emotional investment—for ongoing supervision.

If you discover or suspect that a clinician is using a peer group as a primary source of support and information, you need to wonder why—Are you not available enough? Does the clinician not feel safe with you? To be emotionally bonded to a peer group rather than to you essentially means that the clinician is getting support but not supervision. You effectively are out of the loop and quality control is at risk. Again, it is your responsibility to raise your concerns and gently explore with the clinician her feelings about supervision and possible ways to improve it.

Supervisory Groups

Here supervisors of different teams come together on a regular basis. The purpose of such groups may be any of the functions listed earlier—to discuss the dispensation of new cases, to improve communication and coordination among services and teams, to focus on supervision of supervision, and to develop as a group their own supervisory skills. One person may be a facilitator in a group of peers, or someone higher up the ladder may actually take the supervisory, lead role.

Administrative Meetings

It is a brief daily or weekly touchdown meeting to make announcements, to update staff on ongoing projects and issues, and to quickly set work priorities. A monthly all-staff meeting where announcements are made, good news is shared, updates are provided about budget or audits or staffing changing—the focus here is not on group dynamics, certainly not on supervision, but simply as a forum for communication and connection. It's a meeting, a gathering of the clan, a way of being seen and heard by staff, a means of giving and getting feedback about administrative rather than client-specific clinical aspects of the work.

Box 10.2 is a summary of the different types of groups and their foci and benefits.

Critical Thinking

Practice Behavior Example: *Use critical thinking augmented by creativity and curiosity.*

Critical Thinking Question: Think about your experience with administrative meetings. If you were to plan the ideal administrative meeting, what would it be like?

Box 10.2 • Types of Groups

Case-focused groups	Focus on specific cases; help translate skills to new situations; provide opportunities for leadership and training; interaction of staff of different levels/stages
Training groups	Focus on specific skills; bringing together of staff of similar levels
Staffing groups	Decide on disposition of new cases, initial assessment; provide opportunities for learning
Staff support groups	Focus on support and connection; help reduce isolation, increase staff morale
Supervisory groups	Meeting of supervisors; focus on disposition of cases, middle-management support; provide opportunities for improved coordination and communication among services
Administrative groups/meetings	Staff meetings around administrative issues; keep staff updated; provide opportunities for informal staff interaction

While these are some of the common types of groups, you can probably think of or have been involved in some combination of others. Again, what is important as a supervisor initiating or facilitating any of these groups is clarity of purpose and intent. Without this being clear in your mind, such groups are apt to become rambling, testing, and frustrating for the members.

SETTING STRUCTURE AND FACILITATING PROCESS

Suppose you've decided that you want to have a case-focused group with a mix of staff from different developmental stages and with a variety of different clients and presenting problems. Where do you start?

Format

A good place to start is by deciding about the format. What do you envision the structure and process to be? To use the time effectively and manage the number of potential cases, some supervisors ask members to sign up for presentation in advance, and a certain amount of time is allocated for each case—20–30 minutes, for example, for a new case. Other supervisors may take a tally at the start of the meeting, and still others will take presentations on a first come, first served basis. You can decide on your own personal style, but what you need to make clear to the participants is that they need to prepare in advance. Like individual supervision, you want clinicians to be proactive and responsible, not simply waltzing in and scrambling to come up with an agenda on the spot.

A clear, well-thought-out presentation of a case fosters clear clinical thinking and makes efficient use of the group time. Beginners, in particular, are apt to ramble on about the history of the case, wasting valuable time and making it difficult for other members to determine what these clinicians want help with. You can ask presenters to provide a short written synopsis, similar to the one used for tape presentation presented earlier. This helps contain the amount of information and helps group members focus on the presenter's specific questions and needs.

As with individual supervision, it is important for you not only to be clear about the format, but also to enforce it at the start. If you don't, group members are likely to test— show up without agendas, in a rambling way summarize cases on the spot, ask questions or make comments about issues that aren't relevant.

Recordings

Recordings may or may not be used—that, again, is your decision. The disadvantage of recordings is that they can be time-consuming; their advantage, of course, is that everyone has an opportunity to learn by seeing the actual process. If you feel that understanding process is important for the group members to focus upon, consider including recordings in the format of the group. To be efficient, ask presenters to prepare the tape for viewing by completing the outline discussed earlier.

How the group reacts to a tape or a verbal case presentation depends on your response. If you focus primarily on what the clinician is doing wrong, group members are likely to follow suit, making the experience uncomfortable at best and generally discouraging others from wanting to take advantage of the group process. Some supervisors state at the beginning what type of feedback is permissible—that is, positive comments and constructive suggestions rather than criticism—and then their only concern for the first few sessions is to enforce the rules. If you are supportive, acknowledge the risk taken, and offer constructive feedback to the clinician's questions, your modeling will pay off and members are likely to do the same.

> **Engage, Assess, Intevene, Evaluate**
>
> ***Practice Behavior Example:*** *Use empathy and other interpersonal skills.*
>
> **Critical Thinking Question:** What would you do to help group members feel safe?

Encouraging Interaction

The opportunity to receive input from one's peers, discover new ways to assess a problem, develop creative ideas for working with individuals and family, and hear empathetic stories just when the clinician feels discouraged is what separates group supervision from individual supervision. Hearing multiple ideas and approaches increases the likelihood that the clinician will find what he needs. You want to encourage this group participation. The easiest way to do this is to state this as an objective at the beginning and then making sure that you resist members turning to you for information and advice. For the first few sessions you may find yourself encouraging others to speak—"So what do you all think about . . . ?"— and refraining from giving your opinion until others have voiced their own reactions.

Encouraging group process doesn't mean that you give up your role. A supervision group isn't the same as a peer-support group. The amount of clinical leadership you need to exert will depend on the level of experience in the group. With a mix of experienced and less-experienced clinicians, your primary role may be keeping the process on track. In a more homogeneous group of less-experienced clinicians, you may, as mentioned earlier, wind up doing individual supervision and teaching while others watch.

Some supervisors have a harder time than others shifting gears between individual and group process. Even with moderately experienced clinicians they seem to fall into the role of expert and discourage interaction among group members. This obviously undermines the benefits of having a group, and the supervisor is serving as a poor role model. Even beginners need to feel that they can present their point of view, can offer support, and present highlights from their own experience. Their examples can become a basis for discussion, as well as a contrasting perspective to that of the supervisor.

Focusing on Group Process

Having a mix of perspectives is only one advantage of group dynamics. Another benefit is the opportunity to step back and discuss the group process itself. Similar to individual supervision, you can use the group supervisory process to help clinicians better understand the parallel process by highlighting how it is not only being replicated in the case that is being presented, but by the process in the room—group members are focusing on crisis or context, for example, just as the presenting clinician and ultimately the client are doing. You can use the group as an increasing forum to raise countertransference issues— doing empty-chair work right there in the group, raising questions about the blurring of the professional and personal. These are issues of depth—how you use the group process to illustrate clinician–client process—and this is another issue you need to consider in light of your own style, clinical orientation, and focus of the group.

Group as Family

To focus on group process is also to note how it is different from that of individual supervision. Whereas individual supervision easily replicates a parent–child dyad and dynamics, group supervision recreates a larger psychological family, complete with siblings who must deal with one another as well as with parents.

These family roles create new transference/countertransference reactions within the group itself, and a different side of the clinician may surface. Ellen, for example, who seems always eager to please, may be overshadowed by older clinician Jake and may become quiet and withdrawn. Jamie, an anxious clinician, may unexpectedly take one of the students under his wing; Kate, a more experienced clinician, may openly challenge you for control of the group or serve as spokesperson for the others.

Depending upon your own style and orientation, you may decide to pick up on these dynamics and explore with the group their implications for clinical work. You can raise rhetorical questions: Whom do you feel closer to here? Whom do you feel most competitive with? How is your role here similar to the one you assume with your clients or within your own family? How are your behavior and emotions different from how you present yourself in individual supervision? Or you may focus on the individual: I notice, Teresa, that you seem to have a difficult time confronting clients such as Ms. Jones, but here in group you seem to have no trouble speaking up and asserting your point of view. I wonder why there is a difference. What about the group or about Ms. Jones causes you to respond so differently?

Such questions can increase the group members' sensitivity to these issues and initiate discussion about what is happening in the room. Taking the risk to talk about such issues with the group and connecting the process to clinical work provide a different level of learning and awareness than is possible in individual supervision. But such risk-taking also requires a higher level of trust and intimacy, as well as a willingness on the part of group members to use the group process in this way.

Such trust and risk-taking can occur only if group members believe that you are strong enough to protect them if the need arises. You need not only be a clinical resource, but you must keep a close eye on the pace and depth of the process itself. The group has the potential to become a more powerful, self-generating process than that of the dyad. Without guidance and clear direction, competitive and conflicting cliques can form. The most dominant individual in the group can become the role model who is emulated or opposed, or in the jockeying for position and power, someone can feel left out or ignored. You need to be there to help everyone articulate their needs and reactions, to restate and reclarify goals and intentions, and to keep the process on track.

Having a Vision

You begin with a vision of what the group might ideally be. You clarify goals, expectations, and boundaries: Are cases talked about primarily in terms of clinical options, or is it okay to talk about countertransference issues—the way one is feeling intimated by a father or overwhelmed by a child—or personal reactions—the way, for example, one feels discouraged and depressed by the lack of progress? To what extent should personal news be shared—someone getting married, a recent promotion, another's long-term goals for career? Does talking about such matters help make the group more intimate, less formal, and more supportive? How does it fit with the primary goals of the group? You lead the process by intentionally bringing up topics and raising questions.

The other half of your vision is the atmosphere of the group that you want to create. As with individual supervision, your goals are to reduce anxiety about the content and the group process itself, to encourage everyone to have a voice, and to help everyone feel that their contributions are valued. If you set the right tone and balance, trust and intimacy will deepen, and participants will be able to take greater risks.

Finally, you want to share your vision with the group members and have them be part of the shaping process. Group supervision obviously offers new ways of learning. You may want to explore with the members not only what they want to learn most, but how. You can suggest guidelines, but ask them as a group to decide the details of what the format and the expectations of each member should be. This helps make the process more collaborative, reduces testing behaviors, and better tailors the group to individual needs.

GROUP PROBLEMS: PLAYING OUT ROLES

Even with collaboration, problems can and are likely to arise. Let's talk about some of the most common ones. Basically, most problems have to do with roles, transference issues of control and power, and anxiety and coping styles that come up during the various stages of individual supervision. Even if group members do not focus on roles as part of the learning process, you, like a group therapist, need to deal with role in order to keep the group process working effectively.

Dominating Member

One common problem is the domination of the group by one of the members. Having a rotational system of presentation can help prevent this, but even then you may have one member who is most active, always presenting opinions or asking questions. If you do, the question is why. How is this behavior a solution to another issue? Jake's asking of endless questions about skills or techniques, for example, may cause you wonder whether he is weak in particular areas or whether his clinical foundation is less solid than you originally thought. On the other hand, you notice that Ellen, a new clinician, is always taking notes and asking conceptual questions that she never raises in individual supervision. Is she leaning more heavily on the group for advice because the environment somehow feels safer than that of individual supervision. Your job is to pay attention to these patterns and gently raise your questions and concerns in individual supervision.

But sometimes domination is not about anxiety or skill, but more about a clinician's jockeying for control and power within the group. If the group is a long-term, ongoing group with a focus on group process, you may choose to let the clinician run full course and see how the group members handle it. You can simply point out the process—I notice that Mike has been giving a lot of feedback in the past several weeks and see several of you speaking up less; I wonder if any of you have any reactions to that—in order to give the group members permission to tackle it.

You also need to determine whether the individual's domination truly impedes participation of other members or whether it seems to be a threat to you as supervisor. As in group or family therapy, a coleader often emerges as the group process unfolds. This person can be an additional support and role model for others, and her leadership can represent a further step in the clinician's own development. But if you lack confidence in your own role and skills, you can easily view such challenges as a threat.

You need to sort out whether the problem lies with the group member or you. Bringing the issue to someone you trust—your own supervisor—or having a colleague observe the group or tape the group session and reviewing it with him can raise the questions that you might not consider and help you gain a new perspective.

If you decide that the dominating member is genuinely undermining both your leadership and the group process, and that the group does not have the resources or the time to handle this issue, you will need to take decisive action. One pattern to be particularly alert to is the third-stage clinician's power struggle with you in a group composed of less-experienced staff. The danger here is the replication of family dynamics where the weaker parent—the clinician—joins with the children—the other group members—against the more dominant parent—you, the supervisor. The group members may become swept into the conflict as the clinician and supervisor battle it out. Again, making everyone aware of the process that you see unfolding can not only be an important learning tool, but change the process itself—once you talk about the elephant in the room, it's difficult to continue to ignore it.

A better approach, especially when group members are not at an equal level, is to discuss the group and your relationship with the clinician during individual supervision—I've noticed this . . . you seem to be doing this . . . I'm concerned about this. . . . Action on your part is essential. If this pattern continues for too long, the group members will come to see the dominating member as the true leader, and the group's purpose will be sabotaged.

Quiet Member

The flip side to the domineering clinician is the quiet, lost-child member of the group. Stage 1 clinicians who feel anxious and intimidated by the more-experienced members easily fit into this category, but sometimes even more-experienced staff who are new to the team or those who simply feel awkward in groups can feel this way as well. Often this problem works itself out over time as the clinician begins to feel safe with the other members. Gently and supportively pointing out the person's behavior may be enough to stir him into a more assertive role.

If a person remains quiet too long and always appears to be confused and unable to process the different perspectives that the group offers, you should reassess whether the group is appropriate for his needs. The clinician may need to stay with individual supervision until he becomes more confident and less anxious. Or you may need to determine whether personal issues are being activated by the group process that the clinician needs to sort out. These issues can be discussed during individual supervision.

Group Scapegoat

You, of course, never want to tolerate any scapegoating during group sessions. Fortunately, open scapegoating rarely occurs because group members tend to be sensitive to such issues. However, more subtle discounting of and disregard for a group member sometimes occurs, for example, when someone rolls her eyes or smirks—and others respond, though quietly, in agreement—when a particular member starts to speak. You need to be careful not to passively support such behaviors out of a need to feel part of the group or because of anxiety about raising the issue—again, you have the leadership responsibility to approach anxiety.

SUMMARY

The dynamics of groups are a variation of the larger dynamics of clinical supervision. The themes that emerge when we talk about group problems and process are the same themes we have emphasized throughout our discussion of the supervisory process: the need to begin with a clear vision of what is possible, to be proactive and intentional, to move between learning problems and problems about learning, and to take into account the differing needs of the clinicians at the varying stages of their professional development. Your skills in group supervision can and will develop with increased experience and comfort with group dynamics. To develop a group supervision style, you need to do what you have been doing all along—approach anxiety, trust your foundation of skills, and be willing to make mistakes and learn from them.

The following questions will test your application and analysis of the content found within this chapter. For additional assessment, including licensing-exam-type questions on applying chapter content to practice behaviors, visit **MySearchLab**.

1. The primary function of case-focused groups is to
   a. Discuss and answer questions about clinical cases
   b. Use the discussion of cases to build team support and connection
   c. Develop skills among less-experienced clinicians
   d. Discuss and resolve problems regarding administrative matters

2. It is important to set clear expectations at the start of a supervisory group
   a. So that the group members understand that you are firmly in charge and the leader of the group
   b. To help reduce the members' anxiety and their possible testing of boundaries
   c. To be able to effectively limit the group time to 1 hour
   d. To prevent Stage 3 clinicians from dominating the group

3. Alice is a new clinician. In group supervision she is quiet and rarely presents cases. It would be most helpful to
   a. Use individual supervision with her as a primary source of support and quality control until she feels less anxious
   b. Request that she present a case at least 3 times a month
   c. Have her sit next to you in the group sessions
   d. Suggest that she consider some individual therapy to help her be more open and assertive

4. When presenting cases in group supervision Joe tends to ramble on giving excessive details about the client, takes up a large share of the group time, and asks vague, unfocused clinical questions. What would be most helpful in changing these behaviors?
   a. Do nothing and see if the group members can speak up and give Joe their feedback
   b. Ask Joe to withdraw from the group and instead use individual supervision for clinical support
   c. Set time limits and provide a written outline on the way members should present cases
   d. Ask a colleague of Joe to pull him aside and talk to him about his presentations

5. Nora tends to dominate the group supervision sessions. How would you handle this as her supervisor?

6. Victor consistently brings up administrative questions and complaints in case-focused supervision group. How would you respond?

11

Supervision of Supervision

Competencies Applied with Practice Behaviors — in This Chapter				
☒ Professional Identity	■ Ethical Practice	■ Critical Thinking	■ Diversity in Practice	■ Human Rights & Justice
■ Research-Based Practice	■ Human Behavior	■ Policy Practice	☒ Practice Contexts	☒ Engage, Assess, Intervene, Evaluate

Supervision of supervision—you can almost image a pair of eyes peering over your shoulder as you peer over the shoulder of a clinician. And in its way, the image is accurate—another level is added to the hierarchy of responsibility and quality control. You, as supervisor, must check the work of not only the clinician, but novice supervisors and the clinicians under them as well.

Supervision of supervision, the same word tripping over itself, reflects the awkwardness of the situation. The experienced clinician who doesn't feel like a novice suddenly becomes one again. Becoming a supervisor is mastering a new set of skills, interacting with clinicians in a new way, and thinking about your role in the agency. In this chapter we will talk about this process of moving from clinician to supervisor, and your role in once again taking the lead.

TRANSITIONS AND CHALLENGES

There are several challenges that come with making the transition from clinician to supervisor. The greatest and most common one is that a new supervisor comes to see supervision as merely a higher-octane form of therapy. Rather than understanding and moving toward the new set of skills and perspectives that being a supervisor entails, a new supervisor stays within his comfort zone and essentially sees himself as a senior clinician. Instead

161

of focusing on the development of the clinician, a new supervisor joins with the clinician in focusing on the needs of the clients. Together they agree, for example, to spend the supervisory session talking about Ms. Jones, rather than about what Tom needs to focus on with Ms. Jones at his next therapy session with her.

This challenge is increased in those situations where a new supervisor is promoted out of the clinician pool. While it's best to not have a new supervisor suddenly supervise her former peers, there are times, especially in small agencies, where this cannot be helped. The lack of skill as a supervisor combined with the anxiety of having to focus on the performance of a colleague or friend makes focusing on the client an understandably comfortable option.

Finally, some new supervisors may be able to make the jump and shift their thinking from clinical work to a supervisory perspective, but struggle with other responsibilities and tasks that the new job requires: administrative duties such as quality control, budget formulation, or interagency responsibilities such as serving on community committees or representing the agency or team at state-wide meetings and functions. Wearing these new hats can be uncomfortable or even overwhelming. A new supervisor, lacking skills and confidence in these areas, either falls back into old ways of coping—becoming accommodating and anxious, becoming avoidant and doing little in such settings, or in more extreme cases, deciding not to be a supervisor—or steps down and returns to clinician status after a period of time.

What do you do to help avoid these problems? Here are some of your priorities in helping a new supervisor navigate the transition.

Realize That There Will Indeed Be a Transitional Period

Becoming a supervisor is more than assigning a clinician staff to supervise and telling him to feel free to ask questions as they arise. Just as the new graduate has to make the shift from student to new employee and clinician, the new supervisor needs to make the shift from clinician to supervisor—a step up in the organizational chart. This will take some time for him not only to learn the lay of the land, but to begin to actually think in a new way. This is how the new supervisor begins the developmental process all over again, once again being aware of knowing what he doesn't know.

If you have a long-standing relationship with the new supervisor and served as her clinical supervisor in the past, this foundation will obviously make the transition easier so will her own clinical foundation. While she may feel anxious and overwhelmed about the new job and skills, she already has a strong foundation and self-image as a clinician, one that has moved over time from beginner to experienced. Having grown through this process once makes it easier to do again. As you have done in the past, laying out this new landscape for supervisors, and showing patience yourself with their transition will help reduce their anxiety and enable them to become grounded more quickly.

Realize That Supervision of Supervision Is Different from Clinical Supervision

Just as you don't want the new supervisor focusing with clinicians on their clients rather than on the clinicians themselves, you don't want to make the mistake of focusing on the clinicians that the supervisor is seeing. If you are a relatively new supervisor yourself, or if you lack experience in doing supervision of supervision, you can easily wind up replicating the process, rather than changing it. Your focus is always right there in the room. Your challenge is to help the new supervisor become a competent supervisor, and you do that by dealing with her, rather than with those below her.

If you need support learning and doing supervision of supervision, you need to look up—toward your own supervisor or an outside consultant, who can help you develop your skills and hold tight to this perspective. What you don't want to do is reduce your own anxiety by colluding with the new supervisor in bypassing the process and relationship right there in the room.

Bond with the New Supervisor as Quickly as Possible

While developing a strong relationship of trust is always a primary goal, developing this as quickly as possible is essential when a new supervisor is promoted out of the peer group. You begin this process by welcoming the new supervisor to middle management and explicitly letting her know that you realize that the next few months will be difficult at times. If she must supervise her former cubby-mates, tell her that you realize that this will feel awkward, and that if she has absolutely any questions or problems or needs support in any way, she needs to come to you. She needs to know that you are invested in her and that you have her back.

Why does this need to be stated so quickly and dramatically? Because if you don't—if your welcome is halfhearted, if you are occupied with too many other items and not available, if you seem too harsh and intimidating—the new supervisor, rather than emotionally moving up, will drift back down and return to the comfort zone of her peers. Rather than coming to you with problems and questions, she'll be asking her friends. Rather than feeling she has the support to step up and use her power to set limits and make clear decisions, she will waffle and issue lukewarm, watered-down requests to her supervisees/friends because she is afraid of hurting their feelings and losing their support.

If you fail to bond and help her move away from the peer group, she will fail to grow and you will have no clout. The relationship will never really get off the ground, and your quality control will be compromised.

Have a Training Plan

Just as you need to assess, sort, and develop supervisory goals to address the learning problems and problems about learning of the clinician, you need to do the same for the new supervisor—that is, determine what supervisory and administrative skills he needs to learn, as well as be alert to and address the emotional obstacles that get in the way of the learning. Later we will talk more fully about what you'll want to look for.

The theme that runs through these suggestions is once again leadership. Imagine you and the new supervisor climbing a mountain together. You are taking the lead, and you both are attached by a safety line. The line around her lets her know that you are there and she is not alone. Feeling the tension as you move forward helps her move forward, and prevents her from sliding back if she should slip or get tired. To be successful in her new role, this is exactly the type of active support and direction that she will need from you.

QUALITIES: WHAT TO LOOK FOR IN A NEW SUPERVISOR

Suppose Jodi has moved on to a new job and new agency and you have an opening for a clinical supervisor. Whom do you consider for a promotion?

Your first instincts are probably to think of Ellen, the most senior person among your clinical staff. Maybe a good idea, maybe not. Being a good clinician doesn't mean that someone will automatically be a good supervisor.

And some clinicians won't want to supervise. From their perspective, supervision seems to be too political and too administrative. They enjoy the one-on-one contact with clients, like to flex their clinical muscles, see clinical work as their calling. They appreciate the creativity and flexibility that they, mistakenly, assume is diluted in supervision.

But many others do want to take that next step. In addition to more money and higher status, supervision may appear to be the logical next step for some clinicians, such as those at Stage 3, who are feeling restless or bored with clinical work. Those clinicians who have had a good relationship with you are likely to appreciate the value of supervision and wish to pass on to others what they have received.

This is an important decision. Don't go on autopilot and think of Ellen as the natural shoo-in. Step back and think about the abilities you'd like a new supervisor to have. Not sure? Table 11.1 is a quick list comparing and contrasting the responsibilities and skills of strong clinicians and supervisors.

It's easy to see the similarities, but let's highlight the core qualities that a strong supervisor needs to have.

Table 11.1 Qualities of Clinicians Versus Supervisors

Strong Clinicians	Strong Supervisors
Able to build rapport with a wide range of clients	Able to build rapport with a wide range of intra- and interagency staff
Good clinical assessment skills	Good supervisory assessment skills
Has clear working clinical models	Has clear working supervisory models
Able to define clear clinical goals	Able to define clear supervisory and administrative goals
Able to translate client problems into micro-process	Able to translate clinical/administrative problems into macro-process
Able to be flexible/creative in clinical approach to meet clinical goals	Able to be flexible/creative in approach, able to easily shift roles to meet supervisory/administrative goals
Able to advocate for client	Able to advocate for client, staff, agency
Able to set clear and appropriate clinical expectations and boundaries with clients	Able to set clear and appropriate supervisory/quality-control expectations and boundaries with staff
Able to appropriately utilize community resources	Able to coordinate and shape community resources

The Person Is Clinically Grounded

A new supervisor doesn't need to be a master clinician. What she does need are solid clinical skills commensurate with the level and needs of the staff she will be supervising. A new supervisor who will be directing a new program made up of students or BA level case managers is at a different level than someone who will be supervising a staff with a wider range of experience. A new supervisor who has worked primarily in home-based work may be ideal for heading up a team of home-based workers, but less of a fit if the team will include those doing office-based play therapy or complex outpatient clients.

Engage, Assess, Intervene, Evaluate

Practice Behavior Example: *Develop, analyze, advocate, and provide leadership for policies and services.*

Critical Thinking Question: What do you consider to be the most important quality that a new supervisor should have? Why?

You need to consider your needs, and ideally would choose someone with the most experience and widest range of knowledge. Start with the ideal, but keep your priorities in mind: What is it that you most need from this person in terms of clinical strengths? Knowing this will help you sort through your potential candidates.

The Person Has Insight into His Strengths and Weaknesses

Ellen may realize that while she works well with a wide range of adults, she is weak when it comes to working with children. Her awareness and willingness to admit this weakness is actually a strength. It means that she is less apt to place unrealistic pressure on herself and fall into being the good kid with you and avoid seeking the help she needs, or move toward the other extreme of "don't know what she doesn't know" and assume she can and should do it all. An accurate and open discussion of clinical strengths and weaknesses not only helps you decide how much you need to invest in training or in supplementing her supervisory skills with help from others, but more importantly lets you know that you have a potentially honest relationship on which to build.

This same self-awareness and honesty is important in nonclinical areas as well. A new supervisor who can say that he is effective in organizing teams but knows little about budgeting or community needs is being both open and clear. Such honest communication indicates a good foundation for working together as a team, just as the absence of such insight and honesty would be a red flag and signal larger concerns.

The Person Is Able to Think on a Macro level

What we mean by this is the ability to step back and see the larger picture. Given the strong psychosocial approach that most social workers have, this skill is usually present. But some clinicians who have worked with a narrow client population, or who over time have learned to think in terms of specific clinical skills and techniques, struggle with this. They may be able to see this at the client level—for example, to be curious about the larger family's behaviors and responses on Mr. Smith's depression—but have difficulty applying this perspective in other areas.

A new supervisor who tends to think only in terms of pathology—for example, Tom's problem is that he is passive/aggressive, Shana has a difficult time with authority figures—may be correct, but potentially handicapped. Holding rigidly to one framework suggests anxiety-binding behavior. Just as this is a problem for clinical work, it is even more so for supervision. If you are viewing everything through only a clinical lens, the politics and complexity of problems are missed; solutions lack creativity. It's the old adage that if you only have a hammer, everything looks like a nail.

This is not a question of just knowing content—the role of different community agencies, and the actual unit cost of providing clinical services. What you are looking for in a new supervisor is a curiosity about how elements interact, and an ability to step back and look at problems from multiple angles. Again, to a certain extent this way of seeing can be taught, but the willingness to learn often cannot. You want to know at the front end how much you will need to train, and how well your training will pay off.

The Person Can Successfully Shift Between Multiple Roles

Certainly good clinical work requires an ability to shift gears with a client or shift roles and approaches with different clients over the course of a day. But while roles are different, you are essentially staying within your primary role as clinician, no matter how varied that role may be. A new supervisor is likely to need to shift among various roles—clinical supervisor, administrator, and agency representative. This requires an ability to wear multiple hats in the course of a day, to shift gears rapidly—from an emotional session with a clinician to an analytic, detailed discussion about budget to a stand-at-the-podium presentation before a committee.

Some new supervisors can do this well, while others struggle with such multitasking and transitions. Part of the challenge is content—understanding what is required for each role—but a more important part is emotion—the ability to approach and manage anxiety, to be self-confident, and to handle changes well.

The Person Has Strong Social Skills

Clinicians are by definition sensitive people, but if the work involves community contacts and coordination, or serving on intra- and interagency committees, this requires a potentially different and deeper social skill-set. Does this person perform well in group settings—Is she active? Does he convey a solid professional demeanor? Are you comfortable with this person representing your team or your agency? Is he aware of and sensitive to the political, not just the pathological? Is she clear in thinking, articulate in presentation? Because the work is usually multifaceted, you need supervisors who can successfully meet all the challenges of the work.

Once again, you can start with the ideal, but then be clear about your priorities—what tasks does a new supervisor need to be strongest in? What does she lack in terms of knowledge that can be taught, and what aspects of personality may be more difficult to change? Use your own clinical skills to sort these out.

The Person Is Well Respected Both Clinically and Personally

This is particularly important if you are thinking of promoting someone from within the agency. For example, Ellen may have the most clinical experience and strongest clinical skills, but if other staff see her as defensive or arrogant, this may be an obstacle that is too difficult to overcome. Similarly, if Tom is well loved by everyone on the team but has only a couple of years' experience, staff won't see him as clinically competent. Not only will they wonder why they didn't get the job, they will seek clinical help from each other, rather than turning to him.

Professional Identity

Practice Behavior Example: *Practice personal reflection and self-correction to assure continual professional development.*

Critical Thinking Question: How have your own interpersonal skills changed over time? How have these changes affected your work?

Becoming a clinical supervisor isn't a popularity contest, but after acknowledging that, you need to be aware of the impact of your choice on the rest of the staff. In the long run you may decide that Ellen is the best choice, despite the rest of the staff's perceptions of her. With your coaching and her own self-awareness, you realize that she can change staff perceptions, gain their trust, and overcome their initial resistance. Or, while Tom may not be ready to supervise someone like Ann who has extensive clinical experience, he can head a training group for students, or you can channel his popularity toward serving on a staff personnel committee.

And if you decide to hire someone from outside the agency, you bypass the problem of having someone potentially supervise colleagues, but it also brings new challenges. Some staff will wonder why they themselves didn't get promoted, and everyone may be a bit wary of this new face. Explain to the staff your thinking behind your decision, talk one-on-one with those who may feel slighted, and think about what you might need to do, and what she herself can do, to show that she has strong clinical skills and can be trusted.

The Person Believes in the Team and Agency Mission

Just as you have top priorities, so too do those who apply for jobs—the need for more money and status, the need to move to a different place, the simple need to have a job. Someone from outside the agency may have all the skills and talents described earlier, but if he is not on board with the purpose and vision of the team and agency, you have trouble. Either he will disregard it—focus on what is important to him rather than what is important to you—or he will oppose it—taking an argumentative stand about new programs or budget priorities, all undermining your efforts.

If faced with this, you need to sort out what is beneath the surface. Is the person being oppositional or passive because he doesn't fully understand the mission of the team or agency? Does it reflect a problem in your relationship? Does he tend to be rigid in his thinking and have difficulty incorporating new ideas? Is he passive or oppositional because this is his overall way of coping with change? Once again your clinical skills come into play to determine the source of the problem. If you have trouble unraveling the problem, get help from your supervisor or trusted colleague. Don't spend your time simply feeling aggravated or doing battle.

DEVELOPING SKILLS—THE NEW SUPERVISOR CURRICULUM

So you've finally made your decision and hired the best person you could find. How do you help the skilled clinician become a skilled supervisor?

Box 11.1 is a sample training curriculum for new supervisors that covers the broad supervisory and administrative tasks of middle management. It is divided into 3 phases, much like the beginning, middle, and end stages of clinical work, and like the developmental stages moves from building a strong foundation to increasing responsibility, and from relatively tight oversight to increasing independence.

Box 11.1 • New Supervisor Curriculum

Beginning Phase

Goals
Build strong supervisory relationship
Orient to role/job

Topics/Skills
Teach about anxiety-coping styles/developmental stages
Training—clinician learning styles/parallel process
Training—assessment of clinicians, setting supervisory goals
Training—quality-control issues (e.g., record keeping)
Training—administrative duties (e.g., budgets, committees, functions/roles)

Activities
Set clear expectations for supervision of supervision sessions
Have supervisor observe your supervisory sessions
Attend committee meetings with you
Have supervisor make rounds of community agencies—introduce self, learn about services

Middle Phase

Goals
Develop increased skills regarding supervisory process
Expand supervisory/administrative responsibilities

Topics/Skills
Focus on process—replication of parallel process, clinician presentation in session
Explore impasses (e.g., with particular clinicians, difficulties with administrative duties)

Increase leadership responsibilities (e.g., head committees, represent agency)
Increase administrative duties (e.g., greater input budget, policy/procedure, strategic planning, hiring)

Activities
Observe supervisor's supervisory session/watch recordings
Have supervisor make presentations to other agencies, committees
Share/delegate tasks regarding budget input, development of policy/procedure
Offer specialized training opportunities in supervision/administration

Advanced Phase

Goals
Develop own supervisory/administrative style
Be able to act independently

Topics/Skills
Train on supervision of supervision process
Expand independent responsibilities (e.g., hiring staff, input budget, work with other agencies, community/clinical consultation)
See own role as primarily consultative

Activities
Place in charge of major projects (e.g., revising policy, audit reviews, developing new services)
Assign work at higher levels (e.g., state/regional committees)
Assign to train/consult on supervision/administration
Openly discuss/define challenges to avoid staleness

Running beneath these training goals, skills, and activities are several, even broader, goals that a new supervisor needs to master. We'll talk about content of these now, and in the next section we'll discuss the process—how to turn this information into supervisory knowledge and skill.

Apply Clinical Skills to Clinicians

New supervisors often see supervision as acting as a remote-control clinician— spoon-feeding and telling clinicians how to treat their clients—or essentially giving up clinical work all together and focusing on administrative matters. Neither view is correct. What new supervisors need help realizing is that their clinical experience and skills not only come into play around cases, but in understanding and supporting the clinicians they supervise.

This is where you talk in the language of parallel process. Just as clinicians need to gain rapport and build a sound and safe therapeutic relationship, new supervisors need to use their skills to build a sound and safe supervisory relationship. The assessment of the client that leads to the development of a therapeutic treatment plan has its parallel in the assessment of the clinician and the development of a supervisory plan with goals and objectives. Decisions about pacing, dealing with resistance, and focusing on process are clinical skills transferred to a new arena.

Understand the Developmental Stages

As said at the beginning, the main point in understanding developmental stages is realizing that you can't do the same supervision at Day 1 that you need to do at Day 100; that supervising a new graduate presents new challenges than supervising someone with 20 years of experience. Just as the skilled clinician is able to adjust her style to fit clients of different ages, backgrounds, and problems, the skilled supervisor needs to be flexible to adjust to different personalities and skill levels of clinicians. Knowing the stages helps the supervisor anticipate what may lie ahead.

Understand the Different Roles and Responsibilities That the Work Requires

The ability to shift gears is a quality that you'll be looking for in choosing new supervisors. Teaching them about the various aspects and demands of the work is your responsibility. Some of this will obviously be covered in job interviews and during the first few weeks of orientation. But the real learning comes over those first few months and even years where you flesh out for them the everyday tasks. Some of this will be detailed and mundane— the learning of new forms, the use of new software, the reading of a spreadsheet. Other aspects, however, are foundational skills of management—hiring and firing, maintaining staff morale, effective use of time, weighing service needs to budget constraints—and are ongoing with the increase of responsibility over time.

All this is new information to learn, but it is more a way of thinking to embrace. The clinical world, even with a diversity of clients, can seem homogenous. The world of supervision and middle management is not. This is where some new supervisors have trouble, making this shift, and adapting this broader and more complex perspective. Your challenge is to help them not only understand the specific tasks that make up the work, or learn how to move among them, but understand how they fit together to make an effective supervisor–manager role. Your greatest tool in teaching this is through your own modeling and openness.

Understand the Importance of Quality Control and the Use of Supervisory Power

Responsibility in a clinical relationship is often shared by the clinician and client. The client as consumer ultimately decides what the focus of treatment will be and how far the process and relationship will go.

Supervisors, however, ultimately decide the parameters of the work of clinicians. This can be another difficult transition for some clinicians, especially those whose clinical work was supportive and nurturing. They are apt to carry this over to supervision and become the mother hen type of leader described earlier. The danger is that they struggle with setting limits and boundaries, avoid needed confrontation, and fail to step into the middle-manager role.

While you want to be empathic to a new supervisor's feelings, you also need to be clear with her about the requirements of quality control and the responsibility to ensure effective and efficient clinical practice. This means not only modeling this behavior your-self, but supporting her power to make decisions and set limits.

Finally, with power comes politics, and this too may be new to a new supervisor. He will likely be working with a wider range of nonclinical professionals—the director, other supervisors, personnel directors, as well as those from other agencies. You will need to help the clinician learn how to become sensitive to political issues, and help him learn how to speak the language of this new audience in order to successfully navigate these new waters.

The theme that runs through these areas of content is clearly marking the fault lines between clinical practice and supervision; it is understanding the differences between them that creates the major challenges for new supervisors. Before we talk about the supervisory process itself, let's look at a few scenarios and see where we might focus on a new supervisor's skills and knowledge.

PUTTING KNOWLEDGE INTO ACTION

Sara talked with me about a new family that she just started with, says Jodi, a new supervisor. Actually, I know the family that she is talking about. I worked with them several years ago. The mother has always had problems with medication, and I think that it is important that Sara refer the mother for a psychiatric evaluation right away.

Jason has been coming into work late the past few weeks, and has called in sick 2 Mondays the past month, says Tom. As you know, I used to work with Jason. I know his wife has had problems with depression in the past, and this tends to spill over to him. I'm worried that he is getting depressed himself, is drinking more than he used to, or both. I'm wondering whether I should sit down with him and find out what's really going on.

My staff is unhappy about the new budget cuts, says Ann. At our last team meeting they were clearly upset and hit me with a lot questions about why and how the decision was made. I tried to explain as best I could, but I realized that I don't really understand the why and how myself. I'm wondering if you could come to our next team meeting and answer their questions.

As you read through these different scenarios, what issues and concerns come to mind? If you were the supervisor providing supervision to each of these supervisors, what skills may need to be developed? Let's look at them one at a time and we'll compare notes.

Sara and Jodi

The fact that Jodi is familiar with this family means that she may be able to provide additional information and a different and helpful perspective based on her experience. Her assessment of the mother and her medication may be absolutely correct.

The concern here is that Jodi slips into doing remote-control clinical work, telling Sara what she feels she needs to do with this case. The better questions that Jodi should be asking herself are around how Sara is thinking about this family. What impressions did Sara have of the mother? Is she aware of the mother's past psychiatric history, and if not, why not? If Sara is a new clinician, what does Sara's own assessment of this family tell Jodi about what clinical skills and knowledge Sara might be missing? Is there anything about Sara's presentation of the case that causes Jodi concern about the strength of her supervisory relationship with Sara? Knowing the family and knowing Sara, does Jodi foresee any playing out of parallel process?

It is these types of questions that show that Jodi is thinking like a supervisor and focusing on the problem at hand—namely, not the treatment plan for the family, but the challenges and needs of the clinician with her in the room. If she focuses primarily on the client rather than Sara, she isn't understanding the focus of supervision, or lacking in skills, or is anxious about shifting her focus and needs support to do so.

Supervisory Action

Help Jodi focus on Sara and assess her skills and needs.

Jason and Tom

Like Jodi, Tom's past experience and perspective, in this case, with Jason himself is potentially helpful. But Tom is in that awkward position of supervising someone he has worked with. The problem in situations like this is that he knows, in some way, too much about Jason, and his personal relationship with Jason can undermine his role as supervisor. The fact that Tom is talking about this openly in his own supervision is good sign that he feels comfortable and safe with his supervisor. If he didn't, he probably would not say anything at all in supervision, and approach Jason on his own. His supervisor would be out of the loop, spelling trouble for the supervisor's relationship with Tom and the potential management of the staff.

Talking to Jason about the underlying problems affecting his behavior is appropriate—the lateness and calling in sick are symptoms of something beneath. But there are 2 challenges facing a new supervisor like Tom. One is that the line between supervision and therapy become blurred. Because Tom is more comfortable in the clinical rather than the supervisory role at this point, he may move toward therapeutically treating Jason, his depression, his drinking, his depressed wife—an inappropriate quagmire to say the least.

The other, common to new supervisors graduated from the clinical staff, is that he may talk with Jason about his problems, even suggest that he seek outside help to deal with them, but fail to turn the corner and set clear boundaries and expectations—that Jason needs to come to work on time, that abuse of sick time is not acceptable. This can be difficult because of their past history. He will need your clarity and support to set these limits.

Supervisory Action

Empathize with Tom's mix of feelings and awkward situation. Treat Tom the way he needs to treat Jason, that is, insist that he understand while setting set clear expectations and limits in order to help Tom step into the middle-management role.

Staff and Ann

It's not surprising that the staff are upset about the budget cuts, and the fact that they feel comfortable to raise their questions (and emotions) in a staff meeting is a sign of good relationship between Ann and them. Ann's request that her supervisor come to the next team meeting is reasonable, but the question is why Ann couldn't answer the staff's questions herself?

Is she lacking information? Did her supervisor or those above her do a poor job of explaining the situation and the decision-making process? Did she know the facts, but is she ambivalent herself about the need for the cuts? Is she wanting her supervisor to come to the next meeting to provide support, to explain what she, Ann, doesn't know herself, or to place the supervisor in the role of the bearer of bad news because she doesn't agree with management, or is anxious about taking a stronger stand that might alienate her from her staff?

The supervisory concern is that Ann is not receiving clear information herself and feeling anxious and forced to scramble, is siding with staff and not backing the cuts but not openly saying so, or is anxious about using her power, and wants to stay within her more nurturing comfort zone. All these say something about the relationship with her supervisor or her own problems about learning.

Supervisory Action

Raise all these questions with Ann to find out the source of her lack of understanding. If she lacks knowledge, fill it in and also explore with her why. Given this information, see if she can cover this material herself at the next meeting. If she disagrees with the cuts, discover why, and respond to her the way she needs to respond to her staff, and clearly explain the rationale, options, and implications to reduce her anxiety and help address underlying concerns.

If Ann is anxious about being clear and firm with her staff, again explore what the emotional obstacles may be while also making it clear to her that this is in fact part of her role. Help her see that staff's reactions to her firmness are a separate problem that you can help her with. Finally, if she is on board with all of the above and she just needs your support, or feels that a unified managerial front would be valuable in the staff hearing and understanding the message, then plan to show up.

What we are sorting through here are the same issues that we faced with clinicians—What is their anxiety level and how does it interfere with their learning and practice? What are learning problems and what are problems about learning? How does the supervisory relationship help or hinder the solving of problems and the learning process? And once again we need to be alert to possible dynamics, we need to be proactive and raise hard questions, and we need to be curious about the source of problems and the inner workings of the person before us. Most of all we need to be clear and honest.

SHAPING THE SUPERVISION OF SUPERVISION PROCESS

What do you do to shape and facilitate the supervision of supervision process? The quick answer is do exactly the same as you do when working with a clinician. What is different is only in areas of focus, and the shift in goal to the development of supervisory skills and style rather than clinical ones.

As you do with clinicians, set aside designated times for supervision of supervision. For those supervisors who are still carrying a small clinical caseload, it's a good idea to have 2 separate sessions—one to focus on clinical work, one on supervision. Lay out clear expectations about the process—having agendas, whether recordings are expected, and so forth.

In this new relationship, even if it is with the same supervisor, the developmental tasks so well mastered in clinical work rise up again. This time around, due to having a firmer base of skills, self-confidence, and self-awareness, the process will likely move more quickly. But expect that this new supervisor can once again feel like a beginner who feels anxious about recordings and is worried about how well things are going and what you think. She may at first stumble and become confused. Eventually, however, with your support, things will settle down. She will begin to feel comfortable with the dynamics of this new relationship and perceive you as a source of advice and information. She will, with time, begin to translate her clinical skills and style into a supervisory style of her own.

Your start is like that of supervising the clinician: building a trusting, safe relationship, assessing and determining strengths and weaknesses in terms of knowledge and skills about supervision, looking ahead to possible problems about learning where emotions override what is intellectually known. Together set 6-month goals and objectives. Use your own clinical and supervisory skills to anticipate and manage the developmental challenges that come with each stage of the learning process. Approach your own anxiety so a new supervisor can learn to do the same. Model effective process. Help him understand how you think, how you set priorities, how you address larger systems concerns. Use self-disclosure to help him understand the supervisory life.

The use of recordings and observation is similar to that with clinicians. It helps you and a new supervisor to understand the supervisory process, to train the ear to hear what is being said or not said in a particular session, and to help isolate and eliminate supervisory stuckpoints. Observations can allow you to make suggestions in the session. Consider co-leading a clinical group or training together as a way of learning these skills. Use supervisory sessions as you would use sessions with a clinician—to balance what information you need to maintain quality control with what the supervisor needs for support and training.

Not all training will be covered in the confines of an office session. Just as clinicians can learn from readings, workshops, ongoing trainings, and direct contact with other supervisors, so too can clinical supervisors. One of the better ways to learn about community relationships, interagency committees, and the politics of agency life is to have the new supervisor tag along. He sits in the corner of the room and observes. He sits next to you at a meeting and becomes your assistant. The more public nature of these managerial duties lend themselves to this type of learning and involvement. If you have the time to provide these opportunities, take advantage of them.

The challenges of the learning process are similar to those facing the clinician. Stage 1 supervisors may struggle with anxiety, performance pressure, overresponsibility, and burnout. Stage 2 supervisors may become dependent upon you and more involved with clinicians, though the intensity, given the focus and increased experience, is likely to be less. Stage 3 supervisors are in danger of becoming restless or blind to personal limitations, to misuse power. Rather than seeing clients as resistant and prematurely terminating with them, they may have little tolerance for the antics of various staff and seek unnecessarily severe disciplinary action. Stage 4 supervisors may become bored and go on autopilot, or hopefully realize their strengths and limitations as both seasoned clinicians and supervisors.

Though the content of the work is more varied and expansive, though the responsibilities of middle management require stronger leadership and effective use of power, the day-to-day process remains essentially the same. Your challenges lie in helping new supervisors successfully make the transition, to use their clinical skills and style as a foundation on which to build and broaden their range. You want to help them discover new and untapped aspects of their personality and strengths.

BEING A SUPERVISOR OF SUPERVISORS

In many work settings, being a supervisor of supervisors means reaching the end of clinical line. Those above you may have completely shed the clinical facets of their jobs—they see themselves as immersed in administration and management—even if their roots lay in clinical work. While they are concerned about the quality of clinical work, their world and language are different—one of budgets and efficiency, of community relations and board priorities.

What this means for you is a couple of things. One is that you potentially lack a mentor for yourself in being a supervisor of supervisors. Yes, you have, hopefully, support, someone who can help you think through what is most on your supervisory plate and help you brainstorm approaches and priorities, but the clinical connection has long withered. The coach on how to do supervision, while demonstrating leadership and commitment, may fall short on practicalities and solid advice. The coach empathizes, but you find yourself needing more.

The emotional side of this is that you feel more and more isolated. The loneliness at the top is obviously greatest at the very top, but it seeps down the hierarchy. This too may be something that your supervisor can empathize with even if she, through no fault of her own, is part of the problem.

If you need someone to train you or coach you on the process of being a supervisor of supervisors, you need to be less isolated, seek out outside consultants, meet with other supervisors in your workplace, or look for trainings that can give you the tools or feedback that you may need. You would encourage your clinical and supervisory staff to do this, so why not you? Let your own supervisor know so she is involved and can be supportive, but if necessary, talk her language rather than yours—"I realize that I'm lacking these skills . . . and think that this training would help me be more effective and efficient and help those on my team to be more productive as well." Find the support you need rather than being the martyr and slogging through alone.

Professional Identity

Practice Behavior Example: *Practice personal reflection and self-correction to assure continual professional development.*

Critical Thinking Question: How do you handle isolation and loneliness? What supports do you need to manage these better?

Being a supervisor of supervisors can mean much more than just that you have moved up the hierarchy of the organization. See it as a testament of your own skill and experience. Make yourself as successful in this role as you have in all other roles that you have mastered before.

The following questions will test your application and analysis of the content found within this chapter. For additional assessment, including licensing-exam-type questions on applying chapter content to practice behaviors, visit **MySearchLab**.

1. Supervision of supervision refers to
   a. Making certain that clinicians are feeling supported in supervision
   b. Assessing your own skills as a supervisor
   c. Supervising the supervisory process of another supervisor
   d. Planning how supervision will be provided throughout an agency

2. Supervision of supervision is like supervision of a clinician in that
   a. Your primary supervisory focus is on the clinician, just as the supervisor's primary focus is on the client
   b. Both require that you apply your clinical skills to assess and develop a supervisory plan
   c. Both require budgetary skills
   d. Both focus on the client's problems and treatment

3. Molly is a new supervisor who has many years of clinical experience. When starting your supervision of her supervision, you can safely assume that
   a. The transition will be smooth because she can share her clinical skills with her supervisees
   b. She and you are essentially starting again at Stage 1 in her developmental process as a supervisor
   c. Her strong clinical skills will easily help her take on a leadership role in the wider community
   d. She will quickly become dependent upon you

4. Simon seems overwhelmed by all the new tasks he has as a new supervisor. To help him feel less overwhelmed it would be most helpful for you to
   a. Assess what new skills he needs to learn to better handle the new responsibilities
   b. Reduce his anxiety by reassuring him he is doing a good job
   c. Take over some of the responsibilities from him or assign them to another staff member
   d. Talk with him about stress management

5. Ramon, a new supervisor, is supervising a few of his former colleagues and is having difficulty setting firm limits with them regarding timelines. How, as his supervisor, would you handle this?

6. Maggie, a new supervisor, has strong clinical skills but often seems socially anxious and awkward in community meetings. How would you help her become more comfortable and confident?

12

Management: Hire/Fire and Everything In-Between

Competencies Applied with Practice Behaviors — in This Chapter				
▪ Professional Identity	▪ Ethical Practice	✖ Critical Thinking	✖ Diversity in Practice	▪ Human Rights & Justice
▪ Research-Based Practice	✖ Human Behavior	✖ Policy Practice	▪ Practice Contexts	▪ Engage, Assess, Intervene, Evaluate

As suggested in Chapter 11, the life of a supervisor is rarely just about supervision. There are staff to hire, retain, and sometimes fire; reports to write; statistics to gather and budget numbers to crunch; committees to attend; and staff meetings to plan and run. In this chapter we will cover a range of management topics and tips on how to be an effective leader.

LEADERSHIP ESSENTIALS

You probably know what you don't want to do based upon your own experience with supervisors and bosses—be critical, be micromanaging, be neglectful. But what do you do instead? Here are the skills and tasks and ways of thinking about your job that are essential to good leadership.

Be the Role Model You Are

Like it or not you are a role model for those you supervise and manage. Yes, some staff will be more sensitive to you than others depending on their own stages of development and personalities, but you can't escape having some impact on everyone. You set the pace, and you shape the work culture. So be aware, and be deliberate.

Begin with a vision of who you want to be. What is it that you want your staff to notice and appreciate most about you and your style—your ability to listen, your sense of courtesy and respect, your professionalism, your creativity? What is it that you want your staff to feel most about their jobs—that they can make a difference, that they can clinically grow, that they feel supported, that they are part of a creative team? What you focus upon, what you talk about, what you demonstrate tells your staff what you value. Say it; show it.

Listen and Talk

Just as openness is a sign of a strong supervisory relationship, openness is a sign of a strong team. You need to listen to staff individually and collectively. They need to learn by experience that they can come to you with problems and concerns, which will be heard and understood, respectively, even if not always agreed with. If they hold back or fear criticism, you lose your leadership role. You become the drill sergeant who they may passive-aggressively comply with, but they learn to turn to each other for support and listening. If you seem to listen but fail to understand or act, they see you as neglectful or unreliable and again learn to take care of themselves or get support from others.

You also want to talk. You ask the hard questions so your staff know what is okay for them to talk about—their job satisfaction, their worries about change, their frustrations with new policies and procedures—the elephant in the room that everyone is trying to ignore. Because you are part of middle management, you are the buffer between staff and upper management. Your skill comes in titrating information. You want to let staff know enough about what is happening above them—budget information, staff changes—so they don't become anxious because they don't know what is going on and imagine the worst. You also don't want to be unfiltering—saying too much about things they can't control that leaves them feeling only more anxious. So you need to figure out the balance—a steady stream of updates, letting them know what is and is not happening, information about timelines and deadlines, a reassurance that they need to just do their jobs and that you and others will take care of the rest, that you will keep them informed, and that they can come to you with questions if they get worried.

You also want to tell your staff about what you are doing. It's easy for them to misunderstand what you do. They see you gone for hours to meetings that they have no knowledge of, or out of town for conferences, or holed up in your office as you sift through budget reports and projections. Again, what they don't know they will make up and imagine. So let them know what you do on a regular basis—that you are working on a new interagency committee, that you are needing to write new policies and procedures, that on the state level the focus is on . . . with a deadline of . . . and you are responsible for . . . and the implications for their work are. . . . Let them know how you spend your time.

And let them know how you feel. This doesn't mean that you have to be transparent about your personal life, but define what you sense they see so they don't reach their own wrong conclusions—if I seem a bit preoccupied lately, it is because I'm . . . ; I will be less available in the next few days because. . . . This too helps reduce overall anxiety and serves as a model for their own communication and self-responsibility.

How you carry out this communication depends on your own style and structure of your staff. Weekly emails from you to them updating on you and your work and current concerns may be effective if staff have irregular schedules or are scattered at different sites. If you rely on staff meetings, be proactive in the same way you need to be with group supervision. Meetings that meet only because they are scheduled or pertain to the interests of only a couple of people are seen as boring and a waste of time. Decide on a format, have a clear purpose, and set the pace. Have a way of transmitting information—a follow-up email, posting minutes of the meeting—to those who are unable to attend. If the meeting seems to be not accomplishing what you want it to accomplish—be a forum for open discussion, is poorly attended, seems stiff and boring—talk about the process itself and get feedback about how to make it more effective and efficient.

Have Clear Expectations, Standards, Actions

An inconsistent leader is seen as unreliable, not trustworthy. Staff learn that what you say doesn't really matter because it will change, that what you say you will do may not get done. They learn to be inconsistent themselves and/or turn to each other for support. Like children living with alcoholic parents, they can become both hypervigilant and anxious because there is no clear structure that they can lean on.

So say what you mean and do what you say. This is how staff learn to take you seriously and learn what are priorities. Being consistent doesn't mean being rigid. It doesn't mean that you can't change your mind at times. You can—priorities may shift because of happenings above you, changes may need to be made in routines and procedures because they are not working. Proactive change is part of being responsible. Pragmatism is part and parcel of effective growth. But you need to explain your thinking, give sufficient notice, and provide time for transitions. You don't want to give the appearance of being erratic and emotionally driven. This causes staff to feel crazy and encourages them to do the same.

Be Realistically Optimistic

In *Leading at the Edge*, Perkins, Holtman, Kessler, and McCarthy (2000) explore the leadership style of Ernest Shackleton during the 2 years he and his crew were stranded in Antarctic. High among Shackleton's qualities that enabled the crew to survive was his optimism combined with a realistic assessment of the situation.

Even though you may struggle with getting the support you need from above, you need to be like Shackleton and adapt the right attitude and perspective. This does not mean that you deny or sugarcoat reality—budget constraints, caseload or staffing challenges—but you show confidence that problems can be solved, that obstacles can be overcome. Be positive and give positives to your staff to help them stay creative and focused.

Think Individual, Think Team

Jared seems to be always complaining about something lately—if it is not about the new forms, it is about the mandatory meeting on Friday. As a supervisor you may see this as a morale problem that Jared is having and, you will want to sit down with him to discover what else might be contributing to his change in attitude.

But you also want to wonder if Jared's disgruntlement is being felt by others, though they may be less vocal than Jared. As a supervisor you want to keep your ear close to the ground to detect problems in their early stages. Your skills come into play in sorting out what is an individual's problem and what is a reflection of larger team concerns. The easiest way to determine this is to ask—Are others having problems with the new forms? Is the purpose of the Friday meeting unclear? Is the time particularly inconvenient? If not, the issue is one you need to address with Jared. If yes, you need to gather more feedback from staff, refine your message, and decide what changes and compromises, if any, you are willing and able to make.

As a supervisor working with a range of staff, it is easy to think in terms of the individuals—how Tamara is different from Alan in skill and style, what are the supervisory and clinical goals for Ann. But you also need to think in terms of the team dynamics—What is the level of morale, What are the values and culture you most want to create and foster, What is the overall team atmosphere? You think about them, you say them, and you find ways to put them into action: a sign-out board so that others know when someone is out in the field and can be checked on if seeming to be running late; team traditions of annual picnics or Christmas parties complete with contests for the worst caroling; a quick response to questions and concerns so that staff learn that you are reliable and open. As with other areas of supervision you don't need to have all the answers and details; you need to get the issues and priorities out in the open for discussion and input.

Treat Everyone Equally and Fairly

Or, stated in the negative, don't have favorites. What we are tapping into here is the sibling dynamics that quickly can get played out. Shelly, for example, doesn't understand why Jodi has the cubicle near the window; Tom is upset that Ann is going to the state conference while his request was turned down. The downside of a close team environment is that old family dynamics become stirred, complete with competition, feelings of jealousy, and casting into old family roles. Particularly powerful is perceived favoritism—that you are being biased in your response to some people. It is the type of behavior that can not only hurt morale but cause staff to leave.

What we are talking about here is about ground rules and clear criteria for decisions. Obviously, if Ellen is a new clinician struggling to get her clinical feet on the ground, you are not going to cap the amount of supervision you provide so that others don't get upset. You may need to see her twice a week just to reduce your own anxiety—that's fine. Similarly, you are going to have unique individual relationships with your team members based on personality and role. You may seek out Beth's advice because she is a senior clinician on the staff. You may talk about baseball with Tom because you both enjoy following it. Again, that's fine. What you are looking for is balance—not leaving someone out, not providing perks be they office choices, training opportunities, or time off without clear and consistent rationale and method—you use seniority or specific clinical goals or clear level of need—that you can explain and defend and is perceived as fair.

And if you are worrying that you are being seen by some as biased, you need to pay attention to this perception and address it, individually with the staff who are concerned, or with the team in explaining how decisions are made. Not everyone is going to be happy with your decisions, but that is different from feeling unfairly treated. If someone does, you need not cave in and accommodate, but you do need to do your best to listen and clarify.

TIME AND TASKS

The leadership essentials can be looked upon as a behavioral map of your role. Another way of mapping your work is in terms of time and duties. In his popular book, *The 7 Habits of Highly Effective People*, Stephen Covey (2004) talks about the type of tasks a manager may encounter. He essentially divides tasks into 2 dimensions—tasks that are important or not important according to your job description, and those that are urgent or not urgent in terms of time requirements. The combinations can be represented in the following table.

Here are 4 possible combinations: tasks that are urgent and not important, urgent and important, not urgent and important, and not urgent and not important. This is a handy way of looking at both the tasks that you do throughout a day or week and what your supervisees are doing with their time. As we move through the 4 combinations, think about how you use your time or how you have used your time in past workplaces.

Urgent and Not Important

You get a call from human resources at 9:00 in the morning. For state reporting, they need to know the number of children under 5 years of age whom you served in the past 6 months, and they need the data by 12 noon. Or, you get a call from the city government and they want to know how many clients seen in the last year live in a particular section of the city, and they want the information by 5:00 the next day.

These are urgent tasks in that you are under a deadline. Though they are important tasks of human resources or the city government, they are not important in terms of your own or your staff's primary tasks, such as seeing clients would be. If you find that you or your clinical staff are spending a lot of time on tasks like these—culling through case records, looking up dates on databases—that takes away from clinical work, the question you want to ask yourself is why.

The answer is usually that your team infrastructure is weak. You need more administrative support—hiring an administrative assistant, finding a volunteer—to hand these tasks off to, rather than using up valuable staff time. If you need to make a case for this to your own supervisor, you need to speak her language, that of effectiveness and efficiency, and show how much time is being used for urgent and not important tasks, and how that time can be allocated to clinical work and often clinical fees.

> ### Policy Practice
>
> ***Practice Behavior Example:*** *Understand that policy affects service delivery and they actively engage in policy practice.*
>
> **Critical Thinking Question:** If you discovered that your staff was spending excessive time on urgent and not important tasks, what policy or procedures would you advocate for?

Figure 12.1 • Tasks

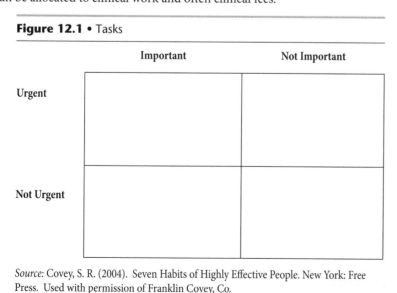

	Important	Not Important
Urgent		
Not Urgent		

Source: Covey, S. R. (2004). *Seven Habits of Highly Effective People.* New York: Free Press. Used with permission of Franklin Covey, Co.

Urgent and Important

These are tasks that have time constraints but are also essential to your and your staff's jobs. The most obvious example is the clinical crisis—a teen who is suicidal, a client who has stopped taking medication and is psychotic, a report of child abuse. Something needs to be done quickly, and this requires your or your staff's primary clinical skills.

But if you or your staff are spending a lot of time on situations like these, and your jobs are not full-time crisis or emergency services, you need to again ask why. There are a few possible reasons. One is that staff are lacking certain clinical skills. Situations turn into crises because the clinicians are missing the signs of potential problems—for example, not catching that the teen is really suicidally depressed, or not tracking whether Mr. Smith is taking his medications or not noticing the initial signs that he is psychologically deteriorating. Look for patterns—are there particular staff who seem to have clients who are in crisis? Is it due to the nature of the caseload or does it say something about skills that you need to address? If it is more wide-spread across the team, you might wonder if there is a need for training across the board.

Or the cause may be something else. It may be that clinicians are too rushed—they have too many other things to do that result in their overlooking signs of impending problems. It may also be that important information is being missed at initial intakes or assessments—that medications aren't tracked at all, for example—or that it is a coordination and communication problem—that the clinician is thinking that the medication clinic is checking Mr. Smith's medication and so she didn't bother to track this information as part of her clinical work.

Or it may be part of the team culture that is being set by you or those above you. One of the leadership styles we discussed initially was the crisis-oriented leader. This is the person who functions well and actually thrives on crisis situations—the urgent and important—but easily becomes bored and unfocused with more mundane situations. This type of leader is always in danger of feeling stretched too far (warranting in his mind the need to unwind in noncrisis times), or has trouble setting priorities, missing the precrisis cues that problems are at hand. The end result is that situations can go unattended until they result in crisis. Because of the role-modeling of the supervisor, this type of leadership often creates a staff who come to respond similarly. The entire team winds up functioning in a reactive way.

If a frequent crisis response is a symptom, step back and figure out the problem. If it is about skill or need for coordination, or about lack of time or reactive culture, determine the source and then focus on changing it. Again, if the problem comes from above—the work demands are unrealistic—or if your supervisor's style is reactive and crisis-oriented, again talk his language, and help him see how his behavior is trickling down and affecting the efficiency and effectiveness of the staff.

Not Urgent and Important

Unless you are doing crisis work as your job, this arena is where you and your staff should ideally spend most of the working time. Important and not urgent tasks are proactive and essential to your job. They certainly will include clinical supervision, but also interagency committees and budget issues. This is also those times where you are stepping back, looking at the big picture, and setting out 3-, 6-, or 12-month goals for you, for your team, and for individual clinicians.

Box 12.1 provides an example of what such proactive, 6-month review and goal setting might look like.

Box 12.1 • Supervisory 6-Month Review and Goal Setting

Clinical Review

Predominate types of client presenting problems. Change?

Demographics of client population.

Wait-list time.

No show rates.

Average length of treatment.

Implications

Need for staff training regarding specific problem areas?

Need for outreach/PR to other populations in community?

Do changes reflect changes in larger community response?

Intake process—need to be more efficient?

Staff not setting clear expectations with clients? Need for appointment reminders?

Are there underlying logistical/transportation problems for clients regarding appointments?

Administrative Review

Budget

Revenues—making targets? If not, why not?

Expenses—within limits? Overages—where? Why?

Receiving data needed for tracking budget?

Quality Control

Clinical records up-to-date and complete?

Client satisfaction evaluations positive? If not, areas of concern?

Community

Coordination with other agencies—communication flow efficient and effective? Areas of concern?

Services—any holes in services, needs not being addressed?

Implications

Revenue—need to coordinate better with billing services. Consider need for staff training. Discuss with management reapportion of revenue to other line items.

Records—need for revising forms? Discuss with staff setting of paperwork deadlines.

Community—need for PR to correct impressions of services.

Staff Review

Staff caseloads—manageable? Evenly distributed?

Staff morale, energy, cooperation—level?

Overall quality of staff clinical work?

Staff satisfaction with supervision/upper management?

Implications

Need to increase staff? Do cost–benefit analysis.

Need to look at shorter-term clinical models.

Improving morale—need for more communication to staff, need for retreats, input on goals.

Supervision—allocation of more time, possible use groups to supplement.

Upper management—discuss value in their meeting with staff on a regular basis.

Obviously, the content will vary depending on the nature of the work setting and your responsibilities, but the purpose is to see what is working well and what is not, and to brainstorm next action steps. This type of focus creates the infrastructure that helps keep priorities clear, maximizes coordination, and helps prevent crises from flaring.

For your clinical staff, important and not urgent tasks will certainly be client contacts. It should also be the paperwork connected to it—charting, billing if those are essential aspects of their jobs. This is where problems sometimes arise with staff. While you realize that paperwork is one of their essential tasks, they do not. If clinicians have this attitude, they are not understanding (or you are not enforcing) the business side of clinical practice. They do not understand that supportive paperwork is what keeps the operation running. Your challenge is to help staff understand that these too are essential aspects of their job.

But like you, they too should have an opportunity to step back and review and plan their own work and goals. This is the purpose of self-evaluation. Such a proactive stance should be part and parcel of their work. Your job is to both model and encourage it in them.

Not Urgent and Not Important

It's easy to cast this combination aside and see it as irrelevant to the everyday work world. After all, even if something isn't urgent, it should at least seem to be important, shouldn't it? What goes in this space are tasks that are, perhaps, more marginally tied to your job description—organizing your cubicle or office, learning a new supplemental software program, reading a book or journal in an area, a bit outside your everyday practice.

But what also goes in this area are opportunities for brainstorming and creativity. These are the times when you put your feet up on the desk and mull over your clinical or supervisory practice. You think and brainstorm about gaps in services or intake systems, about the new, creative ways of training staff or students, and about possible effective time management tools.

This type of off-task, not-urgent thinking often leads to sudden creative insights that can become the precursors for those not urgent and important tasks of formal evaluation, goal setting, and strategy planning. Herbert Benson (2004), the originator of the Relaxation Response, and the Harvard researcher on mindfulness and creativity, talks about this downtime as essential for triggering what he calls *The Breakout Principle* where problem solving can move to a new level and different parts of the brain are actually activated and come into play. You may come up with new ideas that can re-shape how you work. You bring into play other aspects of your personality and creative process.

Mapping out your and your staff work time along these 4 dimensions helps you see where task priorities may fall. As a proactive supervisor or clinician, a majority of your time should be in the not urgent and important arena. Next might come the urgent and important tasks—those work-related crises—but again unless you are in a crisis unit these should be minimal. Next would be the creative aspects—the not urgent and not important tasks—and then finally the urgent and not important tasks—these again should be managed by supportive staff as much as possible.

Where does your own time and tasks lie? Think about how you might reorganize your work to better utilize your own and your staff's time.

HIRING: THE PREPARATION

"Take your time to find the right person for the job" is the sound advice you will often hear from personnel experts. It makes sense. It not only takes time to interview and hire a new employee, but takes even more time and money to train and get him solidly on board. To find out weeks or months later that you made a poor decision is always awkward and costly. Not only is it disruptive to you and the newly hired person, it is equally disruptive to other staff who may have begun to connect to this colleague, as well as to clients who may have formed a therapeutic relationship with the person even if the level of service is not what you hoped.

That said, there are times when reality sets in and you feel under the gun. Luke, for example, suddenly decides to resign because his wife is starting graduate school in another state. Not only do you have his entire caseload to transfer and manage, but you already have a waiting list for services that your own supervisor is feeling none too happy about. You realize that you can't afford to hold out for the perfect candidate.

You need to go into these situations with your eyes wide open. This means not taking whoever you can find, but rather being clear about your priorities. The most important criteria are personality, skill level, and team complementarity. Let's look at each one.

> ### Diversity in Practice
>
> **Practice Behavior Example:** *Understand how diversity characterizes and shapes the human experience and is critical to the formation of identity.*
>
> **Critical Thinking Question:** If you were to create your own "dream team" regarding clinical skills and staff diversity, what would it be?

Personality

If you have to choose between skills and personality, the rule is always go for personality. Why? Because skills can be taught, and personality cannot. If you hire someone who is prone to complaining, for example, not only will he be a drain on you, his attitude is likely to drain or infect others on the team, hurting morale. Your opportunities for changing such behavior are limited and cumbersome. What you are looking for are candidates who seem to have energy, are optimistic, are open, ideally have a sense of humor, and are flexible—showing the qualities of an anxiety approacher. What you want to avoid are candidates who seem overly anxious, are closed, are rigid, are perfectionistic, or have negative attitudes.

You can generally sense these qualities in an interview. If you feel energized, relaxed, and engaged during the interview process, these are good signs that clients are likely to feel the same. If you feel closed or bored, find yourself being careful about how you say things, have difficulty following what the person is saying, or hear a lot of negativity, these are red flags that others too are likely to have the same response.

Skill Level

It is important to decide before interviewing what essential skills the new staff person needs to have, and how much time you or someone else has to train and fill in gaps.

If you're replacing Luke, for example, who worked primarily with adults, you'll be looking for someone with those skills and not worry about whether she is able to do play therapy. Similarly, if Luke was a senior person with supervisory responsibilities, you'll not be interviewing new graduates. Suppose Luke, however, was seeing adults and children and doing supervision. If you find someone strong in 2 out of the 3 areas, part of your hiring decision requires gauging what it might take to fill in that last skill-set.

If an applicant has exceptionally strong clinical skills, for example, could you imagine her moving into a supervisory role in a few months with your support? Do you have time to supervise her clinically and later supervisorily? If not you, who could? If she has solid experience providing supervision and adult work, but is weak in child therapy, would attending a couple of workshops on child work be enough to provide the level of service you need? Could she share a few cases with someone on your staff strong in child therapy as a way of building this skill, or should you perhaps shift child responsibilities to someone else on your staff, or continue looking for someone else?

Obviously you are not going to be able to answer all these questions in advance. You will need to see what your applicant pool offers. What is important is taking the time to think through possible scenarios as a way of becoming clear about your priorities.

Complementarity

Another part of your decision in choosing new staff is hiring those who will be able to add to, adjust to, and ultimately fit into the team or agency culture. This is partially about skills and experience—for example, the ability to work with patients with AIDS, or who can speak Spanish, or have experience within protective services—but also partially about values—for example, a commitment to the psychosocial perspective of social work, or the agency's mission to reduce the causes of poverty, or even a team's belief in flexible scheduling and being a support to each other to alleviate stress. This can be subtle, and though you cannot predict precisely how well someone may or may not fit in, it is another item that you will need to pay attention to when interviewing. Someone with very different values and work culture experience may not only feel out of place, have difficulty connecting with colleagues, and feel frustrated, but may become an undertow to your team process.

But there is something to be said for too much compatibility. Weak, insecure leaders tend to surround themselves with individuals who are clones of their own thinking, while strong, self-confident leaders are not afraid of diversity and welcome staff who have unique points of view. Benson, in applying his Breakout Principle to group creativity, echoes the same idea by urging leaders to "synchronize, not homogenize" their staff. If everyone's point of view is essentially the same, there may be quick consensus and little conflict, but also little energy for new ideas and solutions. You certainly want people who believe in the team mission, but real group creativity, says Benson, comes from the "grating" of different perspectives and personalities.

So look for the mix. If your team primarily comes from one particular clinical orientation—psychodynamic, for example—consider hiring someone who is more behavioral- or systems-oriented just to inject a different way of thinking. If your staff tend to be active and action-oriented, consider adding to the mix someone who is more reflective and philosophical. Avoid polarization but welcome variety. Blend and balance the best of differences.

Critical Thinking

Practice Behavior Example: Use critical thinking augmented by creativity and curiosity.

Critical Thinking Question: Think about your past job interviews. What would you want to incorporate or change to create a more effective process?

Taking the time to do this type of preparation makes the hiring process more effective and efficient by helping you organize and focus the screening process. Now that you know what you need, let's move on to the hiring process itself.

HIRING: THE PROCESS

You've probably personally chalked up a wide range of hiring experiences—the long applications, the never-hear-back-no-response response, phone interviews, group interviews, probing questions, short vignettes, the occasional snap decision. Large agencies often have a formal hiring process that grows in complexity the higher up the ladder you go, while smaller agencies can be more flexible and idiosyncratic in their approach. Whatever the process, the goal is to match candidates with your criteria and needs. Let's walk through the process step by step; once again compare these suggestions against your own experience and preferences.

Screening

You have a stack of applications and resumes. Do an initial sort, eliminating those who do not match the job qualifications—"While I do not have any formal training, I have 3 children of my own and feel I can relate well to them"; "Although I do not have any degree, I believe that my 20 years of addiction can provide a valuable insider perspective to treatment."—Good intentions but not fitting the skill criteria that you have already mapped out.

Next you look for those with the most experience in settings and with services similar to your own—worked at social services in a different state, worked at a community mental health center in the next town doing essentially the same work. You also find those who are moving up—a former case manager who finished her degree and is now applying for a clinical position; a protective service worker with a degree who now wants to move to a mental health agency. You also find new graduates with only field placement experience but strong coursework in your field. Here is where you try and match applications with your criteria. You don't know much about personality at this point, but you can sort through skill level and complementarity.

With this winnowed-down pile, some supervisors move toward setting up interviews, but some winnow further by doing telephone interviews. Why? Because it saves time. With a quick phone call you can provide an applicant with a more detailed description of the job, and answer any make-or-break questions that might eliminate him from the applicant pool—What is the starting salary? If I come in at 6 a.m., can I leave at 2 to pick up my kids from school? Can I start in 3 months after I get back from my cross-country trip? You also can get a sense of the individual's presentation. By calling applicants, you are catching them off guard. You can tell from their voice their energy; by their responses how well they can think on their feet.

You can frame the phone call simply by saying, "Hi, this is . . . from. . . . You have applied for a clinical position with us. I'm just contacting applicants to see if they have any particular questions about the job that they need answered before we schedule interviews," and then you listen for what they say next. Do they sound energetic or depressed and distracted? Do they formulate clear questions, or are they rambling about unable to organize their thoughts? All this obviously doesn't replace a face-to-face interview (unless they live too far to travel), but it does help you screen out those with misimpressions about the work or who may not be a good fit.

Interviewing

The purpose of an interview is two-sided: to help the applicant understand the job, know the work culture, see the work space, and meet you; and to help you understand more about the person's experience and skills, as well as her professional presentation. Some agencies require a structured interview process with each candidate being asked the same set of questions; some even send candidates the questions in advance. Other settings allow for a less formal, more conversational interview process.

Regardless of interview style, you want to map out questions to ask to be certain that you end the interview knowing what you need to know. After describing the parameters and duties of the position, here is a sample of list of typical questions, along with rationale for the question, that you might ask a clinician.

I noticed you have worked at. . . . Can you tell more about your experience there?

You need to know specifics to see how the work and skills compare to your position. If there are any gaps in time on the resume, ask about those as well.

Why are you seeking to leave your current position? (if applicable)

This tells you something about personal ambitions—I want a more clinical position, I want to work more with children—or personal frustrations—I felt too isolated, I had a difficult time with my supervisor, the hours were interfering with my family life—which give you a clue about possible concerns that may arise if working with you.

Why are you applying for this position?

The other side of the previous question. Stage 1 clinicians will often talk about helping others, making a difference, and so on.

Tell me about your clinical orientation and style.

You want to see how they may fit and complement current staff, but you also want to hear how well they can articulate their own approach. Generally, the more experienced, the more clear and detailed the response.

How do you learn best?

Are they self-aware to answer this question well? Does their style fit your own? Does it give you an idea of how much training they might need?

What type of clients and/or problem areas do you work with best? Least?

Here you are learning about strengths and learning problems—I have a lot of experience working with autistic children; I'm interested in working with geriatric clients but haven't had much experience with them—but also problems about learning—I have a difficult time working with victims of sexual abuse because of my own personal history; I have a hard time confronting aggressive men—as well as self-awareness.

What do you foresee might be the greatest challenge of this job for you?

This question again tells you about learning problems and problems about learning. You are also looking for thoughtful honesty—"I think working with the aggressive male clients . . . "—rather than "This sounds great, I can't think of anything!"

What do you need most from supervision? Have you ever had a difficult time with a supervisor? Can you tell me about it?

What they say they need from supervision tells you about learning style, training needs, self-awareness, and anxiety, but also about expectations and whether you can or can't meet them.

Similarly, understanding an applicant's past problems with a supervisor can tell you of needs and dangers. While saying that my past supervisor was too critical or not available says something about needs for positive feedback or availability, you also want to understand how it was handled by the applicant. Did he suffer in silence, pull away, get angry, or approach professionally? Was it one of the reasons he left? Is there a danger that she might be saying the same thing about you 6 months from now?

Again, self-awareness and a balanced perspective are important. To say that my past supervisor was just too controlling is very different from saying that my past supervisor had a somewhat micromanaging style, and while it fine for some, it didn't fit my own way of working.

Can you tell me about a clinical experience you had with a client that you felt bad about? What effect did it have, if any, on your practice?

This is about self-reflection and openness, but it is also about ability to take risks and keep perspective. It's okay to make what later seems to be a mistake, but it's not productive to continue to castigate yourself, or become frightened or too cautious as a result. If the applicant has no regrets, the question is why and whether he tends to be anxiety binding or lay responsibility totally on the client.

Can you tell me about a clinical experience you had with a client that you feel particularly good about or proud of?

How does she measure success in her work? Is it about effort, about outcome? Can she appreciate those moments, or is she prone to perfectionism, self-criticism, or minimizing of her own contribution? This says much about managing stress and avoiding burnout.

What ways do you have of managing your stress?

This is the antidote to burnout itself—playing golf, going fishing, watching kung fu movies. It's less about what he does and more about realizing the need to do something to keep his life in balance.

You can probably think of other questions suitable to your work environment. The theme here is understanding an applicant's skills, past professional relationships, and ways of managing the emotional wear and tear of the work itself. You're listening to the content, but you are also watching the process. Is he overly anxious—tripping over his own words, getting scattered, and having trouble articulating his ideas? Is he too controlled and binding so that you feel little connection, little personality, too little warmth? Is he too hypervigilant, watching you and your reactions too closely, rather than being confident enough to speak his mind?

Is he aware of the process in the room—realizing that he is rambling, saying he doesn't understand, taking the time to be thoughtful. Is he professionally appropriate—not going off into a long emotional story about his own childhood, his string of complaints about past employers? Most of all, how do you feel in the conversation—engaged, interested, bored, concerned, distracted?

Box 12.2 presents a checklist of interview topics and impressions.

Box 12.2 • Interview Checklist

Does the applicant have clinical experience and strengths most needed for the position?

Is the applicant energetic; seem to have a sense of humor, a positive outlook? Does she have healthy ways of managing stress?

Is the applicant able to articulate his clinical style? Define clinical goals?

Is the applicant able to make mistakes, take acceptable risks?

Is the applicant able to define her learning style? Articulate what he needs most from supervision?

Is the applicant able to manage his anxiety in the interview? Able to be proactive and ask questions?

Can the applicant be reflective but not overly critical of past supervisors/jobs?

Do you see the applicant fitting in well with other staff? Does her clinical style offer something new to the team?

Do you feel energized in the interview?

Would you personally go to this person for therapy?

Clinical Vignettes

In addition to these questions, you may want to give applicants clinical vignettes for them to respond to as a way of understanding their skills and orientations. There are 2 types: the short, verbal vignette that you give during the interview, and the longer, written vignette that you have applicants do after the interview itself.

A short vignette might go like this: "I want to give you a short clinical vignette. You are working at a school and a little boy pulls you aside and shows you welts on one of his legs. What would you do?"

The interviewee may go into a long explanation of how she would talk with the boy and help him feel safe, and ask about his home life, but if she doesn't say pretty quickly "and I would call protective services to report possible child abuse," she got the question wrong. This type of short vignette is good for determining awareness of suicidal risk, a variety of abuse situations, and symptoms of major diagnoses such as depression. The answer is less about the candidate's own clinical orientation and style and more about base knowledge and ability to assess and act quickly.

The written vignette does allow for assessing clinical style. Here you have a clinical scenario written out and you send candidates off to a quiet space with pen and paper to write out answers. An example of such questions might be: "The Harris family comes for their first appointment referred by 10-year-old Brian's school guidance counselor. Brian has been having behavioral problems at school—he is aggressive with other children and has difficulty paying attention in class. There is a 14-year-old sister also in the home. Mr. and Ms. Harris have been married for 16 years, and admit to having separated several times in the past, the most recent time was 2 years ago.

Given this background, what are your initial impressions, concerns about this family? What would be your goal or goals for the first session? For subsequent sessions? Who would you see, what information would you gather? What possible diagnosis are you considering? What adjunct services would you consider, if any? What would be your own challenges with this case?"

You could ask a similar question about a couple and their presentation in the first session, or about a seriously mentally ill client faced with an array of environmental stressors. What these longer cases provide is an understanding of the way applicants conceptualize clients and problems. An applicant may focus on Brian with a parenting/behavioral approach, or might wonder about marital stress carrying over to Brian and school, or worry about attention deficit disorder and medication, or doing family therapy, play therapy, couple therapy, or some combination.

Because individuals often write how they think, you can discover not only what they think, but how clearly they think—do they present their ideas about diagnosis or treatment approaches clearly, or is their thinking more jumbled, more vague? You can also note their management of the exercise itself. Do they write 1 or 12 pages? Does it take them 15 minutes or an hour, again reflecting perhaps their anxiety, ability to formulate quickly. Finally, having a written document allows you to compare applicants side by side, or to share assignments with other colleagues to get their impressions.

Second Opinions

Having another set of eyes as part of the interview process can help you sort through those tough choices. How you do this depends upon your own style and time availability of others. Some supervisors may have a trusted colleague sit in on all interviews; some have a colleague sit in on 2 or 3 finalists. Some will do all the interviewing themselves, but if unsure and wanting a second opinion, ask a colleague to do a separate second interview or do a second interview together.

The format is less important than accomplishing the goal of determining the best candidate for the job. If you are going to be the supervisor, it makes the most sense that you have the largest say in who is hired, and that you have a primary role in the interview process, even if someone else may do the initial screening. Again, try to resist feeling boxed in by time and need and avoid simply settling for what you might get.

If you are unhappy with your applicant pool, it's worthwhile to step back and determine why. Is it a problem with how or where the position is advertised? Are there key issues affecting the pool, such as salary or hours, that can be reconsidered? Do you need to rethink how to manage the opening until later—such as late spring or summer when new graduates will be seeking positions? Oftentimes your supervisor or human resources staff can help you sort through these issues.

Some supervisors like to include some or, if a team is small, all of their staff in the interview process. Again, this is a matter of style. What you as a supervisor want to be clear about at the onset is the role staff might take. Are they to actually make recommendations on final applicants, and how much weight does their opinion carry? Are they more consultants to your own decision making? Is their role one of supplementing the interview process by giving applicants a clinician's point of view about the work and the workplace? Is it an after-the-fact opportunity for staff to meet with the new clinician and start the team-bonding process?

Decide what your purpose is so you can be clear with staff and applicants and not set up distorted expectations. Obviously you'll want to consider the time and ultimately the cost of assembling staff together for an interview. Most of all don't abdicate your own responsibility and needs. You are the person who needs to supervise and guide this person toward his own clinical development and your own assessment of team needs. Assume leadership: Be clear in your decisions and be clear about the purpose of staff input. If staff are unhappy with your decision, treat it as a separate problem; don't let it undermine your judgment and needs.

References

References are usually required as part of the application process. But as most human resources specialists will tell you, they have a limited value. If an applicant puts down a professional who also is his friend, what you will hear is what the applicant asked the friend to say, or at best the friend's opinion filtered through the friendship. Contact with former employers also can provide limited information—for example, the dates the person was employed, or impressions from a former supervisor that have grown vague with time or no longer are relevant 6 or 7 years later.

Information from current employers would seem to be the most useful, but here again you need to be careful. A poor employee evaluation is clearly a cause for concern, but so can be a glowing one. A recommendation that is bit too enthusiastic may be the employer's way of fixing a problem, namely, "moving along" a clinician whose work is mediocre or poor. A more balanced appraisal—one that cites the applicant's strengths and weaknesses—is probably not only the most realistic, but ultimately the most helpful to you as a future employer.

HOLDING STEADY: DISCIPLINARY ACTION

You finally hire the best person you can find and feel satisfied in your decision. Now you move on to the stages of development. You take time to orient the new person to the team and to the work, and you focus on lowering her anxiety, creating trust, and teaching skills. Things are overall going well, but then small problems begin to show up—coming in late to work or to meetings, not completing paperwork on time. You need to take action.

While the notion of discipline carries all kinds of parental overtones, in your role as manager discipline is about maintaining standards of job performance and professional conduct, and, as mentioned earlier, ultimately a system of fair and consistent treatment. Agencies usually have a host of disciplinary policies and procedures that apply to all staff, sorted by severity of the offense—from the verbal warning to written warning to eventual or summary terminations. If you are a new supervisor or personally shy away from confrontation, holding staff's feet to the fire can be awkward or difficult. Here are suggestions on ways to keep staff accountable and professional.

Nip It in the Bud

If Jake is coming late to meetings, don't wait until he has done this 12 times before calling him on it. If Tamara fails to turn in her assessment summaries on time, don't let this drag out for weeks or months. You don't need to be a micromanager, but you do want to address issues quickly. Why? One reason is perception of other staff. If it seems like Jake can get away with coming in late and it continues, it will seem like favoritism and unfair to others, affecting staff morale. Another is that once a pattern becomes entrenched, it can become more difficult to break because staff get behaviorally locked into routines, and can feel unfair to them—why are you giving me a hard time suddenly now about assessment summaries, thinks Tamara, when I have been doing this for months and it has seemingly been okay?

Finally, and most importantly, quick action not only stops the behavior so that it is not a source of worry for you, but helps staff learn that you are consistent. Holding staff to clear standards at the onset helps them develop good work habits and helps them understand your role and responsibility.

Give Clear Directives

You approach Jake about his lateness.

"Jake, you have been showing up late for meetings the past 3 weeks. What's going on?"

"Oh, sorry. My wife has started a new job and I have to drop the kids off at daycare, they don't open till 8:00 a.m. and the parking is horrible and it's hard for me to get here on time."

"Oh, I remember struggling with getting my kids out the door. I know what parking in that part of town is crazy. . . ."

"Yeah, my little one trying to dress herself and she. . . ."

This conversation can now spin off into Jake, kid stories, parking dilemmas, and so on. As professional listeners trained to be sensitive to others, it's easy as a supervisor to get caught up in the emotions and problems and miss the point, which will allow Jake to miss the point.

Instead handle the interaction like this.

"Jake, you have been showing up late for meeting the past 3 weeks."

"Oh, sorry. My wife started a new job and I. . . ."

"Jake, I need you to come to meetings on time." And walk away.

Clear behavioral directives tell staff exactly what to do. Your point is clear, and it doesn't get diluted in a context of excuses or emotions. If Jake has a family problem that you need to know about that is affecting his performance, it is his responsibility to come to you about it. If you have deadlines, state them and enforce them—"Tamara I need all the assessments up-to-date and on my desk by 4:00 p.m. tomorrow." Keep it clear, keep it simple.

Get Information and Support

If you are having problems with a particular staff person and are unsure how to proceed, talk with your supervisor and/or human resources department. You want to involve your supervisor for her guidance and backing for whatever you are thinking. You may be unclear about the nuances of disciplinary options—whether, for example, some behavior falls into a Level One Conduct versus a Level Two Conduct Offense—but the human resource department is there to clarify this for you. Always have accurate information and support before acting. If you don't, you risk grievance actions and/or having your decisions overturned.

Document Your Actions

If you talk to Jake about his lateness, make a note in his file. If you talk to your supervisor about Jake, make a note about that conversation and what your supervisor or human resources recommended. You need to have documentation for any disciplinary actions so there is a record of what you did and when.

You also want to state your concerns in terms of behaviors. Jake did this, you told him to do that—behaviors are the best markers of change. This is similar to behavioral goals with clients: To say Mr. Jones needs to increase his self-esteem is vague and unmeasurable; to say that Mr. Jones will apply for 3 jobs in the next months is clear. Apply the same clarity to Jake—that he will be on time for all staff meetings. Setting these behavioral markers avoids any possible conflict of perception where Jake *feels* he is doing better, and you *feel* he is not. This vague feeling stance lends itself to potential misinterpretation and confusion.

There are situations, however, where feelings do seem to be the problem. You are concerned, for example, about Ann's attitude—her seemingly endless complaining, or her resistance to new procedures. You still need to translate change into behaviors—she needs to comply with new procedures on time, she needs to not voice objections in staff meetings, but can talk to you privately—and link these requirements to personnel policies and to her job performance.

What this means is that your concerns need to be grounded within the agency and work standards so as not to be perceived as arbitrary and personal. The agency, for example, undoubtedly has policy statements about staff complying with supervisor directives, which Ann is now violating. Or your concern about her overall resistance is impacting her clinical work—that she is complaining about the agency to her clients, undermining their trust in treatment. State the grounds for your concerns clearly to Ann, and document both your thinking and your directives in her file. Once again, if unclear or unsure, get consultation and support from your supervisor and human resources.

Look for the Problems Underneath

There are times when simply requesting a change in behavior is not enough. You give Jake a clear directive to come to meetings on time, or Ann to comply with new procedures, but if he or she fails to do it, your next conversation is about what is keeping him and her from complying. Jake may not understand why the meetings are important and so ignores them. He may be actually significantly depressed, not sleeping, and is having a difficult time getting out of the house in the morning. Ann may disclose that she is having marital problems that are affecting her overall ability to concentrate on new tasks, or that she really doesn't understand how to fill out the forms.

This type of discussion and information gives you clues to the cause. You can then refer Jake or Ann to the Employee Assistance Program (EAP) for assessment and counseling, or sit down with Ann to show her how to fill out the forms. But again, while you want to empathize with emotions—sorry you are having a difficult time, sorry I wasn't clear enough about filling out the forms—don't confuse means and ends. You don't want to step in and be a therapist for Jake or Ann. You want to be sensitive to the underlying issues, yet clear about the bottom line, namely, that they need to make specific behavioral changes in their work. You want to avoid getting so emotionally swept up that it clouds your goals or hinders your taking action.

So check in with Ann to see how she is personally doing, but also check that her forms are completed. Ask Jake if the EAP referral was helpful, but if you remain concerned that his depression is affecting his clinical work, suggest that he take medical leave until he gets back on his feet. Again, using your supervisor or human resources for support and consultation is often essential.

TERMINATION: MANAGING THE PROCESS

Suppose that despite your best efforts Jake spirals downward rather than improving. Jake's lateness spreads from consistently missing meetings to coming to work late, to missing client appointments even though he says that his depression is under control. Or Tamara's assessments improve, but it becomes clear that her overall skills are not close to matching the needs of the work. After repeated attempts to upgrade her skill base, you realize that gap is too great, and clients are being poorly served.

Human Behavior

Practice Behavior Example: Critique and apply knowledge to understand person and environment.

Critical Thinking Question: What would be your own criteria for terminating someone from a job?

Termination of an employee is one of the most difficult aspects of being a manager. The decision is rarely an easy one, and the process is often emotionally and administratively complex. Key to navigating the process is, as mentioned earlier, getting the support and guidance from your supervisor and human resources staff. This is important with discipline issues, and essential when considering termination. There are potential liability and grievance concerns. The released employee may take legal action against the agency and specifically you, so again it is essential that the process be handled correctly. As with discipline issues, documentation—noting verbal warning, probationary plans, clear deadlines and behavioral directives, referral to EAP—all need to be in writing. You need to show that you were not arbitrary, that your reasoning was sound, that there were options offered and clear mandates prescribed. Without such documentation, the situation collapses into your word against the employee's, a messy situation at best.

But beyond consultation, support, and documentation is the termination process itself. You need to carefully consider how you will terminate the employee, considering both her reaction and the subsequent impact on staff. Let's discuss this starting with a case example.

Back to Sam

We discussed Sam in Chapter 6 on Stage 3 of development. Sam had decided on his own and without his supervisor's knowledge to terminate with a client, and tried to solicit business via email for his private practice, all in violation of several agency policies and procedures. It was also learned after this incident that paperwork was incomplete, and other clients were, though not officially terminated, having their appointments canceled by Sam.

After a meeting of Sam's supervisor with her supervisor and head of human resources, it was decided that these actions were grievous enough to mandate termination. The question was how to best handle this process. Sam was well liked and respected by staff. Not knowing how he would react, it was decided to call him in at the end of the day. He came into the room and present were his supervisor and his supervisor's supervisor. He was showed a copy of the email that he had sent to the outside referral source terminating the case and soliciting business. He was told of the agency policies he had violated. He was informed that he was terminated as of end of the day.

The firing of a staff member needs to be choreographed in that you want to anticipate how the person and fellow colleagues may respond and have a plan to avert any potential problems. It was decided, for example, not to catch Sam after a staff meeting when a number of other staff are still in the office checking messages, gathering their papers. The end of the day when others were gone was considered best. Others were present in the room. You never want to fire someone by yourself. You want witnesses to the process to avoid a "I was never told . . . " situation. You want to spell out reasons for the termination, and state next steps—you need to clear out personal belongings now, you will no longer have access to your computer, you will need to contact human resources regarding certain final paperwork. You want to be sensitive to his emotional state. If Sam, for example, seemed seriously overwhelmed and depressed, or enraged, you would want to consider some follow-up with him as simple concern and to help defuse the situation. Here is where you don't change your mind, but you do use your clinical skills and trust your instincts. When in doubt, once again get consultation.

Once Sam walks out of the room, he is free to talk to anyone he likes and can say whatever he likes about his termination, while you can say virtually nothing. What you can do is send out an email to staff letting them know that today was Sam's last day at work, and that you want to thank for his years of service to the team and agency.

Grief and Loss

Some staff are going to hear about Sam's side of the story. Others will read the email later that day, or notice how his cubicle is suddenly empty of his belongings. This is awkward time for you as supervisor. Sam's friends, hearing only his perspective, are apt to side with his view. Others may feel in shock and have a grief reaction because Sam is no longer there, while some may have no strong feelings about Sam but be shaken by the sudden change. Some will get angry seeing this as confirming whatever negative feelings they had about the team or agency, and a few may, in fact, leave over the next few weeks or months. Others may feel rattled and insecure and anxious about their own work and job security, while still others may find this loss stirring emotions from past personal losses—a divorce, the death of a parent.

You have repairs to make. Because of confidentiality you can say nothing about Sam. You may encourage staff to reach out to him if they are concerned about him or have questions. What you can offer to staff is acknowledgment of their stress, anger, or grief, and support during this change. If any of them feel upset and want to talk, not about Sam, but about themselves, if any are worried about their own jobs or performance, they should absolutely feel that they can come and see you. When they do, listen and reassure.

Depending on the role and status of the person who leaves, the aftereffects may take weeks or months to get over. You need to rebuild trust, be sensitive, but continue to move forward. Think of the aftermath as a new problem that you need to address, rather than doubting your own decision or feeling that you need to overcompensate your management style.

Box 12.3 provides a checklist of questions to help you proactively address staff termination.

Box 12.3 • Termination Checklist

Are the grounds for termination clear—well-documented behaviors, policy violations, and so on?

Do you have supervisory/human resources clearance and backing?

What is the plan in case there is a grievance filed?

Have you choreographed the termination meeting—where, when, who present?

What do you expect will be the staff's reaction—shock, anger, sadness? How will you respond? Is there anyone who will need extra support or attention?

What is the plan for removing personal items from office? Does the terminated person's computer need to be locked down in advance?

What message is the terminated employee likely to convey to colleagues?

What is your message to staff that does not violate confidentiality but acknowledges the change?

What do you expect will be the staff's reaction—shock, anger, sadness? Is there anyone who will need extra support or attention?

What is the expected longer-term impact of termination on staff morale/anxiety?

How can you lower anxiety and rebuild trust among staff—increase supervision, more regular communication, and so on?

Again, these are often difficult and emotionally taxing situations. Preparation is the key. Think it through, seek support and consultation, and base your actions on a firm foundation of evidence and good judgment.

DEVELOPING SKILLS

Like the clinical side of supervision, the administrative/managerial aspects of your job require the building of certain skills that will become honed with practice and experience. Keep your expectations of yourself reasonable. Expect to feel anxious when struggling with budget concerns and spreadsheets for the first time or when handling problem employees. Rather than feeling stuck and overwhelmed, move toward your anxiety and tackle the source of it. Read books, take classes, ask for help, and do your best to avoid self-criticism. Be patient and supportive of yourself in the same way you'd like to be patient and supportive with your staff.

The following questions will test your application and analysis of the content found within this chapter. For additional assessment, including licensing-exam-type questions on applying chapter content to practice behaviors, visit **MySearchLab**.

1. According to Covey's model, urgent and not important tasks refer to

   a. Crisis situations directly related to your job description

   b. Tasks with deadlines but are not essential tasks of your job

   c. Tasks that require you as supervisor to complete

   d. Tasks that can essentially be ignored

2. When hiring a new clinician, it is important to

   a. Look for individuals who are similar to those already on staff

   b. Hire for skill rather than personality

   c. See what the applicant pool offers rather than deciding what you need in advance

   d. Always get a second opinion from a colleague if you are unsure about your final hiring decision

3. Unfortunately, you terminated Bill's employment due to his being found using drugs on the job. Your best response to your staff would be

   a. To send out an email letting them know the circumstances of Bill's termination

   b. Do not bring it up and carry on as usual

   c. Acknowledge Bill's termination, supply no additional information, and empathize with their own reactions and sense of loss

   d. Direct concerned staff to talk with human resources

4. You have been out of the office a great deal in the last weeks working on state committees. You've heard from other supervisors that several of your staff have been complaining about your absence. What would be the best way of addressing this?

   a. Find out which staff members are complaining, and talk with them individually about their concerns

   b. Send out an email or have a short meeting with the entire team just to update them on what you have been focusing upon and let them know who to see for support

   c. Tell your supervisor that your absence is causing a problem and request that she assign someone else to serve on the committees

   d. Continue what you are doing and ignore the complaints since only a couple of people are upset

5. A candidate with a strong resume applies for a clinical position; however, she says that she lives several states away and really cannot afford to travel for an interview. How would you handle this situation?

6. You are considering someone for a position. The person presented well during the interview, but the feedback you received from his references was mixed. What would you do next?

13

Ethics and Liability

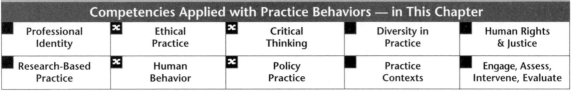

Competencies Applied with Practice Behaviors — in This Chapter				
◻ Professional Identity	☒ Ethical Practice	☒ Critical Thinking	◻ Diversity in Practice	◻ Human Rights & Justice
◻ Research-Based Practice	☒ Human Behavior	☒ Policy Practice	◻ Practice Contexts	◻ Engage, Assess, Intervene, Evaluate

In Chapter 12 we discussed your role as manager and leader. This chapter takes those roles a bit further as we look at ethics and liability. These are essential aspects of quality control as a supervisor, ensuring both high professional conduct and awareness of potential legal dangers. This chapter is divided into 2 parts. In the first part we will look at the National Association of Social Workers (NASW) Code of Ethics (2008), which forms the foundation of professional behavior. In the second part we will look at liability and malpractice issues—the legal concerns associated with these standards and their violations.

Rather than merely re-listing the ethical standards, which are easily available for you to review on your own, we will discuss the way these ethical issues impact clinical supervision and client treatment. We have already talked about several of the major ethical concerns—for example, the dual relationships and potential conflicts of interest that can arise particularly in the first 2 stages of development; the danger of abandonment and abuse in the third stage. Here we will look more closely at the way these issues arise in everyday practice, and how, as a supervisor, you can best address them.

ETHICS: COOPERATIVE, PROTECTIVE, AND INTENTIONAL

The NASW Code of Ethics divide standards by areas of responsibility—to clients, colleagues, the profession, the society. Another way of sorting these responsibilities and behaviors, especially as they pertain to supervision, is along cooperative, protective, and intentional lines. By cooperative we mean those aspects of standards that concern client rights and involvement. Protective aspects refer to those areas where the power differential between you and clients, and again between you and clinicians, has the ability to distort and potentially create harm. Finally, intentional areas are the potential overlap of personal and professional, the ways in which emotions override the clear and clinically based. We'll look at each of these aspects separately and see how they arise in clinical supervision.

Cooperative Aspects

The client has a voice. Clinician and client, as well as you and clinician, work together as a team with clear goals, awareness, and consent. There are 2 main principles making up this aspect.

Self-Determination

The belief in self-determination is deeply woven in the fabric of social work. We, as professionals and providers, serve the clients and follow their lead. We work as a team, helping them develop appropriate clinical goals based upon their needs, not ours. The only time we supersede their desires are in situations of danger to themselves or others—for example, potential suicide, homicide, abuse of children or older people.

These principles seem fairly straightforward and largely they are, but there are few ways this process can go off course. One such instance occurs when clinicians, due to their own anxiety, fail to hear or follow and define what clients are saying. An example of this would be a client who is severely depressed due to an upcoming retirement. Although the clinician senses and says that the client seems very depressed when talking about this and the client agrees, rather than pursuing the issue of depression further, the clinician, because she becomes flooded with anxiety, moves the conversation instead toward retirement plans. Means and ends become confused and unclear. Rather than following the process and listening more deeply to what the client is saying, the clinician moves toward her own comfort zone.

Another version of the same occurs with clinicians who bind their anxiety. Their rigid view of problems and treatment, the danger of taking on a "one-size-fits-all" approach to stress management, obviously prevents them from cooperatively developing goals. But realize that this anxiety-driven stance is very different from the arrogance and abuse of power that we discussed during Stage 3. At that stage the clinician potentially violates client self-determination by taking the mind-set that she knows best what the client needs, or, due to her own blind spots, is cavalier with methods and approach. Such run-over clients are seen as resistant; the problem is seen as lying with them, not the clinician.

Your antidote to these problems begins with your assessment of the situation. You need to sort out lack of skill from anxiety-coping and clinical arrogance. Doesn't the clinician ask about depression because he doesn't know the symptoms, because he is feeling overwhelmed in the session, or is he cocky and impatient and not aware of his blind spots? Look at past patterns, verbalize your questions and concerns, and review together both supervisory and clinical goals and plans.

Informed Consent

Closely related to the notion of self-determination is the area of informed consent. Here the standards spell out helping clients understand in clear language the purpose of services, risks, limits, costs, and alternatives. Some agencies cover this information as part of an orientation at assessment; others cover this information, along with information about confidentiality, in a handout, which is then discussed in the first session.

What's important here is assuring that your information matches the client's level of understanding—about the process, about limits, about client rights, about how the clinician views and thinks about the problem the client is presenting. It's the avoidance of psychobabble language, letting clients know that discussing difficult topics may cause them to feel more rather than less upset at times; that couple therapy is no guarantee against possible divorce; or that clinician interaction with the court, including feedback about client process, is required with mandated treatment. This information also requires being sensitive to and inquiring about cultural boundaries and expectations. What it excludes is assumptions—that the clinician marches ahead, assuming that his and the client's expectations are automatically one and the same. It requires that clinicians understand that clients who are new to therapy, or are easily intimidated by the power of the therapist, may need to be supported in taking an active role.

The parallel process that comes alive is in that you do the same with clinicians as they need to do with clients—clarify their and your expectations about supervision; pick up on any confusion or misunderstandings; don't mistake passivity for consent. Create the therapeutic alliance through open agreement of goals and tasks so that the clinician can do the same.

Protective Aspects

Part of tension that is part and parcel of clinical work comes from the mix of the cooperative aspects of treatment with the protective. If we think of cooperative as clinicians and clients united together against the problem, the protective aspects acknowledge the power differential—that we understand the territory and dangers that come with therapy better than the client because it is our turf. We are the guide, and because we are outside the client's psychosocial system, we have a unique vantage point from which to anticipate what may come ahead. Our responsibility as guide is to protect the client from possible harm. This leads us to several key ethical standards.

Competence

We need to provide treatment and supervision within our competence level. During Stage 1 we talked about the need for providing success experiences for new clinicians. This is in part to help reduce anxiety, increase self-confidence, and build a trusting supervisory relationship. But clearly another ethical reason is that clients are not given

---

Critical Thinking

Practice Behavior Example: *Analyze models of assessment, prevention, intervention, and evaluation.*

Critical Thinking Question: How would you handle the requirement of clinical competency with the clinician's need for growth and challenge?

incompetent treatment. That being said, clinicians, or supervisors, or clients for that matter need to move outside their comfort zones to learn new skills and grow. For clinicians and supervisors this requires both adequate training and support while new skills are learned. For clients it's about support, pacing, and clear understanding of the way the challenges tie into the their goals and problems.

Under this umbrella of competence is also the need to seek consultation when necessary, as well as knowing when to refer a client out to someone with more experience. Again, this is a judgment call, and one that you as a supervisor need to look at carefully and weigh. For example, if Sara feels over her head in terms of helping her client with her history of sexual abuse, can Sara be carefully and closely coached on how to treat the client, or is it better to transfer the client to a more-experienced clinician? Part of the decision is weighing the effects of terminating the relationship between Sara and the client against a new, if more, solid start with someone else. Another part is your understanding of the source of Sara's problem—Is it clearly one of skill or in this particular case one of countertransference and emotion? Can you help Sara understand and move through these challenges, or is it more complex and there is a danger of the client absorbing the brunt of Sara's difficulties?

These are clinical issues that you need to sort through in your own mind, and with help of a colleague if necessary, as well as discuss with Sara, and then Sara with the client. We are returning to self-determination, and also to informing clients of risks and limits of treatment. What you don't want to do is make a simple and quick judgment that leaves the client feeling abandoned or inadequately served.

Abandonment and Dependency

Abandonment and, its twin, dependency are also part of the protective aspects. Dependency falls under the mandate that social workers terminate services to clients when they are "no longer required or serve the client's needs or interests." The relationship is continuing even though no treatment is occurring. As mentioned earlier, this is danger for Stage 2 where the intimacy of the therapeutic and supervisory relationship can be seductive. The relationship goes on and on although the goal and focus has long faded away. Client and clinician meet because they have and because they mutually enjoy the experience.

This once again is a clinical call. For some clients the stability that the therapeutic relationship provides is the treatment. The case is made that without it the client will easily go off course. That said, however, your responsibility as supervisor is to ensure that these goals are still clear, measurable, and continually reviewed. What you don't want are client and clinician, or supervisor and clinician, going on autopilot.

The abandonment concern can arise when termination is instigated by the clinician because of client failure to pay bills, or failure to follow through with program requirements, or because services are not fitting the client's needs. Termination is clearly an option in these situations; the issue is to make certain the client is not in crisis or posing danger to self or others, and that attempts have been made with the client to address the causes of clinician concern. Like the disregard for client self-determination, abandonment can arise out of clinician anxiety, lack of skill, or arrogance.

The anxious clinician may find ways to terminate treatment because he feels clinically over his head. If unskilled or inexperienced, the clinician may fail to accurately assess the client's stability or assume the client will be fine, when, in fact, the client after termination is in danger of decompensating. But it is at Stage 3 where abandonment is more common. The client is seen as resistant; the clinician is impatient and summarily decides that it is best to end treatment. It's not that the clinician can't anticipate the client's reaction; she doesn't really care and rationalizes away any concerns.

Your responsibility in both these situations is to assess the clinician's judgment and to be another set of ears and eyes in evaluating the impact on the client. A subtle but dangerous aspect of this is you, as supervisor, colluding with the clinician. The waiting list for services is long, the client has failed to pay bills or show up for appointments, or the client seems to always demand or require a seemingly out-of-proportion amount of services, and you agreed with the termination without adequate thought to the need or the impact. You can't do this; the therapeutic buck starts and stops with you; you need to be careful not to fall into this trap. If unsure in any situation, seek outside consultation.

Privacy and Confidentiality

These issues bridge both the cooperative and the protective aspects of the standards. The cooperative aspects are the acknowledgment of clients' right to keep their information restricted to the therapeutic relationship. Only by knowing that what you say will not be shared allows you to trust and be open. It is part of the therapeutic compact, and why any sharing, except in clear cases of endangerment, can come only with client consent.

The protective aspects come from the clinician's behavior. It comes with a sensitivity to not talk about clients in public—restaurants, hallways, with spouses. It also comes with a sensitivity to record-keeping. While records need to be accurate, the clinician needs to be always aware that clients have access to their records, and they need to consider how the client might respond to what is included. The standards of NASW and most agency policies include provisions that if it is feared that clients may misinterpret or suffer undue distress by reading what is in a record, that the clinician or supervisor be present to interpret or emotionally intervene. A final subheading under record-keeping is determining the primary client in couple or family therapy, or managing record-keeping as part of group therapy.

For you as supervisor, these issues around records and confidentiality are training and policing issues. You need to make sure staff are documenting their work in a proper fashion, that releases are always secured, and that staff don't talk about cases where others will overhear. As will be discussed later, you are also the guide for navigating the legal issues surrounding record-keeping and limits of confidentiality. Your responsibility is in knowing how and when to act so that staff handle confidentiality concerns appropriately.

The final aspect of the protective standards involves the ones we most associate with client, supervisee, or student harm—sexual relationships and inappropriate physical contact. Not only is this a boundary violation, but the obvious danger comes from the power differential that impinges on the client or supervisee's ability to fully consent. The standards further call for social workers to not engage in sexual contact with client relatives or others close to the client when there is a potential for harm to the client. The clinician is responsible for setting clear and appropriate boundaries.

The danger here once again is rationalization. Client sexual abuse is most likely to occur during Stage 3 of professional development where power is at the forefront and the clinician believes either she won't get caught or that the sexual contact is somehow therapeutic, not harmful. Unlike other ethical issues, sexual contact with clients, supervisees, or students is probably the one most clear and defined.

The issue of physical contact, however, can be more gray. Is gently patting a client on the back as she walks out of your office inappropriate? The perception of appropriate or not is ultimately in the eyes of the client. What is required of the clinician, and of you as supervisor, is clear clinical intention—to once again not go on autopilot, but to weigh out the potential effects given the client's history, personality, perception of the relationship, and cultural background. Sometimes these are relatively clear-cut. It would be hard to find any clinical rationale, for example, for why a male therapist would hug a female client who has a history of sexual abuse, or who clearly has an erotic transference toward the therapist. But other times the holding of a client's hand or patting on the arm when a client is upset can be seen as a simple gesture of compassion. As supervisor you want to help clinicians be attuned to their behaviors, and to their clients' responses in order to make reasonable clinical judgments.

Intentional Aspects

We have been talking about this all along—the notion of making decisions based upon sound clinical thinking, rather than falling into emotions; being proactive, rather than going on behavioral autopilot. These are the situations where the professional and personal can overlap.

Dual Relationships and Conflicts of Interest

I see you as a client, but you are also on the same committee as I am at church—dual relationship. My husband is your supervisor at your job and you come to me for therapy—conflict of interest. In both these situations the personal world is mixing with the professional. These are part of the ethical code because once the personal and professional become enmeshed, the therapeutic objectivity and distance that therapy requires is lost.

The challenges of the different development stages can lead to the blurring of these boundaries. During Stage 1 clinicians may extend themselves in their efforts to manage their anxiety by being "friends" to clients, by feeling the pressure to alleviate the clients' multitude of problems, and by being driven by their idealism to "do what is right." They are overresponsible. They lend clients money, help clients clean up their house, and take clients' kids out to McDonald's because they seem hungry and the parents aren't home yet. Their emotions and anxiety cause them to override appropriate boundaries. At Stage 2 the dangers are less about anxiety and more about intimacy. Sarah and her client, Ms. Williams, have a close and long therapeutic relationship. Ms. Williams invites Sarah to her daughter's wedding. Unlike a Stage 1 clinician who may feel pressure to go in order to please the client, Sarah wants to go because she views it as being therapeutically supportive, and because she truly feels connected to Ms. Williams. She wonders if it is appropriate, worries that other guests may ask her how she knows the family, and is unsure whether to bring a gift. It quickly gets murky.

At Stage 3, blind spots cause clinicians to draft agency clients into their private practice, or invite a therapy-group member who sells flooring to stop over to the clinician's house just to give him an estimate. Rationalization obscures the thought that the client's own professional boundaries may be compromised by the clinician's role. You are the voice of clinical reason and ethical oversight. No, don't take the kids to McDonald's; if you are worried about the kids, either talk to the parents, or if you feel this is part of a bigger pattern, report them to social services. Sure, go to the wedding as a sign of therapeutic support, but sit in the back, say you are a friend of the family, and leave after the ceremony is over. Don't go to the reception, drink too much, and wind up leading the conga line. No, transferring clients to your private practice is against agency policy. No, don't think about involving group members in any area of your private life. Even if the client personally feels that being in the group and potentially making a sale are fine with him, you, the clinician, and me, as supervisor, are responsible for drawing clear lines.

But don't merely be the final word. Help clinicians learn how to clearly and clinically think through nuances of situations that may arise. Discuss the clinical implications of going to a client's wedding. Explore the countertransference issues that arise when a clinician is physically attracted to a client. Discuss the power issues that might arise when you teach a course at the local college and find one of your clients in the class. Help them understand not only the ethical standards but also the intention behind the standard. Help them understand their vulnerabilities as well as those of their clients.

You do all this through the supervisory relationship and process. When a clinician makes a seemingly offhanded comment that her client reminds her of her old boyfriend or mentions that a client wanted to give a clinician a CD of her favorite songs,—you listen and ask questions to help you understand what is occurring—"You've had clients like this before, why does this feel different?" Or, "You seem to be struggling with your feelings here and you mentioned that you have been having a difficult time lately in your own marriage; I'm wondering if this is making you vulnerable to these feelings and behaviors." Your role is not to do therapy, but to help the clinician sort and separate the personal emotions from the clinical thinking.

The danger from a supervisory perspective is that you ignore these issues. One reason you may do this is lack of supervisory skill. Your own anxiety about how to best respond results in you not responding at all—you simply let the comment about the boyfriend go by, and the clinician decides that these feelings shouldn't be talked about in supervision, or are not important to worry about. The other reason is that your own personal life and vulnerabilities become triggered—the clinician's comment about her past boyfriend causes you think about your own past boyfriends, or your own past clients who reminded you of past boyfriends. The uncomfortable emotions that these thoughts arouse cause you dismiss what the clinician is saying.

Your responsibility and challenge is to be self-aware, to do a better job of separating the professional and personal than the clinician may be able to do due to his own less experience and skill. If this is difficult for you, for whatever reason, if you are in doubt, seek support and clarification from colleagues and supervisors.

Being ethical as a social worker, whether it be as supervisor or clinician, is certainly about knowledge—knowing and understanding the values, practices, and boundaries that make up and mark social work as a profession. But it is

Human Behavior

Practice Behavior Example: *Utilize conceptual frameworks to guide the processes of assessment, intervention, and evaluation.*

Critical Thinking Question: How would you do as a supervisor to develop ethical awareness in your staff?

also more than knowledge, more than a checklist of dos and don'ts. It is also about intellect, attitude, and self-awareness—thinking clearly as a clinician and supervisor; adapting a professional attitude that strives to separate the personal from the professional, that serves clients, and that sees them as partners; a self-knowledge that realizes when either the thinking or the attitude is being compromised.

LIABILITY/LEGAL ISSUES

The standards provide the parameters of ethical and sound clinical practice. In this section we will look at the legal implications—the areas where violations can lead to disciplinary action by licensure boards or to legal action by clients. Because regulations not only change over time, but differ among states, the purpose here is not to offer all-encompassing legal advice, but rather alert you to possible areas of liability that as a supervisor you need to be aware of. You should always check your own state regulations and seek legal counsel when legal and liability questions and concerns arise.

The material here is largely drawn from the work of Richard S. Leslie, an attorney who specializes in mental health issues, who writes a bulletin entitled *At the Intersection of Law and Psychotherapy* (2010), as well as the research from the Center for Ethical Practice.

Confidentiality Issues

This is one of the foundational principles of social work practice—that information between client and clinician is confidential.

Records and Informing Clients

As a supervisor, you may need to help particularly new staff understand what does and does not need to be in a clinical record. Stage 1 clinicians, again, often struggle knowing what is and is not appropriate and tend to include too much, nonclinical information in the record.

New staff also need to clearly know how to inform new clients about confidentiality limits—the reporting, for example, of suspected child abuse, that emails are not confidential, or the limits of confidentially by group members in group therapy. Some agencies use a handout of information that is then reviewed with new clients; sometimes an intake staff or department covers this material. Let staff know their responsibilities so that such matters don't slip through the bureaucratic cracks.

Confidentiality in the Workplace

Staff also need to be sensitive to confidentiality in the workplace setting—not talking about clients in hallways, and so on. These slips are easy to fall into as clinicians pass each other in the hall or catch each other between appointments. You need to be the one to make staff sensitive and enforce professional behavior.

In the age of technology, there are new concerns regarding not only online disclosure of client information on computer documents, but also outside the workplace as staff talk about their work in chat rooms, and so on. Again, you need to help staff become sensitive to inadvertent disclosure.

Minors and Confidentiality

Parents have access to minors' records, and states vary as to how liberal they are regarding such access and information. Know your state regulations and know what you can and cannot do if a parent seeing a record could pose potential harm to the child.

Disclosing the "Fact of the Relationship"

Clinicians need to know from clients whether they can leave messages on answering machines about appointments, whether agency letterhead envelopes can be sent to clients, and so on. Clinicians need to ask, let appropriate staff know (e.g., billing department), and document client requests.

Similarly, clinicians need to know how to handle confidentiality and the unexpected caller—the wife, for example, who calls up the clinician asking about the treatment of her husband, or a father about his son. These callers are free to share whatever they want, and the clinician is free to listen, but that is all. The clinician cannot acknowledge the client is indeed a client or share any information if there is no signed release of information.

Confidentiality and Search Warrants

If the police come to a clinician's office with a search warrant, the clinician should ask to see the warrant, object to the warrant, and ask to place the file of the client under investigation in a sealed envelope and brought to a judge. Ask the officers to document the objection and requests. The clinician should then notify the client and document his actions.

Use of Client Information in Public Presentations

Case details need to be masked if used in public presentations. Staff need to be sensitive to these issues particularly in small towns where even broad details can potentially violate confidentiality. For case material for publications, it is best to get the permission of the family. Most publishers have clear protocols for this, and this should be discussed with your editor before writing.

Death and Confidentiality

Finally, confidentiality survives death. Generally, information and records can be passed on only to the executor of the estate. Again, clarify your state laws and document actions.

Child Abuse Reporting

Yes, social workers are mandated reporters of suspected child (and adult) abuse. Failure to do so can lead to disciplinary action with the social work board or potential malpractice liability.

Staff need to know how these reports are to be made. Some agencies are fine with simple documentation of contact with local protective services in client charts; others require that staff send emails to supervisors informing them of reports and establishing a paper trail. New staff often become anxious about reporting processes, and about disrupting the therapeutic relationship with the client. They need clear directives from you—you need to report this today—and clear support—tell me what you think will be the client's reactions; let's talk about helping your client understand why you were concerned.

Finally, staff need to know the requirement for reporting—whom to contact, within what time frame, verbal reports versus written reports. Know your state regulations.

There are several gray areas that commonly arise that you need to be aware of.

Abuse and Culture

What is considered abuse in one culture may not be in another. There are instances, for example, where ritual scarring or burning is used to signify a childhood developmental passage. These still need to be reported, but when making the report social workers should also tell the protective services about the cultural context.

Abuse Across State Lines

Twelve-year-old Thomas reports to his therapist that his father beat him when he visited him last week in another state where the father lives. Should the clinician call protective services in the father's state? No. The clinician should make the report to the local protective services, and they will be responsible for contacting the father's state agency.

Medical Neglect

Suppose a child tells a social worker that his mother stopped giving him his attention deficit disorder medication because she doesn't believe in it. Is this medical neglect? Different locales interpret this differently. Some, for example, require that a doctor must diagnose a condition that if not treated will lead to physical harm. Check your state regulations, and when in doubt have staff consult with protective services. Let them make the decision whether or not a report is needed.

Domestic Violence

When a child witnesses domestic violence, can this be considered emotional abuse? Like medical neglect, it depends on circumstances and interpretation. Sometimes a case needs to be made that the domestic violence is having a long-term impact on the child's functioning. Again, check with local protective services.

Adult Reporting Past Abuse

If an adult reports abuse when he was a child—for example, an adult discloses that his grandfather sexually abused him when he was 10 years old. Is the social worker mandated to report? No, though the adult can be encouraged to report the incident himself.

Staff need to know when and how they should act in these situations and when and how to include you in the information loop. You need to be familiar with the laws and regulations, but when in doubt, have staff contact social services for guidance and recommendations. Make sure they document their contacts.

Child Custody Disputes

Because of the legal complexity and emotionality around issues of child custody and the need for specific training in the area, most agencies avoid getting involved in such situations. If parents come seeking an assessment for custody, many agencies refer parents to outside evaluators who are skilled in this area.

Staff do need to know, however, about custody and its impact on parental approval for treatment of a child. If a parent has sole legal custody of a child, then that parent can consent for treatment of the child. If, however, the parents share joint custody, it is important to know the details of the agreement to know whether one or both of the parents need to consent to treatment. If both parents agree to treatment, but then one wishes to terminate, the clinician needs to consider the impact of abandonment on the child. Finally, know your own state regulations requiring minors' ability to seek treatment on their own. Again, seek legal counsel if you or your staff are uncertain how to proceed.

Subpoenas

Many agencies have procedures and legal counsel in place to handle subpoenas. If a clinician receives a subpoena to testify in court, and the client wants the clinician to testify, then the client is waiving confidentiality and the clinician is free to do so. Problems arise when the client does not want the clinician to testify.

If a clinician receives a subpoena, he needs to first inform the client. If the client has an attorney, then the clinician should get permission to talk to the attorney and then ask the attorney to quash the subpoena. If the client does not have an attorney, the clinician must wait 10 days so that the client has time to file a Motion to Quash. If the client has not done so after that time, the clinician can file a Motion to Quash (see Center for Ethical Practice website for specific information on filing a motion). Finally, the clinician can ask the court to limit the order as narrowly as possible and/or maintain records under seal.

Like child abuse reporting, this is another area that can cause considerable anxiety among staff. Have clear procedures and legal support so that both you and your staff know exactly what to do.

Court Testimony—Guidelines

It's easy to become rattled by having to testify in court, and especially so for the inexperienced. Staff need your coaching to successfully navigate these situations. Here are some helpful guidelines for court testimony.

- Tell the truth—Don't slant information for the benefit of the client or case.
- Don't guess—It's okay to say that you don't remember.
- Prepare—Check notes, have dates of sessions, find out in advance what is likely to be asked, have information on license and continuing education in case there are questions about your qualifications and background.
- Focus on answering the question, not worrying about the effects of the answer—The effects are the attorney's concern.
- Answer the specific question, don't volunteer information—Clinicians think like clinicians, not lawyers, and are prone to try and put information in a larger context. Don't. If the attorney thinks more information is needed, she will ask.

Court Testimony—Roles

There are several roles staff make take when testifying in court and it's helpful for staff to know precisely what their role is. Here are the possibilities.

- Voluntary—Here the client gives permission for the clinician to testify and waives confidentiality. Therapeutically, it's helpful for the clinician to go over with the client in advance what information he may have to disclose so that there are no surprises for the client and potential damage done to the therapeutic relationship.

- Involuntary—The clinician is subpoenaed. Seek to quash or limit disclosure as much as possible. Make sure the clinician does not inadvertently make clinical opinions of anyone else—for example, parents, spouse, or family members—who are not primary clients in treatment with the clinician.
- Expert—The worker testifies as an outside evaluator—custody case, psychological testing—and is not providing treatment. The worker needs to be ready to substantiate her qualifications and answer any possible objections to her "expert" status.
- Court-ordered services—The clinician's feedback is part and parcel of the court order for treatment. It's helpful for a clinician to know clearly at the onset of the referral the court's expectations—that he will need to write a report about treatment progress, that he will have to testify at a hearing, that he will be making verbal reports to a probation officer—and inform and explain to clients at the beginning of services.

Fees

Yes, you can raise your fees; however, it is best to notify clients at the start of the relationship in writing about possible fee changes. You want to give clients plenty of notice and discuss it. Midstream raises in fees could cause clients to feel exploited.

Do not tie releasing of records to payment of back fees—they are separate issues. Be careful about allowing clients to accumulate large balances—this could be construed as a dual relationship problem, where you are creating a debtor–creditor relationship.

Maintaining a License

Licensed staff are responsible for maintaining licensure, but failure to do so has legal and practice implications for you and the agency. Check with staff to be certain that they are renewing their licenses on time (and not necessarily waiting on the licensing board to contact them), have current malpractice insurance either privately or through the agency (absence not only makes them more at risk but can invalidate insurance contracts), and are up-to-date on their continuing education requirements (failure to meet educational requirements can violate a license). Don't assume it is complete—ask for copies of current licenses and supportive information.

Referrals to Physicians

Insurance companies are more routinely asking that therapy services be coordinated with a client's primary care physician. The rationale is to be able to rule out underlying medical conditions—for example, thyroid problems contributing to depression-like symptoms, hormone problems affecting sexual functioning—and to evaluate for medication as adjunct treatment. Some clinicians make it part of their clinical routine to refer their clients for a physical examination at the start of treatment to rule out medical issues, while others obtain a release when any questions or concerns arise. As supervisor, be alert to the medical connection and coordination as staff work with clients.

Advertising

Wording is the key for ethical advertising of services. You obviously can't make false statements about services or qualifications, but you need to be careful that advertising isn't misleading. The bottom line is that you shouldn't say anything that you can't prove. Finally, if you say that you are an "expert" in a certain area, you are setting yourself at a higher standard and your work will be judged at that standard.

Use of Self-Disclosure

A clinician sharing with a client information about his own personal experiences can be a powerful clinical tool, but like other tools it has to be used intentionally. What staff need to be careful of is self-disclosure being construed as personally driven—for example, if a clinician mentions past problems in her own marriage, and the client hears such disclosure as the clinician being unhappy, the self-disclosure may be viewed as an overture.

As with other clinical interventions where the professional and personal can seem to cross (touching a client is another example), you as a supervisor want to be clear that there is sound clinical thinking determining these actions, and that the clinician anticipates and responds appropriately to client reactions and interpretations. This is an issue of training and clinician self-awareness. Your job is to raise these issues and help the clinician sort out the professional and personal intentions.

Termination of Treatment

The concern here is that the client does not interpret termination as abandonment. It is best to clarify in a disclosure statement given to clients at the start of treatment the conditions under which treatment can be terminated—not paying bills, client not getting better, client's problems are beyond the clinician's competence. The clinician needs to make a referral to another practitioner or facility and needs to document.

When clients drop out without notice, staff need to know when and how to close the case and possibly get closure with the client. Some clinicians send a letter to the client stating that since they have not returned to treatment for some time, they are assuming that things are going well and closing the case; the client is free to return at any point; a copy of the letter is placed in the file. Some send these letters by certified mail to have a record of receipt. Others leave a voice mail, again notifying that the case is closed but the client is always welcomed to return, and document the phone call in the client record. Decide on a clear procedure so that staff are consistent and sensitive.

Supervision as an Outside Vendor

If you have staff who are obtaining supervision from someone outside the agency, or if you are a supervisor in private practice who is supervising someone who works for an agency, you need to be clear about coordination to avoid liability. The concern here is that having essentially 2 supervisors—the agency-based one and the outside one—lends itself to each supervisor thinking the other one is "in charge." Potential dangerous situations can fall through the cracks.

Suppose, for example, that John, who works for an agency, tells you about a client he is seeing who is suicidal. You, an outside supervisor, are sufficiently alarmed and you clearly direct John to obtain an emergency custody order immediately. You document your recommendation in your own supervisory records. You want, however, to take this one step further and make sure John's supervisor at his agency is aware as well. Why? Because if John fails to follow through on your directive for some reason, both you and John, and the agency, are apt to be liable for any consequences. You can tell John that he needs to inform his supervisor at the agency about the client and your recommended action. To seal any cracks, you can call the agency supervisor directly, inform him of your conversation with John, and the concerns and recommendations, including that John would see him, so that in case he doesn't hear from John quickly, he can follow up.

To set this all in place, you want to have a clear understanding in writing from the agency supervisor before the start of supervision with John about how such critical situations will be handled. You want to know in advance your role in providing feedback about the clinician's work—for example, is the agency supervisor expecting you to comment on the clinician's performance as part of his annual performance evaluation? All this needs to be spelled out, and the clinician needs to be informed of procedures and roles prior to the start of supervision.

ETHICS AND LIABILITY GUIDELINES

When considering ethical and liability issues, it is essential to keep in mind that the burden of proof rests with the clinician. There is no way to assure that clients won't misinterpret and become distressed over aspects of treatment even years after it is concluded. The responsibility falls upon the clinician to be able to show that her actions reflected sound clinical reasoning and professional judgment. When in doubt, follow these guidelines.

- Do your best to uphold confidentiality.
- Disclose policies, limits, and areas of concern in advance and in writing.
- Obtain client written consent.
- Document in your records your actions and recommendations.
- Obtain consultation.
- Make your decisions based upon sound clinical reasoning.

It is your responsibility as a supervisor to help clinicians learn to think in these terms—to not only know about ethics, but know how to put them in practice; to be sensitive to the impact of their decisions and actions on their clients; to seek consultation when in doubt; to document both clearly and efficiently.

Most of all we are back to relationship. You are responsible for creating the relationship with the clinician that allows for the trust on both sides—that you trust both the skill and judgment of the clinician, and the accuracy and honesty of what he discloses to you—and his trust of you that allows him to not hesitate to seek your counsel when concerns naturally arise. If this trust is solidly in place, you can be confident that you and the clinician can work through these ethical dilemmas together.

Policy Practice

Practice Behavior Example: *Understand that policy affects service delivery and they actively engage in policy practice.*

Critical Thinking Question: If you were to develop one policy to help maintain ethical behavior and reduce liability among your staff, what would it be?

The following questions will test your application and analysis of the content found within this chapter. For additional assessment, including licensing-exam-type questions on applying chapter content to practice behaviors, visit **MySearchLab**.

1. The notion of client abandonment refers to
   a. Your cancelling appointments with clients arbitrarily
   b. The client's perception that you have terminated treatment with him without notice or his input
   c. A client's distorted perception that you don't like her any longer
   d. A clinical technique to raise client anxiety and stimulate change

2. In terms of ethical and liability concerns, good documentation of clinical work needs to show
   a. The number of client appointments scheduled and kept
   b. That the clinician received licensed supervision
   c. The clinicians' clear clinical thinking and reasons for their interventions and decisions
   d. That the client's family was involved in the treatment process

3. Sam has a client who has been complaining about migraine headaches. Sam believes these headaches are caused by stress and wants to teach the client relaxation techniques. Your best response to Sam would be
   a. To ask him to tell you more about the relaxation techniques he wants to use
   b. Suggest that he refer the client to his physician for a medical evaluation
   c. Show him the recent article you read on stress and somatic problems
   d. Explore with Sam whether he himself is feeling stressed

4. Karen has been seeing her client Mr. Jones for a long time and he has been clinically stable for many months. When you bring up Karen terminating with Mr. Jones she balks. How should you respond?
   a. Ask Karen to explain to you her clinical reasons for not seeing termination as appropriate at this time
   b. Tell Karen that you would like to sit in on her next session with Mr. Jones so you can see how he is firsthand
   c. Say to Karen that she is obviously fostering client dependency and that is unethical and will not be permitted
   d. Talk with your supervisor about developing a policy putting limits on the length of clinical services

5. A clinician has seen Ms. Jones for several sessions, but it is clear to you as the supervisor that the clinician does not have the skills to adequately treat Ms. Jones. How would you handle this situation?

6. A clinician tells you that one of her clients bought her an expensive gift and that she is unsure how to handle this. How would you respond to the clinician?

14

Staying Creative: Self-Care for the Long Haul

Competencies Applied with Practice Behaviors — in This Chapter				
✖ Professional Identity	■ Ethical Practice	■ Critical Thinking	■ Diversity in Practice	■ Human Rights & Justice
■ Research-Based Practice	✖ Human Behavior	■ Policy Practice	■ Practice Contexts	■ Engage, Assess, Intervene, Evaluate

Sit down. Make yourself comfortable and take a few deep breaths. Begin to feel yourself settled and relaxed.

Take out a pad of paper. Write at the top of the page "What is my purpose in life?" Begin writing with whatever comes to your mind—to help others, to be a good parent, or even I don't know. Just write down whatever comes to mind, keep your hand moving, and don't censor what comes up. If you feel stuck, write I feel stuck.

Anytime you write down a word or phrase that has some punch—teach others about therapy, help others reach their potential—or that stirs some emotions or some wisp of authenticity, check or circle the phrase. Keep writing.

After about 15 or 20 minutes you will perhaps begin to hit the wall—you don't know what else to write; you are getting bored; the exercise, you say, feels stupid. Keep writing whatever is in your mind—this is stupid, I had enough. Look back at your title. After a few minutes you'll get back on track. Continue writing and circling.

After about another 20 minutes, you may find your thoughts centering around a certain theme or you may actually boil down your thoughts to a coherent sentence—I want to teach others how to manage their lives and reach their potential, I want give my children an absolute sense that life is sacred. Notice any reactions to your phrase—surprise, contentment, excitement.

This particular exercise was developed by Steve Pavlina (2005) and is a variation of cluster writing that has been used as a tool to stimulate creativity for decades. It also harks back to Buckminster Fuller's quote—What is that one thing that no one else can do because of who you are? This is an important question. No doubt you had an answer at some point in your life—as a teenager, in college—but perhaps the answer has changed over time. Your priorities have shifted, or maybe the answer has withered through neglect.

The key to a successful career as a social worker and supervisor is the ability to do for yourself what you advocate to others—an openness to others and yourself, an ability to seek out and handle challenges, the skills and willingness to handle problems and keep them in perspective, keeping your ear close to the groundwork so that you are able to detect changes in needs over time.

What you want to be careful about is falling into all those opposite traits that we have been discussing throughout—going on autopilot, being reactive rather than proactive, being reductionistic in your views and thinking, tolerating stale relationships and emotionally thin or tattered connections to your work—all symptoms that you are choosing the safe over the challenging. Rather than remaining energized, you are simply going through the motions. The heart is leaving the work.

In this final chapter we are going to look at ways you can stay connected to yourself and the everyday work, and define the questions you need to ask yourself to create a fulfilling and successful long-term clinical and supervisory practice. Let's start with supervision for yourself.

> ## Professional Identity
>
> **Practice Behavior Example:** *Practice personal reflection and self-correction to assure continual professional development.*
>
> **Critical Thinking Question:** What is your answer to Fuller's question—what is the one thing you need to do that no one else can do?

SUPERVISION AND SUPPORT

We start here because social work is not a solo act. Not only is the work about people, you need people and their support, even if you work independently, to help you through the emotional stresses and strains that come with the job. Some are able to get this through family and friends, others from close colleagues.

For most of us, particularly in an agency setting, this primary support is going to come, or not, from our immediate supervisor. Not all supervisors, of course, become our mentors, and when they are, we are lucky indeed. Not only do they show us the ropes, we take into ourselves bits of their personalities and ways of looking at the world. They become the role model who can shape who we are for years to come.

But even if we are not fortunate enough to find that right fit of chemistry and needs that creates true mentoring, we may be fortunate enough to have a good supervisor whom we can lean on. As we have been describing throughout, good supervisors for us are someone whom we respect for their skills, compassion, and enthusiasm. Not only are they dedicated to helping us learn, they are dedicated to helping us be who we can best be. They don't have the answer to Buckminster Fuller's question, but they encourage us to discover that answer for ourselves.

Our good supervisor also is able to step in at times of crisis. Rather than replicating the process and becoming anxious herself, she is able to be empathic and enabling, clear and concerned. We know we are not going to be blamed for the problem, or have our own reactions minimized. Rather that focus is on the problem, on putting out the fire as effectively and efficiently as possible.

Finally, like us, the good supervisor keeps us informed about what is happening in upper management so we can inform our staff, but knows how to not overwhelm us with too much information. He, like us, knows how to be a good and appropriate buffer.

The less supportive supervisor struggles with all this. His flexibility is minimal; he is more concerned about doing it right, that is, his way, than our own. He is uncomfortable with new ideas or even new problems. In a crisis, originating from above or from below, he overreacts, leaving us feeling unsupported or burdened. Overall, we feel stifled or bored or criticized. We become avoidant, frustrated, or self-critical.

What do you do if your supervisor gives you less support and guidance than you need? Your obvious first line of defense is to speak up—be assertive and say what you need and how you work best. It may be that her intentions are good, but she is misreading your needs—clarify. Let her know how you learn, how much direction you need, and what helps you most in a crisis. Have these conversations when emotions are flat, when the crisis is over, and when the content is not about cases and staff but about the relationship. These are the meta-conversations of talking about talking.

Professional Identity

Practice Behavior Example: *Practice personal reflection and self-correction to assure continual professional development.*

Critical Thinking Question: Think about your past supervisors. What is the one quality that they had that you most want to incorporate? What would you want to most avoid?

If these efforts have limited results, or if you need support in raising these issues, contact your human resources department or the Employee Assistance Program (EAP). Often they can step in as facilitators for these types of discussions, or if not, at least give you guidelines for other options. Help your supervisor understand your intentions so that your seeking outside support is not seen as a threat, and your concerns are not seen as simple complaining or personal criticism. Connect your concerns with your supervisor's—the overall functioning of your team—and send the message that you both are working toward the same ends.

If these attempts fail, you face the fork in the road administratively and personally. You can decide whether you want to push your concerns further up the chain of command. If you go this route, you are essentially doing a full-court press, choosing your needs and specific outcomes over maintaining the relationship, at least in the immediate time frame. Before you do this, you need to consider your personality and priorities, as well as those of your supervisor, to anticipate the longer-term impact on you and your team.

Of course, you can choose to leave. Simply considering this possibility can be eye-opening—it provides an opportunity for you to reevaluate and redefine your work and career goals—and emotionally freeing—you realize that you are not trapped. If you are invested in the agency, whether due to loyalty, sense of mission, or practical issues such as retirement or health benefits, leaving may not be an option. If you cannot get the support you need at your workplace, then the question is how to get the support you need, rather than assuming that you have to accept none at all.

This is where you consider support from outside the workplace. This may take the form of an outside supervisor-consultant—someone you meet with to help you think through your administrative and clinical issues—or perhaps even individual therapy to help you think about your problems and needs in a new way and give you a different perspective. What is most important is that you do something. Don't feel stuck and resigned to slogging through on your own. Such isolation will take a toll not only on you, but ultimately on your entire staff.

SELF-SUPERVISION

Self-supervision is a strange concept. It evokes images of you looking over your own shoulder, being perhaps scolding and critical, but reflective and supportive. While not a substitute for supervision with someone you respect who can ask the hard questions you are afraid to ask yourself, and see the blind spots you cannot, self-supervision can help you take a closer look at what you have done, or step back and see the larger canvas that is your work.

You can use self-supervision to reflect on a particular session with a client or clinician. Some questions to ask yourself.

What were your goals for the session, and how well did you accomplish them?

Where and how did you get off course?

What was the emotional landscape of the session process—were there times you felt confused, bored, annoyed—why?

How does this session fit into your overall assessment and goals for this client or clinician?

Are you and the client or clinician in agreement about both the ends and means of your work? What do you need to do next?

These questions are like those you ask clinicians about their cases, and their purpose is the same, namely, to help you stay both focused and reflective. Writing down your responses may help you clarify your thinking further.

You can also use self-supervision to look at the larger patterns in your work. The questions you ask yourself are similar to those you ask clinicians to answer as part of their self-evaluation and, in some ways, also similar to the review you do for your proactive supervisory planning. Box 14.1 presents a checklist of possible questions for reflection.

Make time to do this type of review every 3–6 months. Again, write down your answers as a way of clarifying and logging your own internal changes.

Box 14.1 • Questions for Self-Supervision

What is my current theory of clinical work or supervision?

What is the ultimate purpose and focus of my practice? How has it changed in the past year?

What types of clinicians, clients, personalities, problems do I work with well? Why?

What/who are more difficult? Why?

What clinical skills do I need to develop? What emotional triggers do I need to pay attention to?

What administrative/supervisory skills do I need to develop—for example, software training, conducting groups, management courses?

How do I use my own personality to convey your thoughts and ideas effectively to others?

What support do I need from colleagues and supervisors?

Of all the things I do on my job, what do I enjoy the most? When do I feel best?

On a scale of 1–10, how satisfied am I with my work? What could make it better?

What are my goals for the next quarter, and 6 months?

SELF-ASSESSMENT: THE BIGGER PICTURE

Self-supervision helps you stay close to your everyday work. Periodically, however, it's useful to step back even further and look at the ways your work fits into the context of your life. Here is another writing exercise to try.

Sit down with a pad of paper and a pen in a quiet place where you will not be distracted, and where there is no time limit to worry about. Unlike the purpose exercise where you were free-associating, this time write down only what you feel is honest and true. Stay close to yourself and emotions as you write. Be reflective, and take as much time as you need.

At the top of the page write the date and then the salutation—Dear _____ (your first name). Begin writing a letter to yourself as though you were catching up with a good friend on the changes in your outer and inner life: "I know I haven't written to you in the past 6 months. A lot has been going on. I've. . . ." Reflect and write about these past months or year—not only what you have been doing in your work, but how you feel about your work. Talk about changes in your personal life—your spouse, your children, how they've changed, how you feel you have been doing as a partner, a parent. Talk about your successes and frustrations. Talk about your current goals, again both personal and professional, your priorities over the next months, your vision, your life philosophy, how you've changed in the last few years, and what you want most for the next.

See what arises. When you feel finished, end the letter, as you would any other letter, like this—thanks for your support over these past years, will write again soon, Love _____. Read and compare this with other letters you may have written in the past. Consider sharing this with your partner or a good friend.

The goal of this exercise is to help you consolidate your past and reenvision your future by communicating with your inner self. Hopefully it helps you be aware of and possibly reorder what's important to you right now—in your work, in your relationships, in your personal life. And if you discover that your life is imbalanced—that you are not spending enough time with family, are too socially isolated, are not enjoying your work—or find that your priorities have changed, think about concrete ways you can reset it. Change your work hours, make plans to see friends on a weekend, or start taking those music lessons you always wanted to take. Talk to your supervisor about your boredom or aggravation and propose concrete changes for her to consider. Choose action rather than resignation.

RUN TOWARD WHAT YOU FEAR

Just as you want to encourage anxiety-approaching behavior in your staff, you want to make sure you do the same for yourself. And as we have been saying all along, it is about the how, not the what, and you can start anywhere. If you tend to be conservative or cautious in your work life, afraid to take risks and make changes, practice "how you do anything" by taking more acceptable risks in your personal life. Take those clarinet lessons, or have that long-put-off heart-to-heart conversation with your partner. Move toward what feels emotionally difficult in order to increase your capacity for anxiety and change. And if it is easier to begin with your work and move out toward your personal life, that's fine, do it. Again, it doesn't matter where you start, the outcome itself isn't important. What is important is the moving against your own grain.

The Italian artist Michelangelo Pistoletto is known as one of the major shapers of the art world in the past decades. He has led and moved through the Pop, Minimalist, and Conceptual art trends, working in a wide variety of mediums—painting, sculpture, performance pieces. Pistoletto credits his creativity with learning the value of following his passions without questioning where they are leading. He has discovered over time that seemingly unrelated interests will at some point make sense and connect to his work.

Human Behavior

Practice Behavior Example: *Apply theories and knowledge from the liberal arts to understand biological, social, cultural, psychological, and spiritual development.*

Critical Thinking Question: What is it that you most fear? How can you incorporate these challenges into your life?

You too need to challenge yourself to follow your passions and instincts. Learning to trust what you think, say what you think, and see what happens next is what creative therapy and supervision is all about. This is the way you maintain your core integrity, where your outer life comes to reflect your inner one. This is how you increase your emotional flexibility, and most of all, like Pistoletto, how you generate your unique form of creativity.

TRAINING AS EXPANSION

Clinical and supervisory trainings are a good way of translating the process of creativity into concrete action. Go to workshops and conferences and find out about evidence-based and cutting-edge new treatments so your staff doesn't outgrow you, so you can keep your clinical program current and creative. Consider enrolling in a 3-year program in family therapy or intensive supervision. Watch videos of masters whom you admire.

From time to time step outside your theoretical and clinical comfort zone. Consider applying your skills to new populations or problems—children, those with personality disorders, traumatized veterans, those with eating disorders. Read about theories and methods outside your clinical arena—object relations, systems, hypnosis—and find trainers and teachers who can help you learn the skills. By doing so you not only increase your skill base, but stimulate your thinking and reshape your assumptions and core beliefs.

Go Into Therapy

This too is a type of training, or rather, retraining of your mind. Certainly consider therapy to resolve issues that are creating obstacles in your life, but also consider it even if there is no crisis or looming need. Putting yourself in the consumer role may help you clarify your thinking not only about yourself, but about the work.

Teach

As we mentioned in our discussion of Stage 2, teaching is an excellent way of discovering what you don't realize you know. Going to a daylong conference and doing a 2-hour presentation on the information for your staff not only helps you pay attention in the training and share the material with your colleagues, but helps you organize and consolidate the ideas. Offering new staff and students a daylong workshop on your approach to treatment or to supervision helps you articulate what you instinctively have learned to do; case examples help you revisit what works, what hasn't worked, and how your style over time has changed.

MAKING WORK EFFECTIVE, EFFICIENT, AND ENJOYABLE

Supervision and self-assessments help keep you on track and creative. Trainings help you stay skilled and curious. But if life is in the details, then a good part of the work of being a supervisor is in the management of your everyday work tasks. Here are some ways of tackling the day in a life.

Control Your Time as Much as Possible

It's easy to be reactive. You and your staff try to accommodate the demands and needs of clients; you as middle manager are handed tasks, deadlines, and meeting times from upper management. As we have been emphasizing throughout, proactivity is the antidote to going on autopilot, burnout, and sloppy practice. No, you can't reschedule the director's meeting to a time convenient for you, but you can set aside times when you're most alert or relaxed to do strategic planning or to evaluate the program budget. Having as much say as possible over when and where you do something helps you feel that your job is truly your job, and adds enormously to your job satisfaction.

Diversify Your Tasks

The clinician who inadvertently schedules 4 hyperactive children in a row, or spends an afternoon with back-to-back depressed adults is likely to finish the day feeling exhausted or depressed herself. Similarly, if you decide to schedule a full day of policy and procedures review meetings, or 6 straight hours of individual supervision with interns to show them how to do their paperwork, you may find that by the end of the day your job satisfaction rating has gone into sharp decline.

Just as you want to think about how you allocate your time, you also want to proactively think about how you prioritize and set out your tasks. Different problems require different levels of thinking and utilize different aspects of your personality. Such diversity throughout the day in who you see and what you do is key to keeping you alert and engaged. So schedule the staff meeting on Friday not only because everyone is there, but because your energy is at its highest. Follow it with a couple of hours of individual supervision before setting off to that brief training on records, followed by the case observation and consultation after lunch. Mix it up, and build, as much as possible, around your personal higher and lower energy times.

Run Effective and Efficient Meetings

Just as meetings can potentially deaden your own energy, don't have them do the same to your staff. Here are some tips for running successful meetings (Keens, 2010).

- Do schedule for higher energy times of you and your staff—save those afternoon slump times for light administrative tasks.
- Start and stop on time.
- Have a clear agenda. Consider sending it out in advance if more than a few items.

- Convey energy—use your hands, walk around.
- Limit the use of PowerPoint—less than 15 slides in 15 minutes.
- Arrange seating for needs—if a small group, try sitting in a circle; if a large group, consider classroom style; if participants are to interact with each other, make it easy for them to move around.
- If putting notes on a flip chart, keep them succinct.
- Engage your audience—ask others for their ideas, questions, comments. Note areas of agreement.
- If there is a break, sum up after break what went before, say what's ahead.
- Use handout material if there is a large amount of information so participants don't feel overwhelmed and give up listening, and have a way of following along.
- Use humor.
- Thank everyone for coming.
- Have a finale—some closing comment, some statement of appreciation of staff's work, and so on.

Good meetings are their own art form, and like any other skill, take practice. Watch the process of someone who does it well. Ask for feedback on your style from those whose opinion you respect.

Avoid Procrastination

You have 3 months worth of Excel spreadsheets to look over before the next director's meeting, but they keep getting moved to the bottom of your to-do list. Now you're in a panic and angry with yourself because you'll probably have to look at them at home tonight after the kids go to bed even though you're already tired and irritable.

People make up all kinds of reasons to justify their procrastination, but none of them are very good. Sure, you may pull it out and complete the task at the last minute, and even have some sense of achievement in doing so, but over the long haul it takes its toll in stress and work efficiency. The hardest part of particularly boring or dreaded tasks is getting started. Schedule a time to do it when your energy is high, break it up into small time chunks if needed—15–30 minutes—and build in some reward for accomplishment— you'll treat yourself to a double latte after. Think about what you need environmentally— the board room with large table to spread out material and the large door to block out distractions—or what you may need in the way of support—having a colleague to sit next to you to help you stay on task or answer questions.

If procrastination is persistent problem and one that impacts your personal life as well, consider seeking therapy. Often there are underlying issues such as perfectionism, passive/ aggressiveness, or attention deficit disorder. Find out the source, so you can find the solution.

Address Problems Quickly and Decisively

Persistent procrastination can lead to a crisis-like environment on your team that over time contributes to staff burnout. But milder forms of time-mismanagement—problems linger because of indecisiveness and/or poor priority setting—can take their toll as well. Staff feel frustrated and stressed when they can't get answers to their questions and problems in a timely manner. Their work becomes inefficient.

Part of good management is not only making sound decisions, but having an effective and efficient process for making those decisions. You certainly don't want to be impulsive, or act without enough information, but you also don't want to go in the other direction and see every issue as important as the next, or assume that every decision must be backed by only the most extensive research. Here are some important elements of effective decision making.

Make Decisions About Minor Issues Quickly

Maria wants to know if she can be off next Thursday. This question is obviously not on the same level as deciding whether or not to start a new program. Get it off your desk as quickly as possible. Some supervisors designate a particular time of day or time in the week to clear these little decisions out of their in-box. Others set their own criteria for common requests—for example, have in their own minds a policy regarding time off or some spending limit for common staff requests. Such guidelines eliminate having to re-decide the same issues over and over.

Train Staff on How They Should Present Requests to You

Send you an email, talk to you in supervision, put something in writing and put it in your mailbox, tell you their deadline for an answer. Having information come to you in the form that you need it can help you plan your time, and keep you from feeling scattered and rattled.

Have Others Do the Research

Tom wants to attend a 2-day conference on working with trauma. Rather than just handing you a brochure with his request, ask him to work up costs—hotel, registration fees, and so on—along with a clear statement of how this conference fits into his clinical goals and ways he can share this information with staff. Having others do the research for you not only saves you time, but helps them learn how to make sound decisions.

Delegate and Streamline Tasks

Susan wants to know whether another community agency is willing to fund her client's treatment. Typical protocol might be for you to talk to the supervisor at that agency, get his approval, and then inform Susan. You can bypass all this by telling Susan to go ahead and call the supervisor, tell the supervisor that she is calling at your request, and that if the supervisor has any questions she can give you a call. Let Susan do the work on her problem.

Similarly, if you notice that these issues come up frequently, you may want to have a meeting with the supervisor to come up with a streamlined procedure for decision making—for example, submitting a form or the automatic approval under a certain amount—so you both are again not constantly repeating the same tasks.

Break Big Decisions into Small Ones

Not sure whether starting a new program is a good idea? Decide what it is you need to know in order to decide—budget concerns, staffing, community response—delegate out what research you can, and set timelines for gathering this information. Decide at the front end what would be deal breakers—the cost goes over a certain amount, a particular community agency opposes the project—so you don't waste time trying to move obstacles that are not movable. Finally, designate time for decision process—that you will work on a tentative budget Thursday afternoon, that you will meet with community members this coming week and make a final decision by next Tuesday. Be clear and proactive.

Get Support and Advice

Know when you need other perspectives, and know when you need permission. Your supervisor may or may not need to know about Tom's attendance at the conference, but it's important for you to know about it. Have a conversation with your supervisor about information flow—when does he need to be included on decisions, when does he merely need to be informed, when are you free to do what you like—find out. Also know when you need his perspective or when a team approach is necessary. Tom's conference is a solo decision, but the starting of the new program may need a working committee to share tasks or simply to provide oversight and feedback.

Make Your Workspace as Comfortable as Possible

You likely spend a good amount of your time in your office. Like your time, you want to make your space as much as yours as possible. Is the agency chair giving you backache or is the squeak it gives off when you move driving you and everyone around you crazy? Get it fixed, or bring in your own. Beige walls making you depressed? Get some nice pictures, and some plants; throw down the imitation oriental rug over the gray industrial one.

Think about your own needs and wants, but keep in mind others. As it is said about clothes and personal appearance, it is also true about your workspace—you can't avoid making an impression. Others come to you—staff, visitors, maybe your own supervisor— and you want to consider what impression you want to make. If you have stacks of folders on file cabinets and chairs, if you have 20 photos of your dog on your bookcase, or if the papers on your desk are always stacked at a squared 90-degree angle and in a single pile, you create an impression. While you can't control everyone's reaction, you want to be sensitive to the overall appearance and the role-modeling message you are sending to clinicians.

Make an Effort to Spend Time with Colleagues

Therapy and supervision can be isolating work, and isolation can lead to self-preoccupation and burnout. Offset this by building in contact with those like you and those you like— meeting other supervisors in the agency for the third Thursday lunch, an informal complain session with other directors after the weekly or monthly directors meeting adjourns, a regular breakfast with a friend in private practice who has a totally different but interesting approach to clinical work.

Learn to Relax in Sessions

Beginning therapists and often new supervisors falsely believe that they have to be hypervigilant with clients or clinicians—supremely attune their thoughts, ever ready to inject the right uhm or sigh to show they are listening, or offer the insightful interpretation. More experienced clinicians and supervisors learn that it is usually better to allow themselves to relax—to stare off at the space above the client or clinician's head, and see what emerges in their imaginations and emotions, rather than rivetedly making eye contact. Much of the creative process of therapy and supervision is remaining open to yourself and what the words and emotions of others ignite. If you are always poised like a guard dog ready to strike, such creative inspirations can be lost.

Do Something That Helps You Feel Centered

Go to your office a half-hour early and meditate with your chair back (you did get it fixed, didn't you?) and your feet up on the desk. Take time during lunch to go for a walk or go to the gym and pump iron ferociously. Do gardening on weekend, cook a gourmet meal on Saturday nights, and take a writing class that will finally get you started on that novel you've been thinking about.

Therapy and supervision can pull you so easily into other people's lives. The point here is you have something in your life that centers you. An activity that brings you into yourself, to what you are doing right then, that gives you something to look forward to that isn't dependent on strong emotions (other than your own) or a particular outcome, where the doing is enough.

Be Optimistic

Yes, easier said than done. Yes, people have their own temperaments and emotional set points. But optimism can be learned. The positive psychology movement has taught us that efforts to change our perspective can actually change our perspective. Positive thoughts can rewire our brains and replace negative ones. A good outlook improves our immune system, which in turn improves our outlook.

So don't deny or minimize problems, but believe that they are solvable, that things will get better if they are resolved, and that expecting the better rather than the worst prepares you better for what comes next. And as a supervisor, your optimism, still grounded in the facts of the present, can spread to your staff. It is the positive feeling that applicants can pick up when they interview for the job, and that staff can feel when they come back to the building after a long day out in the field.

Box 14.2 is a summary of some of the essential self-care tips.

Box 14.2 • Self-Care Tips

Don't procrastinate—get it done	Make office space your own
Control schedule as much as possible	Run effective and efficient meetings
Diversify daily tasks	Relax in sessions
Have centering activities	Be optimistic
Do self-supervision	Stay close to your sense of purpose
Spend time with colleagues	

STAYING CREATIVE—THE WHY QUESTION

We talked throughout this book about what to do and how to think as a clinical social work supervisor. Perhaps the one question we haven't fully discussed is why. Why become a clinical supervisor?

The quick, flip answer and the one that many unfortunately make is why not? Being asked to be clinical supervisor is, after all, a recognition by others that you have a certain level of clinical skill, a real or potential ability to lead, a way of communicating with others that is effective not offensive, and a social ability that allows you to straddle your middle role in the agency and your multiple roles in the community. And, of course, there's the increased salary. What's not to like?

This all makes sense, of course, but there's another level to this why question. We're back to our purpose exercise at the beginning of this chapter and what you hopefully discovered: How is your sense of overall purpose tied to your being or becoming a supervisor? How does it utilize more of who you are and what you feel you need to do most?

You probably did not think of being a supervisor when you were in college. Yes, you probably made a clear decision to be a social worker—there was something about the values and purpose and focus of the work that ignited some part of you in a way that being a chemist or accountant you realized did not. Yes, you probably made a clear decision to be a clinician. The up close involvement in people's lives, the tracking of their emotions and thoughts, and the intimacy of the relationship may have made you realize that this experience and entrée into people's lives was a unique gift. It spoke to some deeper aspect of yourself. You discovered in others, perhaps, a better sense of yourself.

But why a clinical supervisor? Even though the vision here likely becomes more muddy, asking and answering the why question is important to avoid the simple why not. If your choice of the work is not really a choice, but a default and a going on autopilot, or if it is about money or the bigger office or the title, these will probably fade in value within a few years. You'll be discontent and perhaps leave, or discontent and feel stuck.

Just as you created and nurtured a vision of yourself as a social worker or clinician, create one as a supervisor. Look back at your sense of life purpose, and inventory your talents and passions. Being a supervisor does mean skills and requires leadership. It also requires an ability to motivate others and help them work together as a team. It gives you the opportunity to think macro rather than micro—how to build and shape a program, how to address a community need, how to work with and synthesize your ideas with those of others from different disciplines and perspectives.

These are the challenges and opportunities that clinicians usually never have but are part and parcel of the supervisory life. Do they ignite some new aspects of yourself? Do they stimulate excitement and challenge? If not, why not? Is it a matter of anxiety and lack of skill, the unique qualities not of the work but of the setting, or that your main interests and talents lie elsewhere? Why do you want to be a supervisor today? Discover the answer by asking the question.

Professional Identity

Practice Behavior Example: *Practice personal reflection and self-correction to assure continual professional development.*

Critical Thinking Question: What do you need most to stay creative?

A BIT OF ADVICE FROM BEN

Finally, we'll close this chapter and our journey together with an excerpt from "The Curious Case of Benjamin Button," a short story by F. Scott Fitzgerald (1922). The main character, Benjamin Button, grows younger as he gets older. At midlife he has a daughter but then leaves her because he realizes that as he becomes younger and younger he will not be able to father and care for her. Though he never sees her, over the years he sends her letters. In one he includes this advice about life.

> *It's never too late*
> *To be whoever you want to be*
> *There's no time limit*
> *Stop whenever you want*
> *You can change or stay the same*
> *There are no rules to this thing.*
>
> *We can make the best or worse of it*
> *I hope you make the best of it.*
>
> *And I hope you see things that startle you*
> *I hope you feel things you never felt before*
> *I hope you meet people with a different point of view.*
>
> *I hope you live a life you're proud of*
> *If you find you are not,*
> *I hope you have the strength to start all over again.*

Make the best of it.

The following questions will test your application and analysis of the content found within this chapter. For additional assessment, including licensing-exam-type questions on applying chapter content to practice behaviors, visit **MySearchLab**.

1. Self-supervision refers to
   a. Working in a setting where no supervision is provided
   b. Asking your supervisor to give you feedback about your "use of self," not just your clinical skills
   c. Looking back over your work and assessing challenges, changes, strengths, and weaknesses
   d. A psychological assessment tool that defines particular personality characteristics

2. Having as much control over your work schedule as possible
   a. Is necessary to avoid procrastination
   b. Helps you better maintain your focus and creativity
   c. Allows you to clump similar tasks back to back and more effectively handle them
   d. Has no effect on productivity

3. John asks about shifting more of his clinical cases to work with children. He was hired as an clinician for adult clients. Your best response would be to
   a. Review with John his job description highlighting the adult work
   b. Ask why he is interested in the change and consider it as a possibility
   c. Tell John it would be possible only if he was able to get some training in this area on his own
   d. Wonder aloud if this reflects a larger issue for John and suggest he talk to someone in EAP

4. Gabriele brings up in supervision that she feels that you more often point out what she is doing wrong and say little about what she is doing well. Your best response would be to
   a. Thank her for bringing this up and ask her to tell you more about what you are doing that is upsetting her
   b. Apologize and tell her that you will no longer make critical comments
   c. Say that it seems that the supervisory relationship does not seem to be a good fit and that you both should discuss transferring her supervision to someone else
   d. Explain her that you realize you have been more stressed lately, but that this is essentially how you view your responsibilities

5. You are feeling frustrated because your supervisor never responds to your questions and concerns in a timely manner. How would you handle this?

6. You are feeling tired and burned out. What would you do to handle this?

References

Bandler, R., & Grinder, J. (1979). *Frogs into princes*. Moab, UT: Real People Press.

Bennett, S., Mohr, J., BrintzenhofeSzoc, K., & Saks, L. V. (2008). General & supervision-specific attachment styles: Relations to student perceptions of field supervisors. *Journal of Social Work Education, 44*(2), 47–59.

Benson, H., & Proctor, W. (2004). *The breakout principle: How to activate the natural trigger that maximizes creativity, athletic performance, productivity and personal well-being*. New York: Scribner.

Bernard, J. M. (1997). The discrimination model. In C. E. Watkins (Ed.), *Handbook of psychotherapy supervision* (pp. 310–327). New York: Wiley.

Bernard, J. M., & Goodyear, R. K. (2009). *Fundamentals of clinical supervision* (4th ed.). Upper Saddle River, NJ: Pearson.

Bowen, M. (1978). *Family therapy in clinical practice*. New York: Jason Aronson.

Covey, S.R. (2004). *The 7 habits of highly effective people*. New York: Free Press.

Dziuban, J. I., & Dziuban, C. D. (1997). Reactive behavior patterns in the classroom. *Journal of Staff, Program & Organizational Development, 15*(2), 85–91.

Ekstein, R., & Wallerstein, R. (1958). *The teaching and learning of psychotherapy*. New York: Basic Books.

Ellis, A. (1989). Thoughts on supervising counselors and therapists. *Psychology: A Journal of Human Behavior, 26*, 3–5.

Fitzgerald, F. Scott (2008). *The curious case of Benjamin Button and other jazz age stories*. New York: Penguin Classics.

Frawley-O'Dea, M. G., & Sarnat, J. E. (2001). *The supervisory relationship: A contemporary psychodynamic approach*. New York: Guilford.

Kadushin, A. (1992). *Supervision in social work* (3rd ed.). New York: Columbia University Press.

Karpman, S. (1968). Fairy tales and script drama analysis. *Transactional Analysis Bulletin, 7*(26), 39–43.

Keens, W. (2010). Meetings? How to survive. *US Airways, 8*(10), 27–28.

Leslie, R. (2010). *At the intersection of law and psychotherapy bulletin*. Chicago: CPH & Associates.

Long, W. A. (1985). Adolescent maturation: A clinical overview. *Postgraduate Medicine, 1*(1), 85–90.

Mueller, W., & Kell, B. (1972). *Coping with conflict: Supervising counselors and psychotherapists*. New York: Appleton-Century-Crofts.

National Association of Social Workers. (2008). *Code of ethics of the national association of social workers*. Naswdc.org

Parry, A., & Doan, R. E. (1994). *Story re-visions: Narrative therapy in the postmodern world*. New York: Guilford.

Pavlina, S. (2005). *How to discover your life purpose in about 20 minutes*. Steve Pavlina.com

Perkins, D.N.T., Holtman, M. P., Kessler, P. R., & McCarthy, C. (2000). *Leading at the edge: Leadership lessons from the extraordinary saga of Shackleton's Antarctic expedition*. New York: Amacon.

Ronnestad, M. H., & Skovholt, T. M. (2003). The journey of the counselor and therapist: Research findings and perspectives on professional development. *Journal of Career Development, 30*, 5–44.

Roth, E. (2008). *The curious tale of Benjamin Button*. Paramount Pictures.

Stoltenberg, C. D., McNeill, B. W., & Delworth, U. (1998). *IDM: An integrated developmental model for supervising counselors and therapists*. San Francisco: Jossey-Bass.

Taibbi, R. (2007). *Doing family therapy: Craft & creativity in clinical practice* (2nd ed.). New York: Guilford.

Tudor, K., & Worrall, M. (2004). *Freedom to practice: Person-centered approaches to supervision*. Ross-on-Wye, UK: PCCS Books.

Text Credits

Page 214: Steve Pavlina (2010) Pavlina, S. (2005). How to discover your life purpose in about 20 minutes. Steve Pavlina.com.

Page 220: Keens, W. (2010). Meetings? How to survive. US Airways, 8 (10), 27–28. Originally published as: Herding Cats and Cougars: How to Survive the Meeting You Are Running While Mastering the Art of Facilitation. williamkeens@gmail.com

Index